TEACHING THE WHOLE STUDENT

TEACHING THE WHOLE STUDENT

Engaged Learning With Heart, Mind, and Spirit

Edited by

David Schoem, Christine Modey, and

Edward P. St. John

Foreword by Beverly Daniel Tatum

Published in association with

Association of American Colleges and Universities

STERLING, VIRGINIA

Published by Stylus Publishing, LLC.
22883 Quicksilver Drive
Sterling, Virginia 20166-2102

Library of Congress Cataloging-in-Publication Data
Names: Schoem, David Louis, editor. | Modey, Christine, editor. |
St. John, Edward P., editor.
Title: Teaching the whole student : engaged learning with heart,
mind and spirit / edited by David Schoem, Christine Modey and
Edward P. St. John ; forward by Beverly Daniel Tatum.
Description: First edition. |
Sterling, Va. : Stylus Publishing, 2017. |
Includes bibliographical references and index.
Identifiers: LCCN 2016056705 (print) |
LCCN 2017021400 (ebook) |
ISBN 9781620363058 (uPDF) |
ISBN 9781620363065 (ePub) |
ISBN 9781620363034 (cloth :alk. paper) |
ISBN 9781620363041 (pbk. :alk. paper) |
Subjects: LCSH: Holistic education--United States. |
College teaching--Social aspects--United States. |
Learning and scholarship--Social aspects--United States. |
Engagement (Philosophy) |
Education, Higher--Aims and objectives--United States. |
Service learning--United States.
Classification: LCC LC995 (ebook) |
LCC LC995 .T427 2017 (print) |
DDC 371.102--dc23
LC record available at https://lccn.loc.gov/2016056705

13-digit ISBN: 978-1-62036-303-4 (cloth)
13-digit ISBN: 978-1-62036-304-1 (paper)
13-digit ISBN: 978-1-62036-305-8 (library networkable e-edition)
13-digit ISBN: 978-1-62036-306-5 (consumer e-edition)

Printed in the United States of America

All first editions printed on acid-free paper
that meets the American National Standards Institute
Z39-48 Standard.

Bulk Purchases

Quantity discounts are available for use in workshops and for
staff development.
Call 1-800-232-0223

First Edition, 2017

10   9   8   7   6   5   4   3

To the teachers who changed our lives.

CONTENTS

FOREWORD

Timing, they say, is everything. We live in a time when many people—students, parents, and policymakers alike—are asking fundamental questions about higher education. Is it worth the time, effort, and expense? Do the benefits outweigh the costs? How many of those who begin the pursuit of a college degree will complete it? Will they fall by the wayside with debt but no degree? What will the learning outcomes be? In a world of rapidly advancing technology and globalization, will graduates have the cognitive flexibility and problem-solving skills necessary to address the complex demands of the twenty-first century? Will they be ready for not only the workplace but also life in community with others? Will they understand the crucial responsibilities of citizenship needed to preserve democracy? These questions form the backdrop of *Teaching the Whole Student: Engaged Learning With Heart, Mind, and Spirit.*

In the same week that I read this edited volume, I participated in a meeting of educators and business leaders engaged in dialogue about the urgency of improving higher education. The business leaders spoke of the widespread difficulties they and their peers were having hiring college graduates with the requisite skills. They emphasized that they were not seeking technical skills specific to their various industries; they were prepared to do that training on the job. They were looking for graduates with problem-solving capacity, the ability to communicate ideas effectively, to think analytically, to exercise leadership and work effectively as part of a diverse team. In short, they were looking for holistically educated students and finding them in short supply.

Earlier that week, I had been in another meeting, this time with educational researchers, academic administrators, and funders, again discussing how to improve the outcomes of higher education. This time the conversation was anchored in a discussion of the findings of two multi-institutional research studies—the first conducted by Richard Arum and Josipa Roksa and reported in their influential book, *Academically Adrift: Limited Learning on College Campuses* (Arum & Roksa, 2011). Among their major findings were: little to no improvement during college in critical thinking and complex reasoning as measured by the Collegiate Learning Assessment (CLA) and limited engagement in the academic work of studying and writing.

The second study that was the focus of our discussion was the Wabash National Study of Liberal Arts Education, reported in a 2013 *Change* article by Ernest T. Pascarella and Charles Blaich. It will come as no surprise to the contributors of this volume that a key finding of the WNS project was that *pedagogy matters*. Pascarella and Blaich (2013) reported that "student's exposure to clear and organized instruction enhanced not only their general cognitive skills such as critical thinking but also their orientation toward inquiry and continuing intellectual development." It also increased student satisfaction, which led to higher student retention. They also reported that "*deep learning experiences count*" (emphasis added). Learning activities that require students to apply theories and concepts to practical problems, to synthesize ideas and experiences, and to reflect on the personal meaning of an issue or concept—higher-order learning, integrative learning, and reflective learning—all lead to that elusive intellectual growth a college education should provide. The most positive impact, however, came from what Pascarella and Blaich termed *interactional diversity*, defined as how often students engaged with diverse peers, ideas, and sociopolitical and religious perspectives during college. Of all the things they measured, only interactional diversity had a significant positive impact on all three of their measures of cognitive development—critical thinking skills, the need for cognition (a lifelong learning orientation), and a positive attitude toward literacy activities—a finding that was most evident among White students.

Both meetings, occurring back-to-back that week, underscored the need for *Teaching the Whole Student*. The contributors in this volume understand the importance of clear and organized pedagogy, and know that such pedagogy is at its most powerful when it is *relational, integrative, reflective,* and *in a diverse context*. If we are honest about what is happening in colleges and universities around the United States today, we must acknowledge that not enough of it meets these criteria. But it could. More of our students need the transformative power of the education such pedagogy offers. And our society needs more of the students such an education can foster. *Teaching the Whole Student* offers all of us the *critical hope* that we need to make it so. It is the right book for the right time.

Beverly Daniel Tatum
President
Spellman College

References

Arum, R. & Roksa, J. (2011). *Academically adrift: Limited learning on college campuses.* Chicago, IL: University of Chicago Press.

Pascarella, E. T. & Blaich, C. (2013, March/April). Lessons from the Wabash National Study of Liberal Arts Education. *Change, 45,* 6–15.

PREFACE

The contributors to this book remind us in personal, poignant, and empirical ways of the importance of teaching and of reaching the whole student with heart, mind, and spirit. In the crush of shrinking budgets, technical and corporate efficiencies, and the speed of modern life, we too often lose sight of the basic principles of learning, life, love, and meaning. Our students are our global society's children; they are the very humanity of our present and future. As the contributors to this book remind us, it is our responsibility and honor to treat our students with great care and respect. When we do so, our students flourish as bright, thoughtful, loving, and soulful individuals.

Teaching still matters. The humanity of each individual student and teacher is of utmost importance, and the collective community of students and teachers in our classrooms and throughout our colleges and universities matters, too. Good teaching in higher education necessitates valuing teaching and teachers, giving personal attention to each individual student, and cultivating close teacher–student relationships. Teaching the whole student in this way is a long-standing, core purpose of liberal arts education. In light of the serious challenges facing higher education and its faculty and students today, its importance becomes even more evident and urgent.

Teaching the whole student matters because it (a) contributes to student learning and the core academic purposes of higher education, (b) affirms the humanity of each individual student and helps students flourish and find meaning and purpose in their lives, and (c) contributes to higher education's purpose to strengthen our diverse democracy through the institutions' and students' active participation and leadership in society. The purposes of student learning, student development, and a strong democracy are inextricably linked, but here we also articulate the distinct ways that teaching the whole student affects each.

Teaching the whole student is important for student learning because it affirms the importance of critical thinking above rote, mechanical learning because faculty know, engage, and challenge the individual student. It supports academic freedom and the exchange of contested ideas. It encourages innovation and experimentation in teaching and emphasizes integrative pedagogy and engaged learning. It encourages interdisciplinary collaboration in teaching and thinking across and beyond the disciplines. It increases student commitment to learning because students see themselves as part of an engaged, supportive, and caring scholarly community. Teaching the whole student increases persistence and completion rates and contributes to the academic success of underrepresented students of color and their participation and that of women in science, technology, engineering, and mathematics fields.

Teaching the whole student is critical to student development, as it affirms the humanity of each individual, students and teachers alike. It affirms the importance of human life and relationships above material rewards and helps students (and faculty) find meaning and purpose in their lives. It facilitates the integration of learning with caring, equity, and social justice. Teaching the whole student matters because it helps students find the necessary resources to address mental health concerns and works to build a supportive community in which they learn to thrive and flourish.

Teaching the whole student is essential to a healthy democracy because it calls for open, honest discussion and freedom of speech and thought. Teaching the whole student helps build participation and leadership in civic life, thus serving to strengthen the democracy. It contributes to intergroup engagement in a diverse and sustainable democratic society. It reaffirms colleges and universities as educational institutions, not corporations, and it realizes the potential of higher education as a primary pathway for creating equality in society.

Teaching the Whole Student is a collection of reflective essays by faculty who care deeply about teaching. The idea for this book originated among a group of faculty at the University of Michigan associated with the Michigan Community Scholars Program (MCSP) who worked closely with students in the program as well as provided support for each other as they navigated the complexities of academic life, maintaining their commitments to teaching while dealing with the constant pressures of university life. As we reflected on our shared interests, we realized colleagues across the country were contending with similar issues related to teaching that provided opportunities for a diverse group of students to think deeply and critically, learn about themselves and the world around them, and find meaning and purpose in their lives.

We invited reflective essays from authors who intentionally stretch the boundaries of academic learning and the classroom experience by seeking to identify the discursive space that spans the borders between hard scientific objectivity and lived experiences and core values. These reflective scholars create engaged classroom environments that refuse to detach the brain and course content from the heart, soul, and spirit of the student. Just as they look at the whole of each student learner and the relationships that compose classroom communities, these educators make use of integrative pedagogies that seek to find the interconnectedness of knowledge, understanding, meaning, inquiry, and truth. Each chapter includes a set of reflective questions for readers to consider for their own pedagogical practice; departmental or institutional policy; and broader considerations about approaches to integrative pedagogy, social justice, and student learning and well-being in higher education.

David Schoem, founding faculty director of MCSP and faculty member in sociology, provides an introduction to the book, presenting the case for teaching the whole student, engaged learning, and integrative pedagogy.

In chapter 1, Jerry A. Pattengale, Indiana Wesleyan University's (IWU's) first university professor, explains how, in response to the typically unsuccessful standard approaches to campus retention efforts, he developed a much different, whole person approach to student success. Focusing on students' life calling and purpose, with attention to knowledge, skills, and dispositions, he describes how this integrative approach has not only improved completion rates at IWU but also been adopted at a wide range of different types of colleges and universities.

In chapter 2, Kathleen Manning reflects on her experience teaching social justice to future higher education administrators. As a professor at the University of Vermont, she led one of the nation's outstanding programs for student affairs administrators. She finds that students frequently have had prior negative experiences with dialogues on diversity issues, so they can be defensive and resistant to engaging in open conversations. Manning discusses some of the pedagogical strategies she has used to facilitate successful dialogue about topics related to social justice in graduate classrooms.

In chapter 3, Gillies Malnarich, who for more than a decade served as codirector of the Washington Center for Improving the Quality of Undergraduate Education and faculty member at The Evergreen State College, digs into the links between learning community pedagogy and community change, which she calls "educating for critical hope." Her framing of the challenges that lie ahead is deeply rooted in critical social theory and a commitment to sustainability of the planet. She reflects on curricular and pedagogical strategies that are integral to learning community classrooms that empower students to take on contemporary challenges and the critical hope necessary to persist when solutions are not readily evident.

In chapter 4, David Schoem writes about relational teaching and the importance of community in learning. He goes back more than 50 years to make the case for teaching the whole student, engaged learning, and integrative pedagogy in a foundational academic writing context. He examines his own educational practice in a traditional college classroom and in a residential learning community. In both settings, he has focused on relationship and community building, dialogic instruction, intergroup engagement and diversity, deep learning, student academic success and well-being, and honoring and empowering the humanity of each individual student and teacher.

As a professor and dean at the University of Michigan, former president of Antioch College, and an affiliated faculty member of MCSP since its start in 1999, James Crowfoot has pursued a personal and intellectual passion for and commitment to educating for sustainability. In chapter 5, he describes his experiential and dialogic pedagogy of heart, mind, and spirit for educating and creating a sustainable future. This reflective essay discusses his cutting-edge pedagogical methods of practicing new integrative ways of emotional and cognitive knowing about sustainability involving dialogues about values, psychospiritual processes in the outdoor classroom, and fostering active hope in students.

Adrienne B. Dessel, coassociate director of the Program on Intergroup Relations and faculty member in the College of Literature, Science, and the Arts and the School of Social Work at the University of Michigan, focuses on student-centered experiential and dialogic pedagogy in a religious and ethnic conflict course in chapter 6. She models self-disclosure in the interest of fostering learning about differences in cultures and beliefs. Her reflective essay illustrates the essential role integrative pedagogy plays in creating an open learning environment that fosters critical understanding and an attitude toward peace rather than fostering conflict based on misunderstanding of beliefs.

Joseph A. Galura, faculty member in the College of Literature, Science, and the Arts and the School of Social Work, as well as program adviser for the minor in community action and social change at the University of Michigan, has been a longtime leader in service-learning and a steady partner among the faculty in MCSP. In chapter 7, he reflects on the integrative pedagogy, value, and meaning of service and learning for both students and communities, what he labels as *SERVICE-LEARNING*. He also describes his teaching experiences and strategies for developing deep social and personal reflection in experiential education, emphasizing pedagogy, boundaries, and invitation.

James L. Heft, president of the Institute for Advanced Catholic Studies at the University of Southern California, reflects in chapter 8 on his own approach to teaching that elicits deep encounters in learning through expansive, integrative pedagogy. He discusses his more than 40 years of experience collaborating and facilitating dialogues with people from diverse faith and secular traditions on topics that integrate heart, mind, and spirit. He shares his work in opening communication with students and helping them share their stories. Heft also presents his important work in organizing and leading faculty learning communities to engage in "real conversations about significant questions."

Angela M. Locks, a professor at California State University, Long Beach, is coauthor with Rachelle Winkle-Wagner (2013) of *Diversity and Inclusion*, a widely adopted textbook in higher education programs. In chapter 9, Locks shares her research on the impact of student intercultural engagement with a particular interest in how marginalized and minority students can address experiences of isolation in college in ways that result in their academic success. She discusses her research findings on precollege dispositions, whole student and engaged learning approaches, intergroup interactions in college, and cocurricular diversity programs.

In chapter 10, Kimberly A. Kline, a professor and chair of the Higher Education Administration Department at SUNY Buffalo State; Edward P. St. John, prolific author and an emeritus professor at the University of Michigan's Center for the Study of Higher and Postsecondary Education; and Annie E. Connors, a graduate student in higher education and student affairs administration also at SUNY Buffalo State, provide a framework for the assessment of teaching the whole student, engaged learning, and integrative pedagogy and reflect on how the chapters in this book fit into that framework. In doing so, they explore the intersection among social justice, integrative pedagogy, and assessment.

In chapter 11, the three coeditors, Christine Modey, faculty member in the Sweetland Center for Writing and director of the Peer Writing Consultant Program at the University of Michigan; David Schoem; and Edward P. St. John, conclude this volume with a consideration of the necessity for and implications of adopting a whole student, engaged, and integrative approach integrative approach in college classrooms. They identify the themes emerging across the chapters of these distinguished teachers and authors. In the future, they suggest, there will be an even greater need for whole student education, engaged learning, and integrative pedagogy as a countervailing force to current challenges facing higher education.

We hope this book will serve as a call to action for college educators who share our concerns about education that recognizes and values teachers; supports the academic core of student learning and critical thinking; encourages teaching that honors the humanity, heart, mind, and spirit of our students; and works to strengthen the future of our nation's diverse democracy.

—David Schoem, Christine Modey, and
Edward P. St. John

Reference

Winkle-Wagner, R. (2013). *Diversity and inclusion on campus: Supporting racially and ethnically underrepresented students*. New York, NY: Routledge.

ACKNOWLEDGMENTS

We wish to thank all the authors for their contributions to this book, as well as their enduring commitment to teaching, learning, and students. We are honored by their participation in this project and to have learned so much from their work and writing.

The inspiration for this book came from the Michigan Community Scholars Program faculty who participated in the 2006–2007 Ford Foundation's "Difficult Dialogues" grant initiative exploring the place of religion, faith, spirituality, and meaning in our lives as faculty, staff, and administrators and in our personal lives. The original participants included Percy Bates, Charles Behling, George Cooper, Jim Crowfoot, Frieda Ekotto, Joe Galura, Pat Gurin, Terry Joiner, Heather Livingston, Kelly Maxwell, Louis Nagel, David Schoem, Luis Sfeir-Younis, and Wendy Woods.

Subsequent to the grant activities, a group of faculty continued these discussions every few months over a several-year period with a broader framework, sharing together the deeper meaning in our personal and professional lives and experiences in what became something of a men's group by virtue of the participants. These participants included Charles Behling, George Cooper, Jim Crowfoot, Joe Galura, David Schoem, Luis Sfeir-Younis, and Ed St. John. The group members met for conversations over lunch and also discussed readings and shared their own autobiographical writing.

As the depth of analytic reflection in these gatherings became clear over time, it was Ed St. John's inspiration to consider making these conversations and our writing into a book. There was some resistance at first, because the participants didn't want to risk the informality and depth of the discussions for a focused, formal project such as a book, but Ed's gentle yet persistent encouragement moved us forward. There were a series of stops and starts, proposals advanced, and shifts in chapter authors as a result of negotiations with the publisher, but we did finally arrive at this book that you are now reading. We are indebted to Ed St. John for carrying us through to this moment.

In a book about teaching and engaging students, we can each reach back to thank the great many teachers and students, too numerous to list here, who have mentored, inspired, transformed, and filled our lives with meaning and purpose. We also want to thank the University of Michigan for its support of the Michigan Community Scholars Program (MCSP) and initiatives like it that have been given the space and permission to truly fulfill the promise of deep learning, personal relations, and diversity in higher education in ways that don't always neatly fit into the mainstream practices of institutional life. MCSP has consistently valued in its mission and practice the humanity of each individual teacher, staff member, and student; community building; student learning; intergroup relations, dialogue, and diversity; community outreach; and social justice. As such, it has been a special gift and joy to be part of this program that has allowed so many to flourish personally, socially, and intellectually.

We want to extend our deep appreciation for the editors and staff at Stylus Publishing who have been so supportive of this work. We want to especially thank Sarah Burrows for her guidance throughout the process, as well as Tammy Radford, Andrea Ciecierski, Alexandra Hartnett, Patricia Webb, and Shaqunia Clark.

Finally, we wish to thank our families for their love and support during the process of bringing this book to print. For David, Karyn and our children, Adina and Joe, Shana Garrett, and now Noa Serafina, make everything worthwhile and meaningful. For Ed, Angie has been a source of inspiration, care, and love. For Christine, her family, Barry, Lucy, Aurora, and Ivy, embody the power of learning in love to forge deep relationships that reshape our worlds.

INTRODUCTION

David Schoem

Three powerful approaches to teaching and learning serve as the foundation of this book: teaching the whole student with heart, mind, and spirit; engaged learning; and integrative pedagogy. These educational approaches result in significant positive outcomes for college students, for teaching and learning, for higher education, and for a diverse democratic society (Darling-Hammond, 2010; Deresiewicz, 2014; Kirp, 2014; Kohn, 2004; Kuh, 2008; Nieto, 2015; Palmer, 2007; Palmer & Zajonc, 2010; Schoem, 2002; Schoem & Hurtado, 2001; St. John, Daun-Barnett, & Moronski-Chapman, 2013).

Teaching the whole student involves an approach and mind-set that looks at students with heart, mind, and spirit, including but also extending beyond their intellectual abilities. It includes a focus on both the individual and the community of students and faculty, that is, the scholarly community, and emphasizes relational teaching. *Engaged learning* emphasizes active, participatory, experiential learning that links doing with thinking and learning. *Integrative pedagogy* represents an intentional approach to bridging different and disparate structures of teaching and learning, as well as crossing and stretching traditional intellectual disciplinary boundaries that can limit the breadth and complexity of students' understanding.

The educational outcomes of these three approaches include deep learning, individual well-being and flourishing, and academic success that extends to all students, including students who are traditionally underrepresented in educational achievement and leadership roles in society. Furthermore, the healthy development of a diverse population of well-educated, engaged citizens who are critical thinkers and problem solvers, which is an outcome of these approaches, is critical to the health and vitality of a strong, diverse, and just democracy. These three powerful approaches to pedagogy are widely used, as illustrated by the contributions to this volume, but they have seldom been considered in a cohesive, integrated framework for undergraduate education, which is so needed today in higher education. In this introduction we explain the three powerful approaches and their implications to educational outcomes, with an explicit emphasis on implication for diversity in universities and social justice within America's diverse democratic society.

1

Teaching the Whole Student With Heart, Mind, and Spirit

Teaching the whole student represents recognition and appreciation for the fact that students (and faculty) bring into the classroom their hearts and spirits just as they bring their minds and intellectual capacities (Astin, Astin, & Lindholm, 2011). Students bring to the classroom their life experiences; their social and personal identities; and life's deeper meaning, purpose, and emotions (Chickering, Dalton, & Stamm, 2006; Thomas & Bahr, 2008).

Teaching the whole student affirms the importance of human life and relationships above job preparation and material rewards (Cody, 2014; Giroux, 2012; Lantieri & Patti, 1996). It affirms colleges and universities as educational institutions first and foremost, not as corporate entities (Deresiewicz, 2014; Goodman, 1964). It builds community for students to help find meaning and purpose in their lives and to flourish as individuals and in community (Block, 2008; Newmann & Oliver, 1967). It helps students find resources to address personal, academic, social, and mental health issues (L. Christensen & Karp, 2003; Harward, 2016). It helps students develop, grow, and become thinking and contributing mature adults. It encourages innovation in teaching and supports academic freedom and the exchange of contested ideas.

Faculty who hold a whole student approach bring an appreciation and respect for life and humanity itself, and they affirm the humanity and life of each individual student in the classroom (Block, 2008; Palmer, 2007; Schoem, 2016). They care deeply about their students, and they are interested in creating a classroom community and environment of openness and trust to foster deep learning, academic success, and meaning-making (Ancess, 2003; Nash & Murray, 2010; Palmer & Zajonc, 2010). They value each student in their class, and they explicitly affirm the value of underrepresented students who too often are made to feel invisible, devalued, and marginalized in their classroom and schooling experiences (Eisler, 2000; Hurtado, Milem, Clayton-Pederson, & Allen, 1998; Lewis & Diamond, 2015; Nieto, 2015). Through relational teaching, they seek to challenge and support students as they grapple with intellectual concepts, personal development, intergroup relations, social justice and structural inequalities, and personal well-being (Darling-Hammond, 2010; Kirp, 2013; Palmer, 2007).

What does whole student teaching look like? As a minimal start, it requires that the teacher know each student's name. It involves a heartfelt invitation for students to visit the instructor during office hours, whether for specific course content issues or, more broadly, for the faculty member to get to know the student. It invites students to consider the theory of classroom content and apply it to personal understanding and experiences. It asks students to go deeply and critically into their thinking. It challenges students to interrogate concepts of privilege and power, as well as intragroup and intergroup relationships, while examining their own place in those concepts and structures.

Of course it goes further. It also allows for students to be themselves and to thrive in the classroom. To do so, it requires that faculty build a classroom space based on trust, openness, critical personal and intellectual sharing, and honesty in analysis and critique (Ancess, 2003; Newmann & Oliver, 1967; Palmer & Zajonc, 2010; Schoem, 1997). It allows for students to express love, hurt, happiness, and anger in their personal and social lives (Olson, 2007). It encourages students to search for purpose and meaning in their lives, to wrestle with the big questions in life, and to explore their inner lives and most important relationships (Astin et al., 2011; Chickering et al., 2006). It helps them consider their development as young adults and take ownership of their lives and beliefs with active hope. It helps them listen carefully to new ideas, consider different perspectives, explore vastly different life experiences, and sit with those viewpoints; challenge their own assumptions and views; and reaffirm or reimagine what they believe and think is true and right and just.

Recent research on the mental health of college students reveals alarming data about the students who inhabit our classrooms. As reported by New (2015b), "More than half of college students said they have experienced 'overwhelming anxiety' . . . and 32% say they have felt so depressed 'that it was difficult to function.'" The emotional wounds of schooling, so poignantly described in research by Olson (2007) and depicted in the film *Race to Nowhere* (Abeles, 2010), are the culmination of a lifetime of classroom hurts. These students, who are the academic success stories in that they have made it to college despite these wounds, may be entering our classrooms with a high degree of intellectual curiosity and motivation to succeed, but for too many, their hearts and bodies are necessarily focused more on their emotional health. For some, just getting to class is a huge victory.

Once they enter the classroom, many of our students face a hostile climate based on their social identities. In some cases, whether it is a large lecture class or a seminar, African American students and students with other nondominant social identities may experience feelings of isolation and marginalization as the only member of their social identity group in the room. Women may face a lack of encouragement or outright discouragement in science, technology, engineering, and mathematics (STEM) classes (Pollack, 2015), and microaggressions targeting students from any number of social identities are all too frequent (New, 2015a). The contributors in this volume discuss strategies for creating inclusive climates, developing learning communities, and using dialogic techniques that support learning across cultures.

Apart from emotional health, there is an increasing call from higher education leaders asking if we have put our students on such a competitive and nonstop academic and job-preparation treadmill that they have never asked themselves about the big questions in life, have not been given a space and opportunity to do so in college, and have been actively discouraged from doing so (Deresiewicz, 2014). Whether it is a secular desire to find meaning in life or a need to pursue a more spiritual grounding or to grapple with faith and religion, our students leave college without a fundamental sense of who they are, the purpose of life, and their inner selves. There are many who argue that finding a path to a meaningful life always has been and should continue to be a core value of the liberal arts college experience (Astin et al., 2011; Chickering et al., 2006; Wingspread, 2005).

In contrast, teaching the whole student is not lecturing once or twice a week to a classroom of 250 students who have virtually no personal contact with the faculty member, except perhaps a grade complaint at the end of the semester. It is not a MOOC, or massive open online course, with thousands of students virtually linked but clearly not in relationship with one another, often distracted by texting and games. It is not robotic advising or teaching where no humans need to be present. It is not education that imagines students as disembodied brains, detached from their selves. It is not education that is strictly and exclusively focused on the development of future corporate employees who are technically competent but who are lacking in critical thinking, ethical development, a sense of purpose, and concern for social justice and meaning in life.

Engaged Learning

We emphasize engaged learning, whereby students are actively participating, doing, experiencing, and relating in the service of learning and becoming involved participants in civic and community life (Dewey, 1966). Engaged learning affirms the importance of student involvement in their own learning, clearly prioritizing critical and analytical thinking above rote memorization and passive regurgitation (Block, 2008; Boyer, 1987; Ravitch, 2010). Engaged learning speaks to both engagement with the course content and engagement with the community of their classroom peers and, also, the community outside of campus and the natural environment (Goodman, 1964). By actively doing, students learn and gain new and deeper understandings of course content (Kinzie, 2014; Kuh, 2008).

Engaged learning helps build participation and leadership in civic life. It strengthens democracy through active participation in society, and it contributes to intergroup engagement in a diverse society (Schoem, Hurtado, Sevig, Chesler, & Sumida, 2001). The open learning environment and participation necessary for quality engagement can also facilitate deeper and more critical understandings of social justice and structural inequalities in society. In the field, seeing firsthand the dissonance between theory/research and practice can elicit greater skill in perspective taking through social and personal reflection on one's experiences (Gurin, Dey, Hurtado, & Gurin, 2002).

There are many approaches to engaged learning and teaching. Residential and curricular learning communities immerse students in learning environments that facilitate learning inside and outside the classroom. The residential learning community is lived and experienced on a 24/7 basis and, in a learning community that is diverse, becomes an opportunity to model the ideals of an engaged multicultural community (R. D. Christensen, 2016; Feldman & Newcomb, 1969; Gabelnick, MacGregor, Matthews, & Smith, 1990; Nelson, 2001; Schoem, 2004). Community engagement encompasses a variety of educational practices, including civic education, democratic education practices, learning in and/or from the community, community-based learning, community-based research or projects, and service-learning, among others (Boyte, 2004; Galura, Pasque, Schoem, & Howard, 2004; Saltmarsh & Hartley, 2011). Community service-learning and these other community engagement practices take students out of the classroom into a range of community settings, allowing students to observe, participate in, and reflect on the actual experience of the social scientific readings they do in class (Colby, Ehrlich, Beaumont, & Stephens, 2003; Jacoby, 2009; Westheimer, 2015).

Another form of engaged learning is intergroup dialogue, which provides students with the opportunity to interrogate their own assumptions and social identities, develop active listening skills, build relationships with peers from different social identities or with different viewpoints, consider issues of social justice, and embrace the value of a diverse democracy (Nagda & Gurin, 2007; Schoem et al., 2001; Small, 2011). Other forms of engagement include immersion in the physical environment, whether simply being outdoors in a structured lesson to appreciate and commune with the environment or working on specific projects such as water quality, food safety, vegetable gardening, or natural area preservation (Crowfoot, 2017). Research experiences give students the opportunity to discover, experiment, and practice what they are learning in their textbooks (Locks & Gregerman, 2008). Various types of fieldwork give students hands-on practice and experience in their field of study. Problem-based learning, problem-solving, and case studies are additional examples of engaged learning (Kohn, 2004). Finally, there are classes that engage students in the exploration of one's values and inner self, focusing, for instance, on creativity and/or consciousness (Sarath, 2014). Students can also be positively engaged through creative uses of classroom technology to enhance learning. And, without question, more traditional reading and writing assignments, as well as oral presentations, can be crafted to be highly engaging learning experiences.

Engaged learning very distinctly is the opposite of the banking concept of knowledge (Freire, 1970). It is not passive learning. It is not a traditional lecture course in which students sit for a few hours each week listening to a professor speak. It is not rote memorization of facts and regurgitation of those facts on a multiple-choice exam.

The quality of collegiate learning environments has long been linked to the capacity of colleges to promote engaged learning. For example, the first-year student surveys, started by the American Council on Education and continued at the University of California, Los Angeles (UCLA) (Astin, 1985), and the National Survey of Student Engagement (Kuh, Kinzie, Schuh, Whitt, & Associates, 2005) use indicators of engaged learning and civic engagement to compare institutions. These indicators are included in the assessment information considered by students in searching for colleges. Many selective colleges use this type of information when marketing to students.

Enrollment and completion rates are interconnected with student engagement in learning. Inclusive engagement of diverse students begins with organizational environments that support and encourage engaged learning for underrepresented students. Student support services do much to attract and retain students. At the same time, the underlying issues related to attracting and retaining students in STEM and other fields depend to a significant degree on improvement in relational teaching and the engaged learning within courses, supplemented by research opportunities, learning communities, internships, and service activities.

Integrative Pedagogy

The integrative approach to teaching is built on the intersections and linkages among the many different but often separate educational structures, intellectual conceptual fields, methodologies, and practices in higher education (Huber & Hutchings, 2004). It involves intellectual and structural bridge building and boundary crossing in the service of student learning (Manning, Kinzie, & Schuh, 2006). *Integrative pedagogy* encourages interdisciplinary collaboration in teaching and, by definition and intentionality, calls for a much closer fit between teaching and learning.

Interdisciplinary and cross-disciplinary instruction have become much more common with the advent of curricular learning communities. These programs are one significant and popular example of integrative pedagogy, such as when faculty from English and engineering, or sociology and biology, or business and history coteach or link their courses through common assignments and readings, common themes, and common projects with a single set of students (Lardner & Malnarich, 2008). The faculty might even coteach two distinct courses or guest teach some of the class sessions in each other's classes. The literature on curricular learning communities and linked courses provides extensive documentation on the significant retention and persistence benefits for all students, including underrepresented students, of this form of integrative pedagogy (Tinto, 1998; Tinto & Engstrom, 2008).

Bringing together the separate worlds of academic affairs and student life in higher education's siloed institutional structures is a critical example of integrative pedagogy. For the benefit of student learning, residential learning communities represent an integrative approach that promotes whole student learning through the recognition of the integrated whole of a student's intellectual world and personal and social experience on campus (Smith & Williams, 2007). Other examples involve the inclusion of librarians, enrollment management, financial aid staff, and mental health and academic advisers, programs together with faculty, in the development of holistic learner-focused programs or college support systems.

Service-learning courses are a common example of boundary crossing between academic affairs and student life. Developing community partnerships, classroom readings, and reflection; preparing students to appropriately and respectfully enter the community; providing transportation and discussions en route to the community site; and fostering student relationships with individuals in the community are all boundary-crossing experiences that are best addressed by bringing together the expertise of both faculty and student life's educational staff.

Global education, when conceived broadly, well beyond the parameters of a single study abroad experience, is an important educational example of integrative learning (Bennett, Cornwell, Al-Lail, & Schenk, 2012). Internships, when closely aligned with academic readings, reflection, and study, can offer a significant integrative learning experience (Sides & Mrvica, 2007). A growing number of instructors today ask their students to use portfolios or e-portfolios to integrate their academic and experiential learning with personal and social development during the course of their college experience (Yancey, 2009).

The growing number of intergroup dialogue programs bridges academic literature and conceptual thinking with the direct facilitation and management of intra- and intergroup community, conflict, and relationship building and exploration. Again, the knowledge and skills needed for these critical learning experiences require the jointly shared expertise of academic and student affairs educators (Schoem, 1997, 2002; Zuniga, Nagda, Chesler, & Cytron-Walker, 2007).

Integrative pedagogy is practiced when faculty connect theory to practice, link the theoretical with the personal, and then link the personal back to the theoretical (Taylor, 2011). The academic literature and conceptual understandings come alive when practiced or illuminated in one's own life experience, which helps to make the literature more real and meaningful. Integrative pedagogy also allows students to find deeper meaning, understanding, and insight about their own inner lives and social identities and about the communities, societies, and natural world they inhabit (Gurasci & Cornwell, 1997). When students engage in problem-solving and social or scientific analysis from an integrative approach, they are better able to bring a more complex and holistic lens to their study than if they were limited to a single disciplinary perspective. It is especially important that more serious attention be given to race, ethnic, gender, and class differences in engagement in classrooms. Mentoring junior faculty so they are encouraged to pay attention to diversity matters is especially important.

Integrative pedagogy is the opposite of disciplinary-specific instruction and siloed educational structures. It is not the education that works so hard to keep the intellectual apart from the personal and social, that makes exploration of relationships one-dimensional, that limits a more complete understanding of both content and self. It is not the educational approach that separates students' heart and spirit from their brain and thinking and that is too often representative of higher education today. It is not a place in which students are placed in cutthroat competitive classes with high-stakes, weed-out tests in the classroom and then sent to overflowing counseling centers or given therapy dogs to pet while administrators wonder why so many students seem to be anxious, stressed, and depressed.

Moving Forward

As this introduction and the chapters of this book demonstrate, there is considerable documented, positive evidence associated with the themes of this book: teaching the whole student, engaged learning, and integrative pedagogy. These approaches contribute to student learning and the core academic purposes of higher education. They help students find meaning and purpose in their lives, help strengthen our diverse democracy, and contribute to social justice through diverse students' active participation and leadership in civic life. These approaches have a demonstrated impact on critical and analytical thinking, student retention, and academic success across students' demographic backgrounds, personal well-being, commitments to civic engagement, and social justice. Good teaching in higher education necessitates valuing teaching and teachers and giving personal attention to the individual student, close student–teacher relationships, and the community of scholars. Together, these make a significant and critical positive difference in the core academic mission of colleges and universities, in the lives of students, and in society.

These approaches increase persistence and graduation. They contribute to student learning because students learn in a community. They contribute to intergroup engagement in a diverse society. They contribute to the academic success of underrepresented students of color, other underrepresented students, and majority students, and they also contribute to the participation of women and students of color in STEM fields.

For the benefit of students and at a time of challenge to higher education, administrators and faculty will be wise to carefully consider these powerful approaches to teaching and learning.

References

Abeles, V. (Director). (2010). *Race to nowhere* [Motion picture]. United States: New Reel Link Films.

Ancess, J. (2003). *Beating the odds: High schools as communities of commitment.* New York, NY: Teachers College Press.

Astin, A. W. (1985). *Achieving excellence in education.* San Francisco, CA: Jossey-Bass.

Astin, A., Astin, H., & Lindholm, J. (Eds.). (2011). *Cultivating the spirit: How college can enhance students' inner lives.* San Francisco, CA: John Wiley & Sons.

Bennett, D., Cornwell, G., Al-Lail, H., & Schenk, C. (2012). An education for the twenty-first century: Stewardship for a global commons. *Liberal Education, 98*(4), 34–41.

Block, P. (2008). *Community: The structure of belonging.* San Francisco, CA: Berret-Koehler.

Boyer, E. (1987). *College.* New York, NY: Harper & Row.

Boyte, H. (2004). *Everyday politics: Reconnecting citizens and public life.* Philadelphia, PA: University of Pennsylvania Press.

Chickering, A., Dalton, J., & Stamm, L. (2006). *Encouraging authenticity and spirituality in higher education.* San Francisco, CA: Jossey-Bass.

Christensen, L., & Karp, S. (2003). Rethinking our classrooms: Teaching for equity and justice. In L. Christensen & S. Karp (Eds.), *Rethinking school reform* (pp. 3–10). Milwaukee, WI: Rethinking Schools.

Christensen, R. D. (2016). *Making a difference: Residential learning community students' trajectories toward promoting social justice* (Unpublished doctoral dissertation). University of Michigan, Ann Arbor.

Cody, A. (2014). *The educator and the oligarch: A teacher challenges the Gates Foundation.* New York, NY: Garn Press.

Colby, A., Ehrlich, T., Beaumont, E., & Stephens, J. (2003). *Educating citizens: Preparing America's undergraduates for lives of moral and civic responsibility.* San Francisco, CA: Jossey-Bass.

Crowfoot, J. (2017). Toward a new pedagogy to create a sustainable future. In D. Schoem, C. Modey, & E. P. St. John (Eds.), *Teaching the whole student: Engaged learning with heart, mind, and spirit* (pp. 100–134). Sterling, VA: Stylus.

Darling-Hammond, L. (2010). *The flat world and education: How America's commitment to equity will determine our future.* New York, NY: Teachers College/ Columbia.

Deresiewicz, W. (2014). *Excellent sheep: The miseducation of the American elite and the way to a meaningful life.* New York, NY: Free Press.

Dewey, J. (1966). *Democracy and education.* New York, NY: Free Press.

Eisler, R. (2000). *Tomorrow's children.* Boulder, CO: Westview Press.

Feldman, K., & Newcomb, T. (1969). *The impact of college on students.* San Francisco, CA: Jossey-Bass.

Freire, P. (1970). *Pedagogy of the oppressed.* New York, NY: Herder & Herder.

Gabelnick, F., MacGregor, J., Matthews, R. S., & Smith, B. L. (1990). *Learning communities: Creating connections among students, faculty, and disciplines: New directions for teaching and learning* (No. 41). San Francisco, CA: Jossey-Bass.

Galura, J., Pasque, P., Schoem, D., & Howard, J. (Eds.). (2004). *Engaging the whole of service-learning, diversity and learning communities.* Ann Arbor, MI: OCSL Press.

Giroux, H. (2012). *Education and crisis of public values.* New York, NY: Peter Lang.

Goodman, P. (1964). *The community of scholars.* New York, NY: Vintage Books.

Gurasci, R., & Cornwell, G. (1997). *Democratic education in an age of difference.* San Francisco, CA: Jossey-Bass.

Gurin, P., Dey, E., Hurtado, S., & Gurin, G. (2002). Diversity and higher education: Theory and impact on educational outcomes. *Harvard Educational Review, 72*(3), 330–367.

Harward, D. (2016). *Well-being and higher education.* Washington, DC: Bringing Theory to Practice in partnership with AACU.

Huber, M., & Hutchings, P. (2004). *Integrative learning: Mapping the terrain.* New York, NY: Carnegie Foundation for the Advancement of Teaching.

Hurtado, S., Milem, J. F., Clayton-Pederson, A. R., & Allen, W. R. (1998). Enhancing campus climates for racial/ethnic diversity: Educational policy and practice. *The Review of Higher Education, 21*(3), 279–302.

Jacoby, B. (2009). *Civic engagement in higher education.* San Francisco, CA: Jossey-Bass.

Kinzie, J. (2014). Research on successful learning practices. In B. Tobolowsky (Ed.), *Paths to learning: Teaching for engagement in college*. Columbia, SC: University of South Carolina, National Resource Center.

Kirp, D. (2013). *Improbable scholars: The rebirth of a great American school system and a strategy for America's schools*. New York, NY: Oxford University Press.

Kirp, D. (2014, August 16). Teaching is not a business. *New York Times*. Retrieved from http://www.nytimes.com/2014/08/17/opinion/sunday/teaching-is-not-a-business.html?_

Kohn, A. (2004). *What does it mean to be well-educated?* Boston, MA: Beacon Books.

Kuh, G. (2008). *High-impact educational practices*. Washington, DC: AACU.

Kuh, G. D., Kinzie, J., Schuh, J. H., Whitt, E. J., & Associates. (2005). *Student success in college: Creating conditions that matter*. San Francisco, CA: Jossey-Bass.

Lantieri, L., & Patti, J. (1996). *Waging peace in our schools*. Boston, MA: Beacon Press.

Lardner, E., & Malnarich, G. (2008, July–August). A new era in learning-community work: Why the pedagogy of intentional integration matters. *Change: The Magazine of Higher Learning*, 30–37.

Lewis, A., & Diamond, J. (2015). *Despite the best intentions: How racial inequality thrives in good schools*. New York, NY: Oxford University Press.

Locks, A., & Gregerman, S. (2008). Undergraduate research as an institutional retention strategy. In R. Taraban & R. Blanton (Eds.), *Creating effective undergraduate research programs in science: The transformation from student to scientist*. New York, NY: Teachers College Press.

Manning, K., Kinzie, J., & Schuh, J. (2006). *One size does not fit all: Traditional and innovative models of student affairs practice*. New York, NY: Taylor & Francis.

Nagda, R., & Gurin, P. (2007). Intergroup dialogue: A critical-dialogic approach to learning about difference, inequality, and social justice. *New Directions for Teaching and Learning, 2007*(111), 35–45.

Nash, R., & Murray, M. (2010). *Helping college students find purpose: The campus guide to meaning-making*. San Francisco, CA: John Wiley & Sons.

Nelson, A. (2001). *Education and democracy*. Madison: University of Wisconsin Press.

New, J. (2015a, January 8). Report details microaggressions on campuses for students of color and women. *Inside Higher Ed*. Retrieved from https://www.insidehighered.com/news/2015/01/08/report-details-microaggressions-campuses-students-color-and-women

New, J. (2015b, February 5). Incoming students' "emotional health" at all-time low, survey says. *Inside Higher Ed*. Retrieved from https://www.insidehighered.com/news/2015/02/05/incoming-students-emotional-health-all-time-low-survey-says

Newmann, F., & Oliver, D. (1967). Education and community. *Harvard Educational Review, 37*(1), 61–106.

Nieto, S. (2015). *Why we teach now*. New York, NY: Teachers College Press.

Olson, K. (2007). *Wounded by school: Recapturing the joy in learning and standing up to old school culture*. New York, NY: Teachers College Press.

Palmer, P. (2007). *The courage to teach: Exploring the inner landscape of a teacher's life.* San Francisco, CA: Jossey-Bass.

Palmer, P., & Zajonc, A. (2010). *The heart of higher education: A call to renewal.* San Francisco, CA: Jossey-Bass.

Pollack, E. (2015). *The only woman in the room: Why science is still a boys' club.* Boston, MA: Beacon.

Ravitch, D. (2010). *The death and life of the great American school system: How testing and choice are determining education.* New York, NY: Basic Books.

Saltmarsh, J., & Hartley, M. (Eds.). (2011). *To serve a larger purpose: Engagement for democracy and the transformation of higher education.* Philadelphia, PA: Temple University Press.

Sarath, E. (2014). *Improvisation, creativity, and consciousness: Jazz as integral template for music, education, and society.* Albany, NY: SUNY.

Schoem, D. (1997). Intergroup relations, conflict, and community. In R. Gurasci & G. Cornwell (Eds.), *Democratic education in an age of difference* (pp. 217–225). San Francisco, CA: Jossey-Bass.

Schoem, D. (2002). Transforming undergraduate education: Moving beyond distinct undergraduate initiatives. *Change: The Magazine of Higher Learning, 34*(6), 50–55.

Schoem, D. (2004). Sustaining living learning programs. In J. Levine Laufgraben & N. Shapiro (Eds.), *Sustaining and improving learning communities* (pp. 130–156). San Francisco, CA: Jossey-Bass.

Schoem, D. (2016). Honoring the humanity of our students. In D. Harward (Ed.), *Well-being and higher education: A strategy for change and the realization of education's greater purposes.* Washington, DC: Bringing Theory to Practice in partnership with AACU.

Schoem, D., & Hurtado, S. (Eds.). (2001). *Intergroup dialogue: Deliberative democracy in school, college, community and workplace.* Ann Arbor: University of Michigan Press.

Schoem, D., Hurtado, S., Sevig, T., Chesler, M., & Sumida, S. (2001). Intergroup dialogue: Democracy at work in theory and practice. In D. Schoem & S. Hurtado (Eds.), *Intergroup dialogue: Deliberative democracy in school, college, community and workplace* (pp. 1–21). Ann Arbor: University of Michigan Press.

Sides, C., & Mrvica, A. (2007). *Internships: Theory and practice.* Amityville, NY: Baywood.

Small, J. L. (2011). *Understanding college students' spiritual identities: Different faiths, varied world views.* Cresskill, NJ: Hampton Press.

Smith, B. L., & Williams, L. (2007). *Learning communities and student affairs: Partnering for powerful learning.* Olympia, WA: Washington Center.

St. John, E. P., Daun-Barnett, N. J., & Moronski-Chapman, K. (2013). *Public policy and higher education.* New York, NY: Routledge.

Taylor, S. (2011). Engendering habits of mind and heart through integrative learning. *About Campus, 16*(5), 13–20.

Thomas, N., & Bahr, A. M. (2008). Faith and reason: Higher education's opportunities and challenges. In M. R. Diamond (Ed.), *Encountering faith in the classroom: Turning difficult discussions into constructive engagement* (pp. 3–32). Sterling, VA: Stylus.

Tinto, V. (1998). *Adapting learning communities to the needs of remedial education students*. Stanford, CA: National Center for Postsecondary Improvement, Stanford University.

Tinto, V., & Engstrom, C. (2008). Learning better together: The impact of learning communities on the persistence of low-income students. *Opportunity Matters, 1*, 5–21.

Westheimer, J. (2015). *What kind of citizen: Educating our children for the common good*. New York, NY: Teachers College Record.

Wingspread. (2005). *Declaration on religion and public life: Engaging higher education*. Racine, WI: Society for Values in Higher Education and the Johnson Foundation.

Yancey, K. B. (2009). Electronic portfolios a decade into the twenty-first century: What we know, what we need to know. *Peer Review, 11*(1), 28–32.

Zuniga, X., Nagda, B. A., Chesler, M., & Cytron-Walker, A. (2007). *Intergroup dialogue in higher education: Meaningful learning about social justice: ASHE higher education report* (Vol. 32, No. 4). San Francisco, CA: Jossey-Bass.

PART ONE

WHOLE STUDENT LEARNING
APPROACHES

I

THE WHOLE STUDENT APPROACH AS A RETENTION MODEL

Jerry A. Pattengale

My first major public address on whole person student development was an indication of the battle ahead with the academy's retention status quo. Though I was barely through my introduction, not even 10 minutes into my presentation, an older professor interrupted the packed room when she stood up, about four rows back, just off to my right. Before I could even register a response, she cussed me out. Not a mild curse, but a bitter harangue. She lambasted me and assumed to speak for the masses by asking what in the Sam Hill my research had to do with resolving the acute retention issues on campuses (three expletives omitted).

Her question was a modified and vulgar rendition of Tertullian's "What does Jerusalem have to do with Athens?" Or, restated, "What is a humanities professor doing in a behaviorists' world?" For her, all was vacuous without measurable results, such as learning or living environmental interventions with official retention or graduation correlations.

As an ancient historian, mentored by the esteemed philologist Edwin Yamauchi, I found myself in foreign and often stale territory—conferences dominated by behaviorists. A new language was required: *retention-ese*. At first, I wanted someone to hit me with a frozen salmon and awaken me from what seemed to be educational drudgery. Presentations with no regression studies, however solidly based in classical thought and humanities notions, regardless of their resonance with retention reality, were discarded as speculation. No *T*-factor analysis, no convincing leverage. Conversely, educators with brilliant data analysis on secondary or remotely connected questions were applauded (Elmore & Pattengale, 2009).

Nonetheless, I kept receiving invitations to retention conferences because of our software invention, the Virtual Advising Link System (VAL). It was a ticket to some of the nation's largest colleges and conferences. Everett Webber of Indiana Wesleyan University (IWU) and I led the development of VAL, the first web application that allowed professors to globally link entire rosters to e-mails, photos, and so on. Now, 20 years later, everyone has it, but at the time this simple data dump seemed like rocket science (and it was, based on then-slick technology and detailed assessments of faculty time-on-task in retention efforts). We globe-trotted and gave it away to countless institutions (though a major educational firm, having signed nondisclosure agreements, pilfered it and sold an adapted version under a different name—basic version for only $35,000 and advanced for $70,000). Our solid data sets showed that VAL saved faculty members considerable time. If they were being asked to put more energy into retention efforts, even with handy tools such as the *College Learning Assessment* or *Student Satisfaction Inventory* (SSI) and, later, *StrengthsQuest*, faculty time was the key variable.

During these dozens of engagements, I included a stipulation for keynoting—to give a sidebar session on whole person development. During a 1997 session in Cincinnati with Michigan State's Philip Garner, I also introduced a particular strategy within whole person development: "purpose-guided education" (Pattengale & Gardner, 2000). Although the technology sessions were fun and lively and included conscripted audiences, the purpose-guided education sessions were placed alongside a long list of other options—and yet packed. Eventually, extensive research, funded with millions of dollars from the Lilly Endowment and the Lumina Foundation, led to a robust collaboration with many behaviorists and to my priority of helping students find their "Life Wedge" (Pattengale, 2010a). Extensive research found that most often students dealt with the "purpose" question in their sophomore year, and a wave of books and articles launched from our research (Hunter et al., 2010; Reynolds, Gross, Millard, & Pattengale, 2010; Schreiner & Pattengale, 2000).

Disillusionment With Student Satisfaction as Starting Points

What I had first viewed as stale I soon came to understand as necessary— but the primary questions being researched needed changing. From the start of my new (and lasting) relationships with the behaviorist network, the educational matrix of "knowledge, skills, and dispositions" always struck me as an obvious beacon that most retention approaches avoided. Instead, they focused almost entirely on skills or "at-risk" aspects of the students' profile as determined by behaviorists' instruments. Though important, these research items rarely connected with intrinsic motivational factors—the very aspects of student success and retention—that, because of their emphasis on connecting real-world experience and students' identity and values to course content, engaged learning and integrative pedagogies are likely to enhance.

Next came my disillusionment with student satisfaction approaches, the fulcrum of most responses to attrition woes. For a few years, I gave lectures nationally on the question "Do you have an office of student success or student nondissatisfaction?" The *CPA Inventory* is my simple survey used for years with more than 400 institutions to determine the nature of their retention efforts. It simply helps to categorize institutional efforts by looking at the "*c*ommitment of resources" to student success efforts, "*p*hilosophical commitment" behind the institution's expenditures, and "*a*ssessment" choices. An "Assessment of Assessment Tool" helps with the latter area to determine overall program objectives. The basic categories within the *CPA Inventory* are as follows:

1. Academic Content (foundational facts and/or principles in an academic discipline, e.g., literature, philosophy, history)
2. Ultimate Questions (questions of purpose, life meaning and/or value, and related assignments)
3. The Learning Process (assisting with learning challenges, introducing creative pedagogy, skill sets, etc.)
4. The Learning Environment (dorm, extracurricular, library services, class size, cohort groups, structure of orientation and/or first-year courses, security, parking, etc.)

After listing their institution's top-five retention (or student success) programs based on expenditures, participants were then asked to list which of the four areas most closely aligned with those programs. Ninety-five percent of all campuses represented the third and fourth areas, those related more closely with external factors and not intrinsic motivation. When participants were asked to rank the programs on the basis of faculty or student involvement, the numbers showed little variance on their intrinsic focus (a steady 5%). During various presentations on this subject, we used the slide shown in Box 1.1.

The Assessment of Assessment Tool asks participants to list the top three tools used to measure their programs' effectiveness in assisting with student success, then to list the purpose of each assessment, and once again to see if it's targeting intrinsic or extrinsic factors.

BOX 1.1
Is your "Student Success" philosophy

1. a Student Success model (intrinsic)?
   - Begins with the student's goals in mind
   - Attempts to link student's life passion (purpose) with a vocational path

2. a Student Satisfaction model (extrinsic)?
   - Uses satisfaction surveys to determine the main issues to address
   - Interventions and preventions are focused on satisfaction scales

---

Of the 95% of institutions noted here, the most common basis for retention strategies was an SSI of some type. The results from the 1998–1999 SSI survey of 23,848 sophomores revealed that for public and private schools, content ranked the highest in importance from among dozens of choices. The results also placed three content issues among the top five in importance, similar to the ranking results of 100,000 students from all grade levels. The actual SSI content item the sophomores rated most important was "The content of courses within my major is valuable." Three other content questions rated *very important* related to the quality of instruction and faculty's subject knowledge.

Based on the SSI grid (see Figure 1.1), these high-importance ratings for content would place it and faculty's abilities and subject knowledge at the top. However, if these areas never surface among the areas of least satisfaction, then they are placed in quadrant 2 (top right)—and are never a priority in student success planning. The SSI rationale, which is similar to numerous student satisfaction tools, and very logical prima facie, is to focus an institution's top retention (or student success) efforts on those SSI items that end up in quadrant 1 (top left). It seems sensible: If these items are rated high in importance but low in satisfaction, then we should prioritize these items. In other words, these become our top retention priorities (and often our only ones for years one and two of new retention programs). The SSI protocol next uses focus groups to help reveal more about the issues and how best to address these campus shortcomings.

Any hope that answers for retention woes would come from Maynard Hutchins's (1952) *Great Books of the Western World* list in this schema is rather bleak. Use of values clarification in fueling intrinsic motivation seemed especially unlikely.[1] Colleges and universities seemed reluctant to consider the potential of an approach to student retention that acknowledged the

Figure 1.1. Student Satisfaction Inventory diagram.

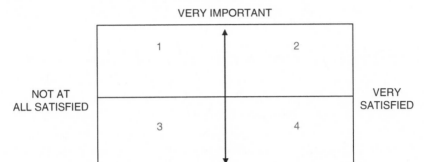

importance of engaged learning and integrative pedagogies for connecting students' values with their course of study.

Educating Faculty Nationally About the Role of Purpose in Retention

My main audience on college campuses was liberal arts faculty members, among most of whom even the definition of *retention* was unknown and, when known, was usually associated in their minds with water. With little knowledge of the issues, many of us are understandably attracted like lemmings to a very user-friendly tool like SSI. I eventually produced a basic quiz simply to help clarify some of this retention-ese for a crowd that often had been conscripted by administration to attend sessions (Pattengale, 2008b).

When asked by staff at *The Teaching Professor* (Magna Publications) to share my list of basic retention principles for faculty internationally through its broadcasts, the basic session set viewership records: "What Faculty Need to Know About Retention" (Pattengale, 2008c). The number-one retention principle, based on years of research with collaborators such as Ed St. John and others represented in this chapter's citations and decided by my colleagues at IWU who had immersed themselves in this field for many years, reflected the key role of "purpose." Their full list follows and varies from other lists but has many items in common with most lists. You will find that our faculty list several principles with purposeful and/or intrinsic motivation aspects, many of which also can be supported by engaged learning and integrative pedagogies.

1. *Life purpose:* Students with an articulated sense of life purpose, or a major life goal, are more likely to succeed in college.
2. *SAT, ACT, and GPA scores:* Students entering with higher normed academic scores are more likely to succeed in college.
3. *The first six weeks:* The first six weeks are the most important in the retention of students to college, and the first two weeks are critical to both their retention and their enthusiasm for a college.
4. *First-year orientation classes:* More than 90% of all colleges have a first-year seminar or class, and these correlate with higher retention.
5. *Student profiles:* Those with certain dispositions are more likely to succeed (i.e., intrinsic motivation, welcoming of help, respect for authority).
6. *Professor connection to orientation outcomes:* Students connecting with at least one faculty or staff member during the first two weeks of college are more likely to stay at that college.
7. *"Intrusive" retention efforts:* Students most at risk of leaving college are often unaware of or not receptive to help needed. Give it anyway.
8. *Student motivation:* Faculty need to learn how to help extrinsically motivated students think about larger questions.
9. *Early college commitments:* Students committing early to a college are more likely to succeed; those committing late in the summer or enrollment cycle are less likely to succeed.
10. *Intentional programs:* The more intentional the program for at-risk students, the more likely they are to succeed.
11. *A plan to persist:* How students complete the phrase "When the going gets tough, I do the following" is highly predictive of students' persistence rate.
12. *Common learning experiences:* Sharing experiences with other students builds needed community and correlates with higher retention.
13. *Integration of the affective and cognitive:* Experiential learning and service-learning helps to build an emotive response to curriculum and also correlates with higher retention.
14. *Student satisfaction:* This is important but is not a panacea or starting point. It's helpful to know if students are satisfied, but this is only one dynamic of student success and not the best predictor.
15. *The last-minute applicants:* Late applicants are less likely to persist.
16. *First-generation students:* Students who do not have a parent or guardian with a college degree are less likely to persist.
17. *Intentional student cohort:* Conscripted groups for learning (and for residential living) directly correlate with persistence (IWU's adult programs

have very high retention and graduation rates and all must be in cohort groups—same 15 students throughout their program).

18. *New knowledge:* New learning is inextricably linked to student motivation and persistence.
19. *First-year seminars with liberal arts basis:* Liberal arts courses assist with intrinsic motivation.
20. *Mission fit:* Students with a connection to a school's mission are more likely to persist.

The value of this list is accented by the selection of IWU into the inaugural group of Foundations of Excellence institutions, a robust external validation process associated with the work of John Gardner, Betsy Barefoot, and Randy Swing.

Lessons in Developing Whole Person Retention Programs

After I gave my first conference presentation on whole person development and key intersections with traditional college sophomores, John Gardner immediately asked me to consider writing a book on the subject in conjunction with the National Resource Center for the First-Year Experience and Students in Transition (University of South Carolina). His staff had realized that many factors occurred within this year, and they were awaiting a researcher with data established. I accepted with the condition that Laurie Schreiner could coauthor or coedit it. This seems contrary to my opening comments about the frustration with behaviorists, and especially with the student satisfaction emphasis, but I had grown to appreciate their skills in assessment. Schreiner is both a psychologist and the codeveloper of the popular SSI. She also was serving as a senior scientist for the Gallup organization (for the StrengthsQuest project) and chair and professor of Azusa Pacific's doctoral studies in higher education.

I had realized that a key both to researching and to implementing whole person development approaches is for humanities professors to work closely with behaviorists. The collaboration continues to be fruitful and enjoyable on many fronts. The first key lesson is that any major effort to address student success issues by liberal arts faculty members needs to include professors steeped in behavioral studies, most likely from psychology or education. On most campuses, the latter (or faculty from science, technology, engineering, and mathematics areas) are critical to help generate often-overlooked empirical research expected by key university stakeholders determining retention programming effectiveness (Braxton, McKinney, & Reynolds, 2006; Patton, Morelon, Whitehead, & Hossler, 2006). One of the crucial early proponents of this collaboration was Edward Zlotkowski, now emeritus professor of English and media arts at Bentley University, and senior editor of the multivolume series on service-learning called Service Learning in the Disciplines, with a volume dedicated to most key disciplines. In developing its student success philosophy, IWU found Zlotkowski's work helpful, particularly his assertion that helping students believe their life's work can improve others' lives is key to student success (Szymanski, Hadlock, & Zlotkowski, 2012; Zlotkowski, 2002). His numerous volumes on service-learning help faculty in many fields, liberal arts and otherwise, find connection with this premise. All of these efforts need benchmarking and assessing, and the collaboration between humanities professors and behaviorists complements this process. In many cases, it's a necessity.

The second key lesson is placing philosophy before logistics. If indeed my philosophical notion is correct that "the dream needs to be stronger than the struggle," then it would take a mélange of discipline experts to help establish both perspective and valid data to test this theory. The questions are different when you begin looking at philosophical starting points, and the logistics reflect how to measure them. As we saw previously in the survey that helps determine intrinsic or extrinsic student success programs, the former starts with students' goals and passions, and the latter tends to put logistics in place for changing environmental issues. These "student satisfaction" items nearly always relate to issues secondary to student goal setting, and yet entire programs become structured around such student satisfaction survey results. Related to this is the important lesson that for people to embrace an idea, they need to be able to get their mind around it. We discovered early on that "whole person" involved many dispositional questions and applications, and many professors simply are not equipped to engage such areas. Nor do many want to. With the increasing pressure by administrators and accreditors to improve retention, uninterested or unprepared faculty are conscripted to assist—often atop other duties. Simple tools are strongly recommended to assist novice retention faculty in both learning and applying effective student success principles, such as the Life Wedge diagram, list of top-20 retention principles, and student retention IQ quiz.

The third key lesson is that campuses endorse a student success philosophy by either design or default. If there is not an expressed and articulated philosophy used by the programs' framers, then the leaders default to the philosophy manifest in their selected tools. There is philosophical underpinning in all retention approaches, including Schreiner's SSI. Campuses employing the SSI as the starting point for retention efforts are likely imbibing its environmental emphasis. It's not a new approach at all but status quo. However, it is a brilliant way to categorize a predetermined list of items and visualize them. Schreiner's emphasis on satisfaction accented some of the most venerated scholars on student success. Upcraft and Schuh (2001) stated,

A third component [of their eight key ones] is assessing first-year student satisfaction, which is the cornerstone of maintaining and improving the quality of services and programs targeted to first-year students. . . . If students are dissatisfied, they will not reuse what we offer, and they will not recommend our services and programs to other students. (p. 9; see also Upcraft & Schuh, 1996)

Really? Is satisfaction with parking as important for a student as excitement for a cause he's come to endorse? Is the dining hall's food really going to trump a student's passion to help change the lives of disenfranchised young men by teaching them the financial literacy practices learned in her major? Is tweaking the options for intramural sports actually going to help a student passionate about national security more than enhancing classroom experiences on the subject?

It took years of robust studies in collaboration with Edward St. John and his colleagues (first at Indiana University and then at the University of Michigan) to collect data and assess this notion of prioritizing purpose over student satisfaction. This is challenging the usefulness of the SSI not as a tool but as the fulcrum of a student success strategy.

As outlined in my *Growth Journal* article, "Student Success or Student Non-dissatisfaction" (Pattengale, 2006), this student satisfaction (or, rather, student non-dissatisfaction) approach uses student satisfaction surveys, quantifies the results, qualifies them through focus group follow-up sessions, and then addresses the specific areas of dissatisfaction. The overarching theory is to remove dissatisfied areas, especially in areas deemed most important to the student (chosen from a preset list on the survey), in order to retain students to graduation.

Addressing student dissatisfaction may nudge retention rates a bit higher, but this approach targets second-rate causes of student attrition. Campuses that begin their retention efforts with student satisfaction surveys often focus on areas of dissatisfaction—aspects of the college experience rarely tied to student motivation. Therein is the main problem facing many well-oiled student success efforts. The removal of dissatisfaction neither guarantees satisfaction nor addresses motivation, an observation popularized by psychologist Frederick Herzberg (Accel Team Development, 2005; Herzberg, 1991; Pattengale, 2006).

At the end of IWU's inaugural year of implementing its retention plan based on the SSI results, we were holding focus groups with a group representing a large cohort of nursing students. The key item that surfaced in the SSI's quadrant 1 (*very important* and *not at all satisfied*) was library services. From all other assessments, our students' library experiences were positive. Keep in mind that we were trying to determine the best intervention based on the SSI's philosophy that would keep these students in school. Turns out, they were frustrated that at high homework times there weren't enough Xerox machines, and the ones present were coin operated. That was the smoking gun we had paid big bucks for, and the number-one intervention according to SSI that would help these students. It was helpful, and we changed the machines immediately. The learning experience for all of us was good. But were the Xerox machines a game changer for any of the students? No. Rather, our hunches (and later research tracking 1,700 students over four years) were that these students were intrinsically motivated at some point to enter nursing. They wanted to help people in times of pain. To bring joy. To assist families on the mission field with basic medical needs. And a host of altruistic notions, of humanitarian goodwill, of their life making a difference. Their life purpose was, in their mind at that point in their journey, tied to nursing. Enhancing that motivation was key. There were still challenges, from learning disabilities to first-generation adjustments, and attentive programs were needed to address them. But the key to persistence was apart from this scaffolding approach. Even when the scaffolding is removed, intrinsically motivated students are more likely to persist than those who are not. And a key correlate with an intrinsic motivation, central to a whole person, integrative approach to student retention, is discovering one's life purpose (see Figure 1.2).

An Unusual Setting for the Formation of Student Success's Success

Halfway between Indianapolis and Fort Wayne, IWU is "the Marion miracle." It's one of the largest Christian universities in the nation, with around 15,000 full-time students, 17 branch campuses, no debt, $10–$20 million revenue over expenses annually, and a gorgeous neo-Georgian campus in the nondescript city of Marion (population 27,000). The endowment has also increased by more than $100 million in the past few years, during a down economy.

Accenting the miracle is the socioeconomic setting. Marion is riddled with urban blight and hundreds of homes on the demolition list. It was fortunate not to have been highlighted in *Roger and Me* (Moore, 1989) instead of Flint, Michigan. It's the site of America's last public lynching in 1930 and an infamous photograph that haunts the great gains in race relations. Suffice it to say, the Marion setting is unlike my graduate alma mater in Oxford, Ohio, where a long tradition of greatness, occasional celebrity alumni, brick streets, and rolling hills rival other college settings like Samford, Hope, and Virginia. Rather, somehow IWU has flourished in a declining city with serious cyclical poverty.

Figure 1.2. *Finding Purpose* by Ron Mazellan.

Note. This illustration is the image associated with the purpose-guided education implemented on IWU's campus. It hangs in the entryway of IWU's Center for Life Calling and Leadership, which was formed as a result of the student success research noted in this chapter. Ron Mazellan is a *New York Times* best-selling author, illustrator, and fine arts professor at Indiana Wesleyan University.

The miracle is that on the southern side of town, a picturesque, vibrant campus continues to draw 4,000 traditional students annually and 11,000 students in various other programs. It has become a founding institution in a purpose-guided approach to student success—a rather intentional manifestation of whole person development, which places a priority on engaged learning to help students integrate their values with their vocational goals.

You don't have to walk very far on the main campus to see thematic signs that begin to tell a remarkable story. From bricks and mortar, literally, to monikers for theaters, majors, programs, and mission statements, whole person attention abounds. *The Purpose-Guided Student: Dream to Succeed* (Pattengale, 2010a) is my college textbook that captures the undergirding philosophy imbibed in these various facets of IWU and reflects the curriculum underpinning IWU's 20% retention and graduation rate increases.[2] IWU's purposeful programming attracted national research projects, tens of millions of dollars in grants, and the inherently good result of the students' success as top priority (Pattengale, 2010a). *Why I Teach: And Why It Matters to My Students* (Pattengale, 2008d) is my short introduction of this purposeful approach for faculty members. Bill Millard (2012), founder of IWU's Center for Life Calling and Leadership, also has a student text used by thousands espousing this same whole student approach: *Explorer's Guide: Starting Your College Journey With a Sense of Purpose.*

And there's the first glimpse of the visual reminder of this approach, a state-of-the-art facility in our massive student center boasting an unmistakable mission, the Center for Life Calling and Leadership. All first-year students take the LDR150 course, assisting them with finding and articulating their life purpose. Other universities, such as the University of Alabama, have benefited from this work (Robinson, 2015).

Across the mall's corridor that parses this modernish interior is the neon sign above the door of the Globe Theatre, one of the main lecture halls that for years housed the first-year course, that says, "Becoming World Changers."

A short walk from the student center is the residence hall village flanked by two extraordinary ventures: the mentor halls. Based on this whole person philosophy, and longevity studies showing their retention effectiveness, are two 300-bed halls that house mentors on one side and protégés on the other (Pattengale, Sprowl, Parker, & Thompson, 2008). And in various corners of academic and residential buildings are "life coaches" (affiliate liberal arts faculty) meeting with protégés.

The Whole Campus and the Whole Person

Upon arriving at IWU 20 years ago, I found a school celebrating a decade of being the state's fastest growing university, which continued for another decade. The president hired me as an internal consultant of sorts to help the university reach higher levels of performance in key dashboard areas (and to create a viable dashboard). Our world seemed to screech to a halt after our first comprehensive self-study, along with a barrage of professional opinions. Although we had an amazing recruiting machine for all programs, we discovered that on the traditional campus, the four-year graduation rates were abysmal, around 36%, and that retention rates were also pitiful for such a remarkable campus and staff, around only 68%.

The president and board immediately demanded fixes, especially realizing the cost of recruiting students only to put them into a revolving door— and the inherently poor approach we were taking to address their needs. The main program targeting the traditionally at-risk students among the applicant pool was the Summer Success program, having finished its eighth year. This intensive program brought these students to campus prior to the start of the semester and worked on skills and weaknesses. If students completed this intentional residential program, they were granted provisional acceptance, and if they showed ability after the first semester, but no later than the second, they were granted nonprobationary status. Our assessment uncovered an ethically gray area: students spending money for a chance that wasn't materializing. After eight years, only one student had persisted past the first college year. The only consolation was that the one student graduated and had a remarkable testimony, but nearly 200 others were out of college and saddled with debt. We closed our main retention program.

During the late 1990s, a confluence of three key things occurred while IWU strategized to address retention woes: an interest in whole person development, an emphasis on finding one's life purpose, and a board of trustees passionate about a rearticulated university mission linked to both of these; that is, developing world changers.

The next fall, in 1999, the course UNV180, "Becoming World Changers: Christianity and Contemporary Issues," became the required first-year course for all students on the main campus (most were traditional-age students). This three-credit liberal arts course met key university mission objectives while addressing student success principles. One of its key integrative components was to help students identify worthwhile causes around their value systems and understand their life purpose and how it relates to their college decisions. The IWU faculty voted unanimously not only to implement this (much to the joy of the board of trustees) but also to make it the fulcrum of the entire traditional campus's curriculum. Three years later, a version was added to the nontraditional curriculum (UNV111).

Simultaneously, the central student success committee, empowered with significant Lilly Endowment funding, led the transition of the campus to outcomes-based assessment. The fulcrum for the campus remains "World Changer Objectives," used to assess the entire campus mission. In short, UNV180 provides a common experience among all new students. It introduces them to outstanding professors (selected from both academic and student development staff with appropriate degrees). And it places them in small sections and thereby they are guaranteed a smaller class and the opportunity to get to know a professor and a peer leader. Students learn the university's mission and how it drives the various academic areas. This includes the integration of faith and learning. One of the key components is to help students integrate their life purpose with their college decisions.

On IWU's traditional campus from 1997 to 2002, our retention rates grew from 68% to 81%. The first-year course was implemented in 1997 and shows the strongest single correlation to this pronounced growth; that is, 8% in one year. Four-year graduation rates jumped as well, growing from 36% to 54% with the introduction of this first-year seminar. The sustained increases reflect remarkable gains in light of the student profile. Average SAT scores fluctuated around 1090, and IWU's first-generation population was more than 30%. The implementation of the UNV180 course also correlated with a 30% drop in academic dismissals among first-year students from first to second semesters.

Among our battery of tools to get a handle on our issues were the NSSE, CIRP, SSI, and Hope Scale and in-house tools. However, in this process we realized a curricular area of inordinate success compared to the rest of the campus, with four-year graduation rates double that of many other cohorts. The outlier curricula focused on helping students find their life passion. A huge boost came in 2002–2003 with our participation in the Foundations of Excellence program through the Policy Center on the First Year of College, now the John N. Gardner Institute for Excellence in Undergraduate Education.

Numerous interventions and preventions were put in place, including but not limited to (a) the Center for Life Calling and Leadership, (b) a dean of mentoring, (c) assistant resident directors with special skills in addressing life purpose discussions, and (d) a central part of our first-year seminar on finding one's life purpose in the context of an introduction to the liberal arts.

The Life Wedge and the Hope Scale: Practical Tools for the Whole Person

Nearly two decades have passed since the professor cussed me out for suggesting this alternative approach to addressing retention needs. The most common outburst I've heard since then is "You're the Wedge guy!" and other such phrases. My concept of the Life Wedge resonated. From large color posters to little handouts, auxiliary items related to the Life Wedge concept had been shared with hundreds of colleges. While I was speaking at a conference in Georgia, a professor from Southern Georgia Technical College brought me a set of heavy Life Wedges that her engineering students cut from metal. The visualization and implication of these whole person ideas remains crucial to its success.

As outlined in *Why I Teach* (Pattengale, 2008d) and *The Purpose-Guided Student* (Pattengale, 2010a), the Life Wedge operationalizes my maxim, based on the research noted in this chapter: "The dream needs to be stronger than the struggle." Much of the curricular and advising efforts around *The*

Purpose-Guided Student are to help identify mature dreams and to self-identify key civic notions and classification of noble and ignoble causes.

Two Life Wedge diagrams are used in this schema. *Your Ideal Wedge* is aspirational based on articulating your dream. *Your Real Wedge* reflects an assessment of what you're actually doing with your time and where such a path leads.

Your Ideal Wedge is usually simple and clean and serves as an articulation of students' life purpose and their goals and dreams. It also provides "an uncluttered outline of the skills, activities, and experiences you should pursue to keep your wedge sharp and narrow, and keep you moving toward those goals" (Pattengale, 2008d, p. 7). Figure 1.3 shows the Life Wedge diagram used by students to plan their top priorities. Although a series of steps helps them to do this, the basic formula begins with their focus on a life purpose (number 1 on the diagram). If that is not known, then they are asked to put a general cause that they find appealing.

The difference between Your Ideal Wedge and Your Real Wedge is that of starting points. Your Real Wedge fills in the wedge (number 2 area on the diagram) based on actual time allotments from a self-study of time usage, and these activities drive the wedge (one's life path) toward some (usually

Figure 1.3. Your Ideal Wedge, where the goal or life purpose (number 1) drives one's planning.

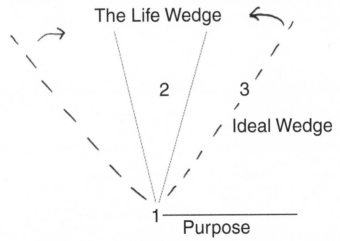

Note. The hash marks show the need for individuals to narrow their life wedge for more effectiveness in reaching their goal. From *The Issues Affecting Sophomores: How to Help Students Make Successful Transitions From First to Second Year*, by J. A. Pattengale, 2009b March, presentation at Southeast Missouri State University, Cape Gerardo, MO.

haphazard) target (number 1) instead of the ideal philosophy that has the goal of determining the priority of activities.

Figure 1.4, on noble and ignoble causes, helps students self-select such commitments and begin thinking of worthy causes. On the Your Ideal Wedge diagram, number 2 (inside the wedge) are the top five commitments needed to help get to number 1, which is the students' key goal. Those activities in number 3 are helpful but not as high of a priority. Often, the process helps students discover that many items in number 3 of Your Ideal Wedge are actually in number 2 of Your Real Wedge, and vice versa.

Your Real Wedge reflects more of what's on your Outlook calendar and list of actual activities at day's end. "Committee meetings, errands, social commitments, doctor appointments, grocery shopping, paying the bills, and all the other responsibilities of real life can easily fill up your wedge, dulling and widening it. The challenge is to bring the two as close together as possible" (Pattengale, 2008d, p. 7). In Your Real Wedge, the starting point is not at the bottom of the wedge like in Your Ideal Wedge but often inside the diagramed wedge (number 2) or outside (number 3). Serendipitous or nonstrategic commitments often drive one's Life Wedge and will likely lead to a target. In Your Real Wedge, students look at their actual commitments (taken from a time assessment exercise tracking the largest blocks of times outside of sleeping), then envision where their wedge is pointing and where they'll likely end up by default (see Figure 1.5).

Of the battery of tools used, the one that most resonated with our work was the Hope Scale (Ihrke, 2000; Snyder, 1994; see also Curry, Snyder,

Figure 1.4. The student's rating of causes.

Rating of Causes					
A significant waste of resources	Definitely unimportant	Appears to be unimportant	Somewhat important	Definitely important	An optimum use of resources
Only causes at least "definitely important" and "definitely positive" can also be "noble."					

Ignoble	Definitely negative	Somewhat negative	Somewhat positive	Definitely positive	Noble
Only causes at least "definitely negative" and "definitely important" are usually considered "ignoble."					

Note. From *The Purpose-Guided Student: Dream to Succeed,* by J. A. Pattengale, 2010a, New York, NY: McGraw-Hill, p. 55.

Figure 1.5. Life Wedge concept adapted for first-year student posters at Indiana Wesleyan University.

Note. From *The Purpose-Guided Student: Dream to Succeed*, by J. A. Pattengale, 2010a, New York, NY: McGraw-Hill. Copyright Jerry Pattengale and Gary Philips.

Cook, Ruby, & Rehm, 1997; Pattengale, 2003a, 2003b; Snyder, 1995, 1996, 2002). The late C. R. Snyder, my friend through mutual research interests, expended much of his career looking at student motivation—a key to our whole person development interventions and preventions. Snyder (1995) noted that the common process among interventions promoting positive growth is that "they attempt to increase the sense of agency and pathways that people have for the goals in their lives" (p. 359). Our team found his

Hope Scale to be one of the simplest tools in targeting students who are at risk because of low motivation. Research has shown how students complete the following statement is an indicator of their success prospects: "When the going gets tough, I _____." Snyder's work sheds considerable light on this response. And he gave the Hope Scale free to help structure responses.

Underpinning his research was the notion that "high-hope individuals" typically

- clearly conceptualize their goals;
- envision one major pathway to a desired goal and can generate alternative pathways, especially when the original one is blocked; and
- perceive that they will actively employ pathways in pursuit of their goals (Snyder, 1996).

In my curriculum on motivation, I use the actions of heroes to help students understand the dynamics of their passion and direction (Pattengale, 2010a). Likewise, Snyder studied what high-hope people say and do.

The Hope Scale contains a total of 12 items, a fraction of the lengthy student surveys. The following eight items are the ones actually measured within the instrument. The designation of questions is in parentheses. Following the essence of Snyder's (Snyder, 1995) philosophy, the questions related to willpower are labeled "agency," and those related to waypower are labeled "pathways."

1. I can think of many ways to get out of a jam. (Pathways)
2. I energetically pursue my goals. (Agency)
3. There are lots of ways around any problem. (Pathways)
4. I can think of many ways to get the things in life that are most important to me. (Pathways)
5. Even when others get discouraged, I know I can find a way to solve the problem. (Pathways)
6. My past experiences have prepared me well for my future. (Agency)
7. I've been pretty successful in life. (Agency)
8. I meet the goals that I set for myself. (Agency)

Participants rate each item from 1 (*definitely false*) to 4 (*definitely true*) and are given a Hope Score. The Hope Scale's simplicity, reflecting one of the lessons noted about clarity, continues to be a valuable resource in this journey to assist students with their sense of life purpose, for the most part in our approach, by helping them visualize how they are going to stay with Your Ideal Wedge (see Figure 1.6).

Figure 1.6. Michigan State University mural based on Jerry Pattengale's mantra, "The dream needs to be stronger than the struggle."

Note. In an open competition for students involved in the programs of MSU's Career and Placement Center, this mural won first prize for visual representation of the center's mission to help students visualize and realize their dreams. It was hung in the center's entryway, which was also home to the Collegiate Employment Research Institute under the directorship of Philip Gardner.

Conclusion

The interest in the whole person approach to student success continues to show measurable retention results at IWU, with its record retention rate set in fall 2014. The faculty continue to find multiple ways to address the questions and issues noted in this chapter related to life purpose, particularly through the use of engaged learning and integrative pedagogies across the curriculum. Though this campus approach is complex and has 20 years' worth of research and measured interventions, the philosophy is certainly transferable to any campus. Some of the tools, such as the Life Wedge and Hope Scale, may help, and some iteration of the Center for Life Calling and Leadership may be adaptable.

Any student success council (or board or steering committee) will likely read a wide swath of books and studies and hopefully will also consider the sources noted here. It is incumbent on these leaders to involve a healthy mix of professors from both the humanities and the behavioral sciences. From benchmarking to tracking measurable aspects of objectives within the dispositions area, the purposeful philosophical approach noted in this chapter needs valid assessment measures—and this faculty collaboration can help ensure them. It's imperative that a well-informed student success council embraces a philosophy and doesn't let logistics determine its course. By design or default, its plans will espouse a philosophy. And if it's attached to aspects of the students' journey that intersect with intrinsic motivation, with intentionality in helping them find goals integrated with their passions, our research shows that such an approach has a viable chance of being successful.

Reflection Questions

1. What student success or retention strategies does your campus currently use? How has your campus assessed the effectiveness of these strategies?
2. As an instructor, in what ways have you seen the impact of students' sense of life purpose on their ability to be successful in postsecondary education? What other dispositions, in your view, seem to make a difference in student success?
3. As an instructor, what opportunities do you provide students to integrate course materials and their interests and values into a larger sense of life calling or vocation? In what ways have you found such integration to be valuable to students?
4. How might faculty in the liberal arts and faculty from the behavioral sciences collaborate on your campus to develop and, just as important, assess your student retention efforts? What promising opportunities exist for these efforts? What are potential barriers or obstacles to them?
5. What is the difference between student satisfaction models of retention and whole person development models? How might these models enhance or compete with each other?

Notes

1. For more of my thoughts on this matter, see "What Are Universities For? The Contested Terrain of Moral Education" (Pattengale, 2010b) and "The Big Questions: Have Our Colleges and Universities Lost Sight of Their Purpose?" (Pattengale, 2009a), a review of Anthony Kronman's *Education's End: Why Our Colleges and Universities Have Given Up on the Meaning of Life* (Yale University Press, 2008). See also Pattengale (2008a), "Motivating Millennials and Digital Natives,"

and Pattengale (2008c), "What Faculty Need to Know About Retention." See more at www.facultyfocus.com/articles/teaching-and-learning/the-student-retention-iq-quiz/#sthash.CdT8zgIE.dpuf.

2. This is well documented at IWU and is also discussed in *Exploring the Evidence* volumes (Millard, Garner, & Pattengale, 2007), the *Indiana Project on Academic Success* reports and presentations (Bloomington, IN: Education Department, 2004–2006, funded by the Lumina Foundation), and regular grant reports to the Lilly Endowment, Inc. (2000–2007).

References

Accel Team Development. (2005). Frederick Herzberg. Retrieved from http://www.accel-team.com/human_relations/hrels_05_herzberg.html

Braxton, J. M., McKinney, J. S., & Reynolds, P. J. (2006). Cataloguing institutional efforts to understand and reduce college student departure. *New Directions for Institutional Research*, *2006*(130), 25–32.

Curry, L. A., Snyder, C. R., Cook, D. L., Ruby, B. C., & Rehm, M. (1997). Role of hope in academic and sport achievement. *Journal of Personality and Social Psychology*, *73*(6), 1257–1267.

Elmore, T. (Moderator), & Pattengale, J. A. (2009, June). *Understanding the philosophy behind* The purpose-guided student [Film]. Atlanta, GA: National Leadership Forum.

Herzberg, F. (1991). *Herzberg on motivation*. New York, NY: Penton Media.

Hunter, M. S., Tobolowsky, B. F., Gardner, J. N., Evenbeck, S. E., Pattengale, J. A., Schaller, M., & Schreiner, L. A. (2010). *Helping sophomores succeed: Understanding and improving the second-year experience*. San Francisco, CA: Jossey-Bass.

Ihrke, H. L. (2000). *Hoping and coping: Exploring the relationship between a new model of hope and successful transition to college life* (Unpublished junior thesis). Indiana Wesleyan University, Marion, Indiana.

Maynard Hutchins, R. (1952). *Great books of the Western world* (Vols. 1–54). Chicago, IL: Encyclopedia Britannica.

Millard, B. (2012). *Explorer's guide: Starting your college journey with a sense of purpose*. Dubuque, IA: Kendall Hunt.

Millard, B., Garner, J. B., & Pattengale, J. (2007). The exploration of purpose. In *Exploring the evidence III*. Columbia, SC: National Resource Center, University of South Carolina.

Moore, M. (Director). (1989). *Roger and me* [Motion picture]. United States: Dog Eat Dog Films.

Pattengale, J. A. (2003a, April 17). Shooting for the right goals: Keeping students satisfied not the same as helping them succeed. *Chronicle-Tribune*. (Republished in *Buck Creek,* pp. 23–26, by J. A. Pattengale, 2013, Oklahoma City, OK: Dust-Jacket Press)

Pattengale, J. A. (2003b, February). *Student success or student non-dissatisfaction: Building dreams stronger than struggles*. Plenary address at the Indiana Project on

Retention Conference, Indiana University and the Lumina Foundation, IUPUI, Indianapolis, IN.

Pattengale, J. A. (2006). Student success or student non-dissatisfaction. *Growth Journal, 6*(1), 13–25.

Pattengale, J. A. (2008a, May). *Motivating millennials and digital natives.* Online seminar, Magna Publications, Madison, WI.

Pattengale, J. A. (2008b, December). The student retention IQ quiz. *Faculty Focus.* Retrieved from http://www.facultyfocus.com/articles/teaching-and-learning/the-student-retention-iq-quiz/

Pattengale, J. A. (2008c, November). *What faculty need to know about retention.* Online seminar, Magna Publications, Madison, WI.

Pattengale, J. A. (2008d). *Why I teach: And why it matters to my students.* New York, NY: McGraw-Hill.

Pattengale, J. A. (2009a, November–December). The big questions: Have our colleges and universities lost sight of their purpose? [Review of the book *Education's end: Why our colleges and universities have given up on the meaning of life* by A. Kronman]. *Books and Culture.* Retrieved from http://www.booksandculture.com/articles/2009/novdec/thebigquestions.html

Pattengale, J. A. (2009b, March). *The issues affecting sophomores: How to help students make successful transitions from first to second year.* Presentation at Southeast Missouri State University, Cape Gerardo, MO.

Pattengale, J. A. (2010a). *The purpose-guided student: Dream to succeed.* New York, NY: McGraw-Hill.

Pattengale, J. A. (2010b, July–August). What are universities for? The contested terrain of moral education [Review of the book *Debating moral education: Rethinking the role of the modern university* by E. Kiss & J. P. Euben (Eds.)]. *Books and Culture.* Retrieved from http://www.booksandculture.com/articles/2010/julaug/universitiesfor.html

Pattengale, J., & Gardner, P. (2000, November). *Intrinsic motivation.* Seminar at the National Conference for Students in Transition, Cincinnati, OH.

Pattengale, J. A., Sprowl, D., Parker, K., & Thompson, R. (2008, January). The purpose-guided campus: Homework to mentoring hall. *Recruitment and Retention in Higher Education.*

Patton, L. D., Morelon, C., Whitehead, D. M., & Hossler, D. (2006). Campus-based retention initiatives: Does the emperor have clothes? *New Directions for Institutional Research, 2006*(130), 9–24. doi:10.1002/ir.176

Reynolds, P. J., Gross, J. P. K., Millard, B., & Pattengale, J. (2010). Using longitudinal mixed-methods research to look at undeclared students. *New Directions for Institutional Research, 2010*(S2), 53–66. doi:10.1002/ir.372

Robinson, B. (2015, Spring). Guiding light: Ellen Pate helps students find passions, develop career paths. *Capstone: University of Alabama,* pp. 16–17.

Schreiner, L., & Pattengale, J. (Eds.). (2000). *Visible solutions for invisible students: Helping sophomores succeed* (Monograph 31). Columbia: University of South Carolina, National Resource Center for the First-Year Experience and Students in Transition.

Snyder, C. R. (1991). *Conceptualizing, measuring, and nurturing hope*. Retrieved from http://onlinelibrary.wiley.com/doi/10.1002/j.1556-6676.1995.tb01764.x/epdf

Snyder, C. R. (1994). *The psychology of hope: You can get there from here.* New York, NY: Free Press.

Snyder, C. R. (1995). Conceptualizing, measuring, and nurturing hope. *Journal of Counseling and Development, 73*, 355–360.

Snyder, C. R. (1996). To hope, to lose, and to hope again. *Journal of Personal and Interpersonal Loss, 1*, 1–16.

Snyder, C. R. (2002). Hopeful choices: A school counselor's guide to hope theory. *ASCA Professional School Counseling, 5*(5), 298–307.

Szymanski, D. W., Hadlock, C. R., & Zlotkowski, E. A. (2012). Using public sector research projects to engage undergraduates. *Council of Undergraduate Research Quarterly, 33*(2), 19–26.

Upcraft, M. L., & Schuh, J. H. (1996). *Assessment in student affairs: A guide for practitioners.* San Francisco, CA: Jossey-Bass.

Upcraft, M. L., & Schuh, J. H. (2001). Assessing the first-year student experience: A framework. In R. L. Swing (Ed.), *Proving and improving: Strategies for assessing the first college year* (Monograph 33, pp. 7–9). Columbia: University of South Carolina, National Resource Center for the First-Year Experience and Students in Transition.

Zlotkowski, E. (Ed.). (2002). *Service-learning and the first-year experience: Preparing students for personal success and civic responsibility* (Monograph 34). Columbia: University of South Carolina, National Resource Center for the First-Year Experience and Students in Transition.

2

INCORPORATING SOCIAL JUSTICE INTO TEACHING

An Integrative Pedagogy Approach

Kathleen Manning

A s professors and instructors, we have deep-seated ideas about how to generate high-quality teaching and learning. These ideas come from our personal experience as students, particularly the lecture, an instructor-centered approach to teaching and learning. In contrast, "integrative learning requires new ways of thinking about teaching, learning, and assessment and the development of new skills" (DeZure, Babb, & Waldmann, 2005, p. 28). In integrative learning, the passivity of the lecture is supplanted with the activity of engaged learning. Detachment is foregone in favor of meaning-making, and the isolation of higher education's ivory tower fades as students make connections to their communities through practice and experience.

In this chapter, I use my 25 years of teaching graduate students in a higher education and student affairs program and undergraduate students in race and culture classes to illustrate integrative learning concepts. Using ideas similar to the integrative pedagogy goal of promoting coherence across the learning experience (DeZure et al., 2005), I sought to infuse social justice ideas across the students' experiences in the master's program. During my journey as a professor, the master's program in which I worked evolved from attracting majority-White cohorts to a proud record of enrolling extremely diverse cohorts by race, class, gender, sexual orientation, religion, and diverse identities. In this chapter, I use vignettes to illustrate the ways integrative pedagogy was and was not incorporated into my teaching and learning in a social justice context. Integrative pedagogy is a particularly apt approach to social justice because of the emphasis on student centeredness; interdisciplinary subject matter; and the current societal need for greater understanding of different cultures, backgrounds, and ways of being.

The vignettes offered here are composites of experiences from my teaching in several classes at different institutions. They do not represent any one student, university, or event but instead illustrate common dilemmas and situations I encountered as a professor. The observations I make here should be understood in the context of the standpoint from which they were written. As a White, heterosexual, middle-class, highly educated woman, I possess privileges that many others do not have. If we are to make any progress on social justice, we must be clear about the contexts from which we speak. The following vignettes are mine alone. I do not claim to speak for others, including those with backgrounds and sets of characteristics similar to mine. I do not speak for the students in the classes from which I draw these experiences. Any observations about their reactions and behavior are made from my perspective alone.

Through these vignettes and the chapter narrative, I seek to convey the joys and sorrows of teaching from social justice and integrative pedagogy perspectives. The joys come from opening up conversations often taboo and commonly painful in U.S. society. The sorrows come from the struggle to move beyond the blindness of privilege integral to my White racial identity and the occasional hopelessness that can arise from the struggle to teach from a social justice perspective.

Integrative Pedagogy Defined

The integrative pedagogy initiatives, most notably spearheaded by the Association of American Colleges & Universities (AAC&U) and the Carnegie Foundation for the Advancement of Teaching, arose from undergraduate curriculum reform efforts. These two organizations described the purpose of integrative pedagogy as an effort to develop students as

> "integrative thinkers who can see connections in seemingly disparate information and draw on a wide range of knowledge to make decisions," students who can "adapt the skills learned in one situation to problems encountered in another" [AAC&U, 2002]. . . . [They are] learners prepared for the twenty-first-century world: who are intentional about the process of acquiring learning, empowered by the mastery of intellectual and practical skills, informed by knowledge from various disciplines, and responsible for their actions and those of society. (Huber & Hutchings, 2004, p. iv)

Ferren and Anderson (2016) further defined *integrative learning* as "an empowering developmental process through which students synthesize knowledge across curricular and cocurricular experiences to develop new concepts, refine values and perspectives in solving problems, master transferable skills, and cultivate self-understanding" (pp. 33–34).

In this chapter, concepts from these authors are paired with vignettes to highlight the use of integrative pedagogy in the classroom. Because the techniques and practices of integrative pedagogy situate the student as the focus of the educational effort, they are particularly applicable to teaching in student affairs and other professional education curricula. At the heart of integrative pedagogies is the effort to meet the needs of students—to start where they are rather than where a professor might imagine or want them to be. When using integrative learning, students are placed in the center with their development and ability to make meaning as primary. Instructors and students collaborate so that students can employ their skills and abilities to make crucial connections (Gale, 2006). This approach is apt for student affairs graduate programs that use theory to practice as a means to advance professional education. Integrative learning urges students to "draw connections between concepts, integrate multiple skill sets, and offers practical learning tools that can be applied to a variety of academic and professional contexts" (Ferren & Anderson, 2016, p. 37). The practice opportunities in student affairs professional preparation programs through internships, assistantships, work experience, and volunteer experiences, coupled with theory gained through academic study, closely align with the goals of integrative learning.

Although integrative pedagogy and engaged learning can occur through a variety of means, common undergraduate-related integrative practices include first-year seminars, capstone seminars, service-learning, cocurricular activities, and cross-campus initiatives. Graduate education classroom activities and assignments use these and other techniques such as portfolios, journal writing, and self-assessment to achieve integrative learning. Through these practices, students connect and apply learning across different contexts and times with the goal of inspiring personal liberation and social empowerment (Huber & Hutchings, 2004). The liberatory and empowerment goals of integrative pedagogy make it a challenging yet particularly appropriate approach to teaching from a social justice perspective. The emphasis on personal meaning-making and the goal of "addressing major issues that challenge students" (Ferren & Anderson, 2016, p. 37) further connects integrative learning and social justice. Often in classes taught from a social justice perspective, the professor's and students' emotional and personal perspectives are challenged by class content and practices. Students' needs, identities, and beliefs clash with those of the other students and the professor. Students' levels of awareness regarding their and each other's identities and histories can create class dynamics that require a pedagogy that can flexibly meet the needs of students wherever they are in their development. Students' level of commitment to social justice issues and the extent of their knowledge about history and current events create a complex mix of competing demands and priorities. The professor's characteristics including age, generational status, race, sexual orientation, and a host of other personal identifiers further add to the mix.

Vignette Number 1: "I'm Not Here to Brainwash You"

Experience teaching a graduate-level class, "Cultural Pluralism in Higher Education," and conducting antiracism trainings hadn't eased the anxiety I experienced in the first few classes of a new section of the undergraduate class "Race and Culture." The students' obvious suspicion and defensiveness made it clear that they were skeptical. Race is often a taboo subject in the United States, and here we were, talking about race. Nothing in their previous educational experience prepared them for this. Students of color feared being offended and abused by students who were either aware and insensitive or unaware and naïve about their privilege; White students feared being called "racist." All students most likely wondered why this White woman was teaching a class about race.

After several years of teaching, I had developed an introduction intended to create a spirit of openness in the class. I announced that I was there not to "brainwash" anyone but instead to share information often disregarded from history and social sciences books. At the end of class, it was up to them to make a decision about where they stood. This announcement was accompanied by a personal confession— one likely rarely heard from a professor. I revealed my upbringing by parents who daily used racial slurs and hateful depictions of African Americans. When a student claimed, "Racial slurs were never used in my home," I disclosed that those hateful expressions were part and parcel of my everyday childhood existence. Each time I made this confession, students of color appeared to be more curious and less skeptical about my motives. The shoulders of White students dropped, and their bodies relaxed more. To the students of color, I hoped to become more authentic, someone who was trying to honestly unlearn her oppressive ways. Someone working to confront the horrors of race relations in the United States. To the White students, I hoped to convey that I wasn't merely a racial justice crusader but a person who struggled with the same questions they had. Questions they had but did not feel safe to raise in previous classes.

For all students with targeted identities, I hoped my openness would create a classroom climate that enabled us to have authentic cross-racial dialogue. Although I believed the information they learned and exercises they undertook in classes like "Race and Culture" would place the White students "on the right side of history," my approach to fairness and equality meant that this was a journey only the students could take. By connecting my background and personal history with the goals and content of the class, I wanted to help students "see connections in seemingly disparate information and draw on a wide range of knowledge to make decisions" (Huber & Hutchings, 2004, p. iv). I did not want the students to simply take my word regarding the need for all to work on social justice. I wanted them to learn the information and make their own choices about how the history and concepts we studied connected to their personal experience.

Theory to Practice

Like other professional education, higher education and student affairs master's programs were founded with theory to practice as central to the educational effort (Evans, Forney, Guido, Patton, & Renn, 2009; Parker, Widick, & Knefelkamp, 1978; Patton, McEwen, Rendón, & Howard-Hamilton, 2007; Upcraft, 1994). These programs combine administration, teaching, human development, and other content in ways that ask students to balance theory and practice. The student who would become a practitioner in higher education and student affairs cannot be successful without an understanding of theory and practice. As professional education with an experiential, practical component, the integrative pedagogy goal of applying the classroom learning to "outside" contexts was embedded in the original curricular design of higher education and student affairs programs.

For graduate programs with theory to practice and social justice as components of the curriculum, integrative pedagogy is a powerful method. Higher education and student affairs professionals work with students, faculty, and administrators from a wide range of identities, backgrounds, and experiences. Knowledge of how to interact in this rich environment is crucial for success in today's higher education world. The globally connected approach of integrative pedagogy provides means to draw experiences into the classroom that allow students to engage with the content in unique and meaningful ways.

> Integrative learning comes in many varieties: connecting skills and knowledge from multiple sources and experiences; applying theory to practice in

various settings; utilizing diverse and even contradictory points of view; and, understanding issues and positions contextually. . . . Integrative experiences often occur as learners address real-world problems, unscripted and sufficiently broad to require multiple areas of knowledge and multiple modes of inquiry, offering multiple solutions and benefiting from multiple perspectives. (Carnegie Foundation & AAC&U, 2004, p. 1)

From an integrative pedagogical perspective with a social justice foundation, students can integrate their learning across the theoretical and practical aspects of the curriculum. The theory component emerges from the classroom, assignments, literature, and research. The theories in use by the practitioner partners are an additional source of theory for the students. The practice part of the theory-to-practice continuum entails assistantships, practicum, experiential classroom exercises, and prior work experience. Students in higher education and student affairs master's programs have firsthand experiences and practice with initiatives that increase social justice in higher education settings. When one incorporates integrative pedagogy techniques into social-justice-oriented classrooms, the theory can be readily applied to practice in the assistantship and practica contexts. Likewise, their practice can be readily applied to content and theory discussed in class. Students cannot learn social justice from a book; in the same vein, practice alone does not provide students with the depth that places their practice in theoretical and historical contexts.

Higher education and student affairs is a field where easy answers do not exist. The personal and professional lives of graduate students and their more-seasoned practitioner partners intertwine and combine with the complexity of the learning environment to challenge teaching and learning. The experiential and personal nature of these graduate programs combine and enable students to reflect on their professional lives, identities, and commitment to social justice. Subject matter covering human development, leadership, and social justice makes individual reflection commonplace. This type of professional education and the integrative learning incorporated means that application to their personal lives is inevitable.

Similar to the students' reflection on how the personal is reflected in the professional, my personal feelings, as a professor, were intricately entwined with my professional sensibilities. Although this was true for all classes, courses such as "Cultural Pluralism in Higher Education" and "Race and Culture" were opportunities for significant reflection, personal challenge, and the dynamics emphasized by integrative and social justice pedagogies. In these classes, it became necessary to pursue the integrative pedagogy goal described by Huber and Hutchings (2004) to help students see that they are "responsible for their actions and those of society" (p. iv).

Vignette Number 2: Why Social Justice? Why You?

Prior to teaching, I had been a student affairs administrator for 10 years. Although I enjoyed administration, I was enticed into the faculty by my desire to infuse more *cultural diversity* (the term used in the late 1980s) into the pedagogy of my teaching and the student affairs national curriculum. My desire to introduce what I came to call *social justice* into the student affairs curriculum emanated from several places: an upbringing in the racially charged New Jersey of the 1960s, an overwhelmingly White upbringing by education and community, a doctoral-driven reading of Paulo Freire's (1997) *Pedagogy of the Oppressed*, and a personal background that made me relate to and want to keep company with those who experienced profound hurt. Although I considered myself an unlikely faculty candidate upon graduating from my doctoral program, I respected my faculty advisers who urged me to apply for open faculty positions.

Throughout my 25 years of teaching, I found that each class session was a time for reflection and self-doubt. Was I providing enough new content and knowledge for the students of color in the class? Did they feel supported? Did I adequately address the microaggressions that inevitably occurred as we all learned new ways to address injustices? Could I have done more? Was it my place to confront the microaggressing student, or should I encourage others to do the confronting? What was an appropriate balance between personal reflection and content? How could I, a White, heterosexual, cisgendered woman from a working-class family, relate to students with such different experiences from mine? What did I add to the conversation about oppression and justice?

Building Trust

Trust is a particularly thorny issue when incorporating social justice into any curriculum. In class everyone is on edge as the instructors and students learn aspects of each other's identities not previously exposed. Racial dynamics as practiced and expressed in the United States mean that an integrative-pedagogy-related technique such as intergroup dialogue is new for most students. Misinformation, social class backgrounds, and various expressions of privilege combine to make class conversations, exercises, and assignments challenging and potentially oppressive. Family backgrounds and home communities that limited interaction between different groups make class dialogue difficult for many. Students and instructors enter the classroom with entrenched preconceived notions or inevitable unacknowledged prejudices. To meet the integrative pedagogy goal of preparing students to work and learn in today's world, instructors must build trust within classes such as "Cultural Pluralism in Higher Education" and "Race and Culture," which takes enormous skill; skill that I often doubted I possessed.

The following vignette recalls my early experiences teaching the "Cultural Pluralism in Higher Education" and "Race and Culture" classes. It's an experience similar to those often relayed to me by people attempting to teach these types of classes for the first time.

Vignette Number 3: The Two-Week Stomach Knot

This was it. The reason I went into teaching. Early in my career as a faculty member and without opposition, I proposed a summer class called "Cultural Pluralism in Higher Education." Taught over two weeks, four hours a day, the class was intense, to say the least. Although some questioned what I could accomplish in two weeks, subsequent years of teaching the class on a semester schedule convinced me that the intensive version worked best. We had to come back and face each other the next day—regardless of what happened in the previous class. There was no cooling-down time, no forgetting. The next day, we were right back into the discussion, agreements and disagreements, working through our differences.

If infusing more cultural diversity into the student affairs curriculum was why I switched from administration to faculty, why did I have this knot in my stomach? Why did my hands shake before every class? Why was I plagued with doubt about the choice of books?

Several years and many students later, accompanied with some unbelievable successes and some utter failures in similar classes, I concluded that we must have passion to do this work. There is no half-teaching, no hiding, no facade of detachment. When I asked a cherished colleague why we fight for social justice, he replied, "Because it hurts more not to do it."

Bringing Your Whole Self Into the Classroom

The proposal for this volume described the authors as faculty who "don't detach the brain and subject matter from the heart, soul, and spirit (reality) of the individual student." The student affairs field has whole person development as a foundational value (American Council on Education, 1937, 1949). Integrative pedagogies entail a process whereby students and professors bring all of themselves into the classroom. The artificial boundaries of subjectivity and objectivity blur as the personal and professional become fodder for learning and development. This personally oriented aspect of integrative pedagogies is especially important when incorporating social justice into an academic curriculum. There is nowhere to hide in a social justice classroom where individual identities are an integral part of the curriculum and learning process.

As demonstrated by the previous vignette, you must share yourself—even if that sharing is uncomfortable, risky, or out of character. Teaching from social justice involves an acknowledgment of identities and coming face-to-face with oppression and privilege. Because everyone has what Jamie Washington called "targeted" and "dominant" identities, the classroom dynamics related to identities is complex and, at times, painful.

In 2007, Sue Borrego and I (Borrego & Manning) compiled a collection of narratives written by the NASPA Undergraduate Fellows Program (NUFP) in a book we titled *Where I Am From: Student Affairs Practice From the Whole of Students' Lives*. Sue had collected the reflections through an exercise with the NUFP fellows. She asked them to write short accounts of "where I'm from." The results were powerful accounts of the joys and sorrows these students from underrepresented groups faced in getting to and staying in college through graduation.

When teaching from social justice and integrative pedagogies, students share their identities and perspectives. It is only fair that the professor do the same. The following vignette is an account of my experience of including my "where I'm from" story in the *Where I Am From* book and using that exercise in a course.

Vignette Number 4: Where I Am From

Coediting the book *Where I Am From: Student Affairs Practice From the Whole of Students' Lives* with Sue Borrego was supposed to be easy. NUFP fellows had written the narratives that we were to collect into a book. Sue and I sat in her kitchen as she cooked or paced around the room, and I recorded the ideas she recited on my computer. When she brightly commented, "We should include narratives about where we're from," I thought, "I'm not sure I signed on for this." But write the narrative I did—about New Jersey, growing up working class, having siblings with issues of alcoholism and depression, and finding a home in New England, a place considered "cold" by many.

In the first day of a "Cultural Pluralism in Higher Education" class, I followed Sue's format from NUFP. Student volunteers read several sample narratives from *Where I Am From* as an introduction to the exercise. Then, students wrote their own narrative and were given the opportunity to read it aloud. As we read our narratives aloud, tears, silence, laughter, wonder, and disbelief filled the room. No discussion—just read the narratives, let them soak in, and move to the next volunteer.

My Catholic elementary and high school educations and college science major underprepared me for student affairs classes where feelings, emotions, and personal accounts were de rigueur. But if I was going to ask students to write and read their narratives, I would do the same. I read mine despite the lump in my throat and break in my voice when I read. Only some of us read our narratives, yet the exercise brought the class closer than expected all the same. There's something powerful about knowing where people are from, what has made them who they are.

Reflection Is Key

Although I attempted to use social justice and integrative pedagogies in all my classes, "Cultural Pluralism in Higher Education" provided the most difficult and meaningful challenge. Journals, class discussions, affinity and inclusive group discussions, immersion exercises, and readings were several ways that my coinstructor, a woman of color, and I built the self-reflection necessary to achieve course goals. Setting ground rules in the first class was another technique we used to build an open, nonthreatening environment where social justice work could occur. We were, after all, speaking about topics of identity, history, and background that hit close to home for all of us.

Ground rules are useful only if the people in the course have ownership for them. The process of developing ground rules took a different form each semester. Often, my coinstructor and I offered ground rules compiled by Jamie Washington; these were pearls of wisdom that Washington had developed through years of antiracism training. Sometimes, the students and instructors developed the ground rules from scratch. In both cases, there were themes that ran through the ground rules that we committed to one another: trust the process; confidentiality; we all make mistakes; be open; listen; all of us have something to learn.

An interesting aspect of the ground-rule-setting process was the way that the rules were forgotten or neglected by all of us on a regular basis. It was not that any of us wanted to forget the ground rules but simply that our commitment to openness and confidentiality was often tested as we pursued topics that were difficult, even hurtful. Pitfalls regarding this process were everywhere.

Ground rules provided yet another opportunity to use integrative pedagogy concepts in the classroom. Students were challenged to engage in the context by generating and committing to a set of ideals. Theirs was an active involvement built through creating both the content and the process used in the class. Faculty were challenged to build an environment that was a safer place to explore challenging topics. Teaching in multi-identity pairs, using experiential learning, and asking for student input when the class process faltered were additional ways to encourage integrative pedagogy and social justice.

Lessons Learned

My goal in teaching from a social justice perspective was to work with graduate and undergraduate students to promote fairness and justice within the classroom and eventually across all aspects of society. Together, in and out of class, we challenged the traditional ways that privilege was expressed in society. Integrative pedagogy relates closely to this goal because there may be no better definition of *social justice* than the goals of personal liberation and social empowerment (Huber & Hutchings, 2004). Attempting those goals meant adopting new ways to teach and learn. Several classroom practices, outlined next, were tested in the process.

Managing a Powerful Classroom Environment

When you step aside from the traditional professorial role and exercise authority differently, tensions inherent in the classroom become apparent. Previously silenced students from historically oppressed identities open up and say things that may be painful and uncomfortable to instructors and students, particularly those with privileges that enabled them to be oblivious to those viewpoints. Classroom dynamics, between and among students and the instructors, must be managed in ways that empower all students to speak and be heard. Trust and authenticity are two extremely important aspects in this process.

In the classes discussed in this chapter, the coinstructors and I used discussion groups to create a safer place to build trust and promote authenticity. Two styles of discussion groups were established: affinity and inclusive. To form the affinity groups, we asked students to identify themselves by race, sexual orientation, or other salient identities and group according to that identity. Inclusive groups, on the other hand, asked students to form groups that were diverse across their multiple, intersecting identities. These groups were not assigned by the instructors but formed by the students. As the groups took shape in the classroom, students could visualize the dynamics of affinity and inclusivity. The absence of some identities became apparent; the presence of previously invisible identities was revealed. The limiting dynamic of "checking off one box" was made visible as students refused to prioritize one identity over others. Nuances were revealed as students discussed their identities openly and enacted them visually.

Calling Out Racism, Homophobia, and Other Isms

If faculty members are going to promote social justice, we must create a just classroom environment. Although both students and instructors are involved in this process, I believe the professor bears a definitive responsibility. As the person who organizes and manages the class, the instructor must confront micro- or macroaggressions so the learning environment is maintained. Although these aggressions can be viewed as learning opportunities for majority students, they are another oppression in a long line of many for students from historically oppressed groups. When these aggressions are expressed in the classroom without a response from the instructor, that offensive point of view is validated, and targeted students are doubly oppressed by the original comment and the lack of challenge about the offense. Ignoring the comment is guaranteed to shut down the learning, particularly for students from the targeted group. After several failed attempts and justified, critical feedback from students, I learned to adopt the phrase "Let me share why someone might find that comment offensive." Commenting on the remark or action meant embarrassing a student, but I erred on that rather than ignore the oppression of underrepresented students.

Working With the Social Justice Police

The nature of student affairs programs means that some students believe they are at the pinnacle of social justice development. Through undergraduate training, personal identity development, or other means, they learn the language and practices of social justice. Despite their training, they may fail to see the full range of the history and challenges inherent in building a just world. Identity development models provide insight into these students who may be in the encounter stage (Cuyjet, Howard-Hamilton, & Cooper, 2012; Wijeyesinghe & Jackson, 2012). When they are empowered by their new knowledge, emboldened by privilege, and/or angered by oppression, self-righteousness may result. In lieu of self-reflection about how all of us collude in individual and institutional oppression, these students turn their attention to the transgressions of others. Managing the different levels of awareness, knowledge, and development present in the room and teaching to these differing levels of awareness is daunting. I admit that I never reached the skill I would have liked when working with students who failed to see their shortcomings and areas for growth when they were pointedly fixed on those of others.

Integrative pedagogy may provide some insight into the challenges of simultaneously teaching students with a lack of awareness and students who believe they are the most aware person in the room. Panels of outside presenters from a range of identities and life experiences can help students gain perspective about their identity development. Presentations by community activists who have experienced cycles of success and failure can help students envision a more complete understanding of how institutional oppression works. Assignments that require students to interact with people working to promote social justice can help them better understand the actions necessary to build understanding and promote transformation.

Better in Intention Than in Practice

Like my students, I struggled to achieve theory to practice regarding social justice. It is one thing to claim to work on social justice; it is quite another to do it. A concept related to integrative pedagogy that is helpful in this regard is to think of teaching as a spiritual act. Teaching is not something learned once and perfected. The ever-changing nature of students, theory, and your personal and professional cycles as a person and professor make teaching an art. Because you are affecting people's lives, approaching teaching and learning as a spiritual practice places it in the realm of transcendence. Particularly when using principles of social justice to work toward a more just world, faith, trust, and authenticity must be part of the teaching and learning processes.

Despite the challenges of teaching from a social justice perspective and the difficulties of incorporating integrative pedagogy, the goals of fairness and justice are worth the effort. If nothing else, that effort can move us closer to the end goal of individual and institutional transformation.

Conclusion

In this chapter, I shared some joys and sorrows from my 25 years of teaching graduate and undergraduate students. Although this work is difficult, even painful at times, the goal of using integrative and social justice pedagogies to transform the world is worth the effort.

Reflection Questions

1. In what ways have you encountered questions or self-doubts when teaching from a social justice perspective? How have you addressed those concerns?
2. This chapter notes that trust among class members is essential to raise issues and talk about social inequality and social justice. What other qualities have you found to be important for tackling these difficult topics in classrooms?
3. Thinking about your major program or courses, what are the values, knowledge, dispositions, and skills you hope students will integrate at the conclusion of the program or course? How do you facilitate that integration?
4. This chapter suggests that reflection is important for effective integration of course materials and experiences. What kinds of reflective activities have you pursued with your students? Which ones have you found to be most effective?
5. What does it mean to you to bring your whole self into the classroom? What parts of yourself are you more and less comfortable revealing during classroom discussions? Why?
6. Near the end of this chapter, teaching is described as a "spiritual practice." What is your understanding of this phrase? Do you see your own teaching as a spiritual practice? Why or why not?

References

American Association of American Colleges and Universities (AAC&U). (2002). *Greater expectations: A new vision for learning as a nation goes to college.* American Association of Colleges and Universities: Washington, DC.

American Council on Education. (1937). *The student personnel point of view.* Washington, DC: Author.

American Council on Education. (1949). *The student personnel point of view.* Washington, DC: Author.

Borrego, S., & Manning, K. (2007). *Where I am from: Student affairs practice from the whole of students' lives.* Washington, DC: NASPA.

Carnegie Foundation and Association of American Colleges & Universities. (2004). *A statement on integrative learning.* Washington, DC: Author.

Cuyjet, M. J., Howard-Hamilton, M. F., & Cooper, D. L. (Eds.). (2012). *Multiculturalism on campus: Theory, models, and practices for understanding diversity and creating inclusion.* Sterling, VA: Stylus.

DeZure, D., Babb, M., & Waldmann, S. (2005). Integrative learning nationwide: Emerging themes and practices. *Peer Review, 7*(3–4), 24–28.

Evans, N. J., Forney, D. S., Guido, F. M., Patton, L. D., & Renn, K. A. (2009). *Student development in college: Theory, research, and practice.* San Francisco, CA: John Wiley & Sons.

Ferren, A. S., & Anderson, C. B. (2016). Integrative learning: Making liberal education purposeful, personal, and practical. In M. M. Watts (Ed.), *Finding the why: Personalizing learning in higher education: New directions for teaching and learning* (No. 145, pp. 33–40). San Francisco, CA: Wiley.

Freire, P. (1997). *Pedagogy of the oppressed.* New York, NY: Continuum.

Gale, R. A. (2006). *Fostering integrative learning through pedagogy.* Integrative Learning Project. Retrieved from gallery.carnegiefoundation.org/ilp/uploads/pedagogy_copy.pdf

Huber, M. T., & Hutchings, P. (2004). *Integrative learning: Mapping the terrain.* Washington, DC: Association of American Colleges & Universities and the Carnegie Foundation for the Advancement of Teaching.

Parker, C. A., Widick, C., & Knefelkamp, L. (1978). Editors' notes: Why bother with theory? In L. Knefelkamp, C. Widick, & C. A. Parker (Eds.), *Applying new developmental findings: New directions for student services* (No. 4, pp. vii–xvi). San Francisco, CA: Jossey-Bass.

Patton, L., McEwen, M., Rendón, L., & Howard-Hamilton, M. (2007). Critical race perspectives on theory in student affairs. In S. R. Harper & L. D. Patton (Eds.), *Responding to the realities of race on campus: New directions for student services* (No. 120, pp. 39–53). San Francisco, CA: Wiley.

Upcraft, M. L. (1994). The dilemmas of translating theory to practice. *Journal of College Student Development, 35,* 438–443.

Wijeyesinghe, C. L., & Jackson, B. W. (Eds.). (2012). *New perspectives on racial identity development: Integrating emerging frameworks.* New York, NY: New York University Press.

PART TWO

ENGAGED LEARNING AND TEACHING IN PRACTICE

3

LEARNING COMMUNITY CLASSROOMS AND EDUCATING FOR CRITICAL HOPE

Gillies Malnarich

We need critical hope the way a fish needs unpolluted water.

—Paulo Freire (2004, p. 2)

Twenty-five years after writing *Pedagogy of the Oppressed* (1970), Paulo Freire wrote *Pedagogy of Hope*. The Brazilian educator revisited his earlier work to clarify what progressive educators should do to make the world more just and equitable. He argued that one task is "to unveil opportunities for hope, no matter what the obstacles may be. After all, without hope there is little we can do" (2004, p. 3). A critical theorist and popular educator, Freire knew about the political, economic, and social circumstances that harbor hopelessness and despair. His is not a naïve hope. Instead he equates a fish's need for unpolluted water to humans' need for *critical hope*—solution-oriented action informed by truth telling, clear analysis, and compassion.

I discovered *Pedagogy of Hope* when I was rethinking my purpose as a teacher after a deeply disturbing event. In summer 2004, I attended an institute on Whidbey Island, cosponsored by Schumacher College, an international center for ecological studies in England, and the Whidbey Institute in Washington State. An assigned reading, *Water Wars: Privatization, Pollution, and Profit* (Shiva, 2002), by one of the institute's facilitators, the physicist and ecologist Vandana Shiva, documents the erosion of water rights in the world. The push to privatize water while denying access to the poor, along with escalating conflicts over water scarcity, underscored a World Bank vice president's prediction: This century's wars would be fought over clean water, not oil.

Shiva's book is a sobering read and so was our extended seminar discussion. The grief and despair, especially among the institute's younger participants—many recent graduates in environmental studies and related fields—stunned me into silence. Later, I tried to make my way back to speech through memories:

> I remember the rusty-red creek behind my friends' houses in the mining town where I grew up and how almost all those kids died from cancer before they turned 40.

> I remember the town where I was born and how we girls who lived downwind from the site of heavy metal production could not carry a baby long enough to be mothers.

> I remember the dairy where cows died of lead poisoning, spines twisted, and how the company bought the farmers' silence but years later their children's spines twisted too.

During the night I woke with this question in mind: *What does it mean to educate for hope?*

That fall I wondered what my students in Evening and Weekend Studies, a program for working adults at The Evergreen State College, thought about the state of the world. Despite our different personal histories, our conversations surfaced a common sentiment: People yearned for a less troubled and damaged world, most assumed technology would rescue us, and a surprising number said they kept "positive" by blocking out bad news. Freire would equate this disengaged optimism with naïve hope, which, easily bruised, turns to cynicism.

After similar conversations with many students at Evergreen and other schools, I remain convinced that we educators need to learn how to educate for hope—an essential student learning outcome in our times. Honest engagement with the challenges before us, as well as with our own intellectual, emotional, and spiritual responses to those challenges, requires an approach suggested by this book's subtitle: *Engaged Learning With Heart, Mind, and Spirit.* Freire, who tells us he wrote *Pedagogy of Hope* (Freire, 1994) "in rage and love, without which there is no hope" (p. 10), made room for raw, angry, heartbreaking, life-affirming hope: I wonder if we can, too, especially in our classrooms.

But how might we do this hard work? What basic curricular and pedagogical moves will give our students the know-how to take on contemporary challenges and the critical hope to persist when solutions are far from obvious? How might we help students understand that to do so will require the integration of past experience and present knowledge, deep engagement with self and community? In this chapter, I address these questions by drawing on insights from my teaching experience and my work at the Washington Center for Improving the Quality of Undergraduate Education, the national resource center for learning communities located at Evergreen. Before doing so, I return to the Whidbey Institute, postseminar, and what the young people there taught me about the Freirean task of unveiling opportunities for hope.

Essential Knowledge: Finding One's Place in History

In the evening, a new graduate from a well-known West Coast environmental studies program asked Satish Kumar, founder of Schumacher College and cofacilitator of the institute, how he became an environmental activist (and, by implication, how she might too). The highlights from this conversation begin with his story, then take a very different turn.

Satish grew up in a religious family in the northwestern part of India on the border with Pakistan. He became a Jain monk when he was 9 years old and left the monastery when he was 18 after reading a book by Mahatma Gandhi, who believed individuals could pursue enlightenment not by removing themselves from the world but by being in it. Satish joined the walking university led by Gandhi's follower and successor Vinoba Bhave, who walked throughout India for more than 20 years, organizing around the issue of land ownership. Always joined by 50 to 100 students, Vinoba's message was simple: Just as air, sunshine, and water are nature's gifts that cannot be owned, so too is Mother Earth. Satish described how Vinoba met with landlords and made this proposal: If you have five children, consider me, a representative of the poor, as your sixth child, and give me one sixth of your land to distribute to the poor. Using this approach, Vinoba secured five million acres of land for the landless. This lands-gift movement—supported by doctors, lawyers, students, professors, and businesspeople—educated Satish about the power of nonviolence.

And so Satish's account unfolds. In the early 1960s, at a teahouse in Delhi, Satish read a newspaper report about an antinuclear demonstration in Trafalgar Square in London, England, where 12,000 people demonstrated, and Bertrand Russell, the famous 90-year-old philosopher, was sent to prison for civil disobedience. Inspired by Russell, Satish, now in his mid-20s, and a friend decided to walk with a message of peace to Moscow, Paris, London, and Washington, D.C. Their journey begins at Gandhi's grave and ends at John F. Kennedy's, assassinated one month before they arrived in the United States.

On Vinoba's advice, they took no money so they would learn to accept people without judgment. They met heads of governments and thousands of people. In the then-Soviet Union, a group of women workers, attracted to their banner, invited the two Indian men for tea at the tea factory where they worked. Satish described how over tea one woman jumped up, rushed to the factory, and came back with four packets of tea. She asked Satish and his friend to give a package to each leader with this message: If you ever get a mad thought to push the nuclear button, please stop, and make a fresh cup of tea. Think about the ordinary people who produce this tea, work in factories, work in the fields, lead a normal life; think of these people who are not your enemies. We are ordinary people, and we have done nothing to deserve nuclear attack. Satish said this encounter gave their journey a purpose, for now they had a message to deliver.

The spellbinding, heroic stories this humble man told are powerful and instructive. But they turn out to be from too distant a place and an experience too unlike what the young people at Whidbey know to move them from hopelessness to hope. The paralysis in such moments is profound and paradoxical: Highly skilled graduates who care deeply about the environment aren't sure how to *use* what they have learned to make a difference. They are uninformed about grassroots social change.

To educate for hope, we need to know our own people's history. This country, like all others, has stories as inspiring as the walking university and the walk for peace. For instance, well before Satish and his friend arrived in Washington DC, a handful of women stood outside the Kennedy White House to protest the dangers to children's health of radioactive fallout, which was found in mothers' milk and, subsequently, their babies' teeth. These women, who belonged to Women Strike for Peace, participated in a worldwide demonstration of 50,000 women in November 1961, and they, with others, eventually won a ban on aboveground nuclear testing in 1963. One of the women who stood vigil outside the White House—and later believed her efforts were futile because underground nuclear testing continued—heard the famous pediatrician Benjamin Spock, a high-profile activist in the antinuclear movement, tell the story about how he first became involved. She was in the audience when he talked about the daily presence and persistence of a handful of women (*her* presence and *her* persistence) that prompted him to stop his car one morning and find out what mattered to them so much. Rebecca Solnit (2004), who told the story of these women's vigil in *Hope in the Dark: Untold Histories, Wild Possibilities*, reminded us "to hope is to give yourself to the future, and that commitment to the future makes the present inhabitable" (p. 5).

Other stories, equally powerful, begin locally. The story of the Citizenship Schools is but one example. In *We Make the Road by Walking: A Year-Long*

Quest for Spiritual Formation, Reorientation, and Activation, Myles Horton (Horton & Freire, 1990), founder of the Highlander Folk School in Tennessee, in conversation with Paulo Freire, described how these schools grew out of the grassroots movement for racial justice in the South. The idea for the schools came from Esau Jenkins, a bus driver from Johns Island, South Carolina. He was attending a Highlander workshop on the United Nations and pointed out that it was fine to talk about the world, but he had problems at home. While busing folks to and from their jobs in the city, he was trying to teach them to read so they could pass the voter registration exam, vote, and exercise political power. He asked for Highlander's help to set up a literacy school. It would become the prototype for Citizenship Schools.

Bernice Robinson—a beautician, organizer for the National Association for the Advancement of Colored People, and niece of the activist educator Septima Clark—taught the first class. She decided to use the Declaration of Human Rights to introduce the theme of democracy and citizenship to keep adult learners inspired while they struggled to read words and write their names. Because she did not want people to be stigmatized, she turned the literacy class into a community organization—a Citizenship School—where people could plan what they would do *as a community* when they got the vote. A decade and a half after the first class met in January 1957, around 100,000 people had learned to read and write at Citizenship Schools, setting in motion a nationwide agenda for social justice.

By summer 2004, none of the young people who heard Satish's stories knew about the Citizenship Schools. And they did not know about Highlander's integrated residential institutes in the 1950s that brought together African American southerners and Whites to discuss community organizing, union rights, and civil rights activism. And they did not know that Martin Luther King Jr., Rosa Parks, and John Lewis attended workshops there and that Eleanor Roosevelt, among others, came as a guest speaker. Minus historical grounding, how can we imagine the radical possibilities when diverse people take on the problem of segregation by beginning the painful work of learning to *trust* the other—the precursor to truth telling and courageous action?

The Highlander story is so unlike the accounts of Black History Month. So, too, did adult educators in North America envision a version of democracy in 1946, when racism was rampant, the threat of nuclear annihilation was real, and the carnage of war, the Holocaust, Hiroshima, and Nagasaki seared the public conscience. Yet, the statement of beliefs they adopted in Ottawa, Canada's capital, begins with these words: "We believe . . . that quite ordinary men and women have within themselves and their communities the spiritual and intellectual resources adequate to the solution of their own problems."[1] These adult educators appreciated the difference between an informed citizenry and empowered citizens, as did the bus driver and activist, Esau Jenkins. They referenced an *imaginative citizenry* where people are the subjects of their own lives—where *we* have the capacity to grapple with life-threatening problems.

Still, communities are far from idyllic: Class, race, gender, and status inequities prevail, and those with power exercise it. Even so, everyone living in a mining company town isn't a company booster. In Nanaimo, British Columbia's first mining settlement, some folks left the coalfields after a nasty strike to build the utopian community of Sointula on Matthew Island, establishing cooperatives—industries, community gardens, schools, a library, a health clinic, an orchestra, and a theater troupe. Some stayed put. And like folks would eventually do in other mining towns, they organized unions, challenged company doctors' complicity, and founded environmental organizations. Others kept silent, didn't balk, settling into naïve hope. As Solnit (2004) pointed out, "Hope just means another world might be possible, not promised, not guaranteed. Hope calls for action; action is impossible without hope" (p. 5). Without action—informed by clear analysis—the creek runs rusty, loaded with carcinogens. Friends die too soon. To lose hope is to lose one's place in history, to miss history-making possibilities.

I return to the young people at the Whidbey Institute. We walked and talked, and I asked a series of questions: Where do you live? What do you like best about this place? Tell me about the people. What matters to the community? Tell me what worries you. Does anyone share your concerns? What do you think needs to be done? Tell me how you might include folks. We sketched out a Venn diagram of possibilities, including the gaps between what they knew and what they needed to know to make a difference. I told them how in one strife-ridden community on the West Coast, a logging company, a First Nations tribe, and environmentalists reached a compromise on how to live on the land. But before this happened, a leader from each group—CEO, tribal chief, and activist, respectively—met for two years on their own, away from the glare of publicity. These three women learned how to *hear* one another. When they figured out a wholly new way to talk about their differences, representing a synthesis of former ways of knowing, they invited all their constituents to the first of many town meetings.

I offer these stories and memories to remind us that more than intellect is involved when learning and teaching. Emotions are too—heart and spirit are perhaps less visible than mind, but always present. The prior knowledge we bring to learning something new includes home-based, local knowledge where places are populated by ordinary people and shaped by their choices. If this knowledge—steeped in heart, mind, and spirit—is systematically discounted, as it often is in the academy, our collective ignorance makes history-making possibilities unimaginable.

After the Whidbey Institute, I began to explore what learning community practitioners, myself included, might do to turn our classrooms into sites for learning how to reclaim our place in history, a first step toward turning despair or disengaged optimism into critical hope.

Learning Communities' Potential: Rediscovering Radical Possibilities

Although some folks may bristle at the language, Freire most likely would regard learning community practitioners as among those "progressive educators" he addressed in *Pedagogy of Hope*. When thinking about *learning communities* as sites for integrating knowledge and action, though, our frame of reference must be learning communities done well—a necessary qualification if we are to act on learning communities' radical possibilities. After a brief overview of learning communities, I turn to the curricular and pedagogical moves embedded in learning community practices that are especially relevant when our aim is to educate for hope.

Learning Communities' Basic Components

Since the early years of implementation, learning communities signal intentional structural reform, a radical break with one teacher teaching one subject to one set of students. As Patrick Hill (1985) argued in "The Rationale for Learning Communities," the essential benefit of learning community design is "to make structural changes which release, for faculties and students, the powers of human association, . . . the stimulation of thought, the exposure to diversity, the need to clarify one's own thinking in the community." He also emphasized that once people are put together, they need "real time and space to learn from each other" (pp. 4–5).

Although learning communities take many forms, a standard definition captures the commonalities: Learning communities link or cluster classes, typically around a theme or question, and enroll a common cohort of students in two or more classes (Smith, MacGregor, Matthews, & Gabelnick, 2004). An influential monograph, *Learning Communities: Creating Connections Among Students, Faculty, and Disciplines* (Gabelnick, MacGregor, Matthews, & Smith, 1990), highlighted the purpose, namely, to give students "opportunities for deeper understanding and integration of the material they are learning and more interaction with one another and their teachers as fellow participants in the learning enterprise" (p. 19). In both two- and four-year schools, faculty from different disciplines and fields—often with librarians, student affairs professionals, and administrators—work together to recast students' learning experiences.

As practice evolved, a field-based definition of *learning communities done well* includes other core components: at least one intentionally designed integrative assignment for all students in the cohort, robust and collaborative partnerships between student affairs and academics (essential if we are to teach the whole student), ongoing professional development for teaching teams, regular assessment from the classroom to program levels, and sustained learning-centered administrative support (Lardner & Malnarich, 2008a, 2009; Matthews, Smith, & MacGregor, 2012).

The impetus for initiating learning communities has also evolved. At most institutions, faculty organized learning communities around topics and themes they found interesting. Their infectious enthusiasm, emphasis on collaboration, and active classroom learning strategies engaged students. Retention rates were impressive compared to those of stand-alone classes, leading some schools to bundle general education requirements into learning community options.

Within the past decade, learning communities have been reconceptualized as an intervention strategy for student success. If previously neglected students are to earn a credential—today's version of passing the voter's exam—purposeful collaboration among faculty, student affairs professionals, and administrators is required. The field now pays far more attention to locating learning communities in relation to students' needs, including at critical transition points (e.g., high school to college); along curricular pathways; and at "curricular trouble spots" where institutional data indicate that students, especially first-generation students and students of color, flounder and frequently fail (Malnarich, 2005). Recasting learning communities as a student success strategy has underscored learning communities' potential to become a credible strategy for institutional change and broad educational reform (Lardner & Malnarich, 2008b).

On campuses across the country, multiple learning community designs are in play: first-year interest groups, paired or linked classes, coordinated studies, interdisciplinary studies, federated learning communities, and living–learning communities. Designs vary based on institutional constraints, degrees of curricular integration, and teaching teams' composition. Strong programs foster social and intellectual connections among people and ideas, practice active engagement and reflection, and encourage students to collaborate and take charge of their learning.

Simply put, learning communities free educators from fealty to a one-course model where entry points for learning are limited. They also offer educators the means to implement a consensus regarding twenty-first-century liberal education where national reports and initiatives such as *College Learning for the New Global Century* (Association of American Colleges &

Universities, 2007) and "The Degree Qualifications Profile" (Schneider, Gaston, Adelman, & Ewell, 2014) identify broad integrative knowledge as an essential student learning outcome. But can learning communities give educators the latitude needed for students to tackle tough issues while learning the practice of critical hope—the antidote to disengaged optimism?

Learning Community Curriculum: Developing Students' Integrative Habits of Mind and Skills

Structural changes associated with learning communities free up classroom time and space to rethink curriculum—what we want students to do *out there* that we are responsible for *in here* (Fink, 2013; Wiggins & McTighe, 2005). This focus on student learning—coupled with research on how people learn (Bransford, Brown, & Cocking, 1999) and the implications for teaching (Ambrose, Bridges, DiPietro, Lovett, & Norman, 2010; Donovan, Bransford, & Pellegrino, 1999)—departs from a curriculum-as-coverage approach. Less stuff, but more is expected. As Lee Shulman (2004) observed in "Toward a Pedagogy of Substance," "The outstanding pedagogue recognizes that you can't teach everything, and so understands the subject matter deeply enough to be selective, to be simplifying, to be structuring and organizing" (p. 131).

The less-stuff challenge for learning community practitioners also includes three additional moves, all related to integrative learning: first, to bring to integrative curricular design key dimensions of disciplinary understanding and field expertise (Boix-Mansilla & Gardner, 1998); second, to design integrative curriculum for deep learning (Marton, Hounsell, & Entwistle, 1984) so students can experience shifts in thinking and practice worthy of protracted self-reflection; and third, to craft assignments so students can develop the habits of mind associated with skillful integrative thinking (Huber & Hutchings, 2004; Lardner & Malnarich, 2009).

Even though several generations of education reformers have been preoccupied by the limits of highly specialized knowledge given the complexity and interdependence of "problems" since the Second World War, designing assignments so students develop integrative habits of mind remains the least developed aspect of learning community practice (Lardner & Malnarich, 2008–2009). Yet understanding the moves of integration, including when a strife-ridden community needs to reimagine its social contract or young environmentalists need to know how to step outside the familiar territory of their training, is learning that will make a difference in the world.

But some of the graduates I met at Whidbey had been in programs where integrative learning is highly valued. What might be missing in their education that would exacerbate a lack of awareness about grassroots social change referred to earlier? The move that stymied these young people is the very move crystallized in Alverno College Faculty's (1994) classic prompt for designing abilities-based curriculum: What do we want students to *know* and be able to *do* (i.e., the explicit shift from *possessing knowledge* to *using knowledge*)? And it is also the move that Alexander Meiklejohn (1932/1981)—who crafted University of Wisconsin at Madison's Experimental College, which influenced Tussman's Berkeley experiment, the Arts One program at the University of British Columbia (UBC), and Evergreen—expected educators to facilitate. He wrote, "The chief task . . . is to get [students'] minds active, to give them a sense of urgency of human need, to establish in them the activity of seeing and solving problems" (p. 25). Meiklejohn's insistence that our job is to instill in students a proactive capacity to see "in every new situation . . . an object of active inquiry" (p. 25) complements Freire's notion of educating for critical hope.

Interviews I had with Evergreen students as part of a Washington Center assessing complex learning project illuminate the difference between possessing knowledge and using knowledge in relation to scientific literacy. Here's what emerged: For Evergreen's equivalent of science majors, scientific literacy meant you should be able to make science accessible to others—to take complicated scientific ideas and, without dumbing them down, be able to explain a phenomenon so nonscientists could understand the implications of a certain course of action. The proof of science literacy is to be an able communicator of what you know. For nonmajors, an exposure to science should affect their stance in the world—they should be able to internalize the scientific method whereby they would appreciate that whatever they thought to be true was probably false. In other words, the proof of science literacy is the capacity to question assumptions, one's own in particular. If we agree with these students' nuanced articulation of what they should know and be able to do in the context of science literacy, we need to craft assignments that give students practice *using* what they know outside the academy. Perhaps the young people at Whidbey had few or no opportunities to translate their knowing, including "broad integrative knowledge," *for use* in a contemporary world dominated by scientific ignorance and naïve hope regarding technology.

When Meiklejohn was president at Amherst, he set up adult education classes with the help of local textile unions from Holyoke and Springfield to teach mill workers reading, writing, economics, and history. Then, after the experiment at the University of Wisconsin at Madison came to an abrupt end, Meiklejohn left and re-created the Experimental College as an adult education center, the San Francisco School of Social Studies. Designed around the theme of contemporary American society, the school offered not individual courses but a curriculum based on poetry, prose, fiction, and nonfiction by leading thinkers—a reading list selected because of its potential to challenge students' assumptions. People met weekly to discuss and debate the values and problems of San Francisco, their studies leading to informed analysis, the basis for collective action. This format was repeated in other locations, and by 1949, 40,000 adult learners across the country were meeting in Great Books adult study programs to figure out how to change people's and communities' circumstances for the better.[2]

In Meiklejohn's version of learning communities, learning inside the academy intentionally develops people's capacities to address complex real-world challenges from the vantage point of contextualized, historical thinking and does so in the company of others who most likely will have views quite different from their own.

Learning Community Pedagogy: Learning How to Learn Across Significant Differences

We teach people, not curriculum. This insight inspired Bernice Robinson to turn a literacy school into a citizenship forum and Meiklejohn to design a program where investigating public issues became the means for improving reading, writing, and, ultimately, one's community. It's also reflected in the questions Myles Horton asked Paulo Freire when they began their conversation on education, social change, and Citizenship Schools in *We Make the Road by Walking* (Horton & Freire, 1990): How do you treat people with respect? How do you build and maintain a program that treats people with respect?

After the Whidbey Institute, my sense of urgency about educating for critical hope was countered by a wary reluctance to make room in unpredictable classroom settings for what I described earlier as "raw, angry, heartbreaking, life-affirming hope." But until I invited emotion into the classroom (not just during faculty–student conferences), the possibilities for educating citizen leaders in here for out there would be limited. I began to experiment on how to create *community*—what Hill (1991) defined as a place or process by which diverse others engage in "conversations of respect" (p. 41). Or, in the context of one of Evergreen's five learning foci, to develop students' capacity to *learn across significant differences*; that is, "to learn to recognize, respect and bridge differences—critical skills in an increasingly diverse world."[3] In effect, this is what the activist, tribal leader, and CEO learned how to do during the years they met prior to modeling the practice for their constituencies.

In our classrooms, the stakes are not so high as those in the small coastal town, but in the long run, students' ability to practice what Terry Tempest Williams (2004) referred to as the *open space of democracy*, "a landscape that encourages diversity and discourages conformity" (p. 9), matters; that is, the ability to know how to make room for dissent and differences. So what might this look like in a classroom setting? I turn to an account of a recent teaching experience—a yearlong Evergreen Evening and Weekend Studies program I taught with Joli Sandoz from fall 2013 to spring 2014 called Building Resilient Communities (BRC)—to illustrate a few pedagogical moves we might consider.

Although a program description attracts a majority of students interested in a particular inquiry, what happens when students first gather sets the tone, expected behaviors, and nature of individual and collective engagement for subsequent classes. By the end of the first BRC class, we wanted everyone to know that *real people* are in the room whose unique contributions are essential to creating a vital academic community. We spent the majority of time on introductions where students in pairs talked about where they grew up, where they went to school, and why they chose BRC with reference to the program description. We heard what people have learned from others, then reviewed upcoming assignments: to read a few chapters from our first book, prepare notes on especially significant passages for our first BRC seminar discussion, and write a version of the "I am from" poem.[4] By evening's end, most people know 20 or so classmates' names and contact information for a few people.

Next class, students arrived, poems in hand. Poems were read and heard multiple times in twos, followed by a choral reading. The students chose one of their stanzas to read aloud: the first on familiar items found in their home; the second on the sights, sounds, and smells from their neighborhood; the third on their family's favorite foods; the fourth on family sayings; and the fifth on people's or relatives' names, a generational link. We heard all readers for stanza one, then stanza two, and so on. Some students sent their poem to parents and siblings; some turned the assignment into an extended family activity. The power of the "I am from" poem, brought to my attention by David Schoem during a plenary he gave at the national summer institute on learning communities, is its evocative quality, as well as its pedagogical value for revealing unsuspected diversity. Within the bonhomie of our collective reading, we detected commonalities and differences. In one student's family, a saying is a threat: "If you don't study, you'll end up earning the minimum wage." But, for another, everyone in her family has always earned just the minimum wage. The possibility of learning across significant differences, an outcome essential to the practice of critical hope, can happen only if classrooms truly give students and faculty (typically through ongoing seminar discussions) the time and space to explore the implications of *exposure to diversity* and *clarifying one's thinking in community*, the cornerstones for learning communities done well.

Hill (1985) was actually for *uncongenial diversity*, a provocative phrase he defined as "diversity which discomfits and which calls into question . . .

existing standards, understandings of self and other, and distributions of resources and privilege."[5] In fall 2003, I sat in on a class taught by Hill where students, in preparation for their weekly seminar, identified not only several passages from assigned reading they found compelling but also a passage that made them want to fling the text aside.

Among the books we discussed in BRC, Staughton Lynd's (2013) *Accompanying: Pathways to Social Change* suggested how we might work with our students. In analyzing his own extensive involvement in grassroots social change, Lynd distinguished between two theories of social change: *organizing* and *accompanying*. He described organizing as a "process whereby person A decides what would be desirable for person B to think and do, and then seeks to bring about that predetermined result" (p. 1), an approach he likened to trade union organizing (and faculty–student relationships in many classrooms). In contrast, Lynd forwarded the idea of accompaniment as articulated by Paul Farmer, cofounder of Partners in Health, which has projects in several countries including Haiti and Rwanda. Farmer described accompanying as "to go somewhere with him or her, to break bread together, to be present on a journey with a beginning and an end. . . . There's an element of mystery, of openness in accompaniment. I'll go with you and support you in your journey wherever it leads" (p. 2). Accompanying our students as we learn how to *really* learn across significant differences makes sense as a predictable practice, given the necessary (yet unpredictable) responsibility to educate for critical hope.

In BRC, conversations typically followed a protocol: In circles of no more than five students, each person read aloud a passage from the assigned book and explained why the passage was selected, and, without interruption, everyone heard everyone's contribution. Then each circle did its collective best to identify questions or themes for a seminar discussion; these were posted, and then everyone chose a seminar to join. Sometimes several themes or questions were clustered together. Faculty also posted questions or a single focus for seminar discussion if students' assumptions needed to be challenged. Some students joined seminars that attracted fewer students, the experience of voicing one's views in a larger group being too intimidating an experience early on in the program. Over time, students became better at identifying and sharing passages that they found puzzling and/or that made them angry. In seminar discussions, we practiced using the ladder of feedback (see Appendix 3A), learning to ask clarifying questions first, all the way up to respectfully voicing disagreements (not always successful). As people became more impassioned and comfortable, seminars sometimes erupted into emotional exchanges. We learned how to make room for our and others' feelings by adopting a method for stopping conversations that are no longer respectful. In brief, any seminar participant can hold up his or her hand with the palm outward, signaling "stop talking." In silence, students did reflective writing. And when people finished writing, the conversation continued. Students were also intentional about assessing their participation (see Appendix 3B).

Some faculty may regard protocols as overcontrolling, but the purpose is to focus attention on the substantive and genuine differences present in any community. Inequities among students' circumstances in BRC mirror those in most communities. Studying income inequality, as we did, reveals class and gender differences; studying wealth inequality reveals systemic racism and the generational consequences of practices such as redlining. When adults returning to formal schooling read that the American dream is now out of reach for people like them, the data and analysis are unbelievable, crushing, infuriating: We learn to navigate the difference between social analysis and individuals' experiences, between public issues and personal troubles.

Contrary to BRC students' first impressions, they learn from unlikely teachers and classmates once they replace an unspoken in-the-head judgment ("That's a stupid thing to say") with intellectual curiosity ("Why might this be a reasonable thing for him or her to think?"). Repeating the moves of listening attentively, asking questions, making room for democratic deliberation, figuring out what to do when conversations erupt, and coaching individuals on how to return to difficult exchanges is the work of accompaniment. The emphasis is on *practice*, the moves we need to learn if we are to replace naïve hope with critical hope.

In Here–Out There Possibilities: The Blue Dot Tour

When I was a student in UBC's inaugural Arts One program, David Suzuki, the Canadian environmentalist and broadcaster, then a young genetics professor and upcoming research scientist, was a frequent lecturer and visitor. He'd drop in and join seminar discussions, and by listening to him, I learned the value of questioning assumptions. In late spring, Suzuki invited students from his lab, graduate classes, and Arts One to attend a science symposium at Rosario on Orcas Island. Early findings about extensive environmental degradation were known (and a few of Suzuki's graduate students had already left the university to become ecoactivists). We sat cross-legged in a circle with a few professors and Suzuki to talk about his dilemma: Should he stay at the university or leave to become a science educator in the service of a broader public? He was asking students to advise him. He talked about the role of expertise in a democracy, arguing that scientists had an obligation to make scientific knowledge accessible to the public (Vinoba's belief, too, and that of Evergreen science students). He told us that specialized knowledge represents only pieces of a puzzle and that ordinary people need to draw on multiple fields of study before we decide what to do. Suzuki left UBC a few months later.

The Blue Dot Tour in Canada is the Rosario circle writ large and David Suzuki's final national tour. Named after Carl Sagan's reference to Earth as a "pale blue dot" when seen from space, the purpose is to mobilize Canadians to amend their constitution, the Charter of Rights and Freedoms, so it includes people's right to live in a healthy environment. "What's more important," Suzuki asks, "than the right to breathe fresh air, drink clean water, and eat healthy food?" In each of the 20 Blue Dot stops, Suzuki calls on Canadians to protect the places and people they love and "for ordinary people to come together to take extraordinary action." Local community leaders and groups, First Nations, and celebrated musicians and writers join him. The plan is to push municipal governments to adopt declarations, then municipal mayors to push provinces to adopt bills of rights, then provinces to push the federal government to change the charter.[6] Suzuki told a crowd in Manitoba, "Science shapes our stories; the environment is embedded inside, within us" (Yarmie, 2014). Suzuki wants to shift the way we see the world, to challenge assumptions.

From the classroom out there to the classroom in here: To be precise, I am referring to the classroom of Susan Smythe, my friend and colleague whose field of study, biogeography, means she and her students at Douglas College cannot turn away from bad news. She told me about inviting a newly minted master's-level graduate to give a guest lecture. He spoke for an hour about a climate-modeling program that predicts how the Amazon Basin will change and what the consequences are. "The particular things he was talking about looked pretty dire," she told me, "not a lot of good news." Students slumped in their seats. The lecture ended, and he left. She felt depressed, and the students did too. After a 10-minute break, Susan made room for her feelings and theirs. In her gentle and precise way, she began to probe and reframe the data as a call to action, her question "So what are *we* going to do about it?" deeply serious and heartfelt.

The radical possibilities for educating for critical hope are present in teaching done well and learning communities done well.

An integrative pedagogy asks us to accompany our students—to walk alongside them as we model a way to be fully present in the world in rage and love. This passage from *Hope in the Dark* by Rebecca Solnit (2004) is what I think we would want all our students to win for themselves:

Causes and effects assume history marches forward, but history is not an army. It is a crab scuttling sideways, a drip of soft water wearing away stone, an earthquake breaking centuries of tension. Sometimes one person inspires a movement, or her words do decades later; sometimes a few passionate people change the world; sometimes they start a mass movement and millions do; sometimes those millions are stirred by the same outrage or the same ideal and change comes upon us like a change of weather. All that these transformations have in common is that they begin in the imagination, in hope. To hope is to gamble. It's to bet on the future, on your desires, on the possibility that an open heart and uncertainty is better than gloom and safety. To hope is dangerous, and yet it is the opposite of fear, for to live is to risk. (p. 4)

For educators, taking the risk to educate for critical hope begins by opening our classrooms to all the "I ams"—whose knowledge, limited by background and experience, serve as foundational stories for becoming compassionate, able analytical thinkers who know how to learn across significant differences. And as we puzzle through questions and issues together, we need to coach our students in the moves associated with truth-telling, solutions-oriented, integrative thinking. And finally we need to ensure that students learn how to use what they know in the broader community so "we, the people" can do the work of an imaginative citizenry. Simply put, recall the First Nations leader, the activist, and the CEO and how we might give our students the *practice* in here to do what is so necessary, and so essential to democracy, out there.

Reflection Questions

1. What role does personal and public history play in your students' engagement with course material and in your own thinking about course design and curriculum?
2. What opportunities are your students, or the students in the programs with which you are affiliated, afforded to use their knowledge to address real-world social issues?
3. In what ways might you as an educator—whether a classroom teacher, a program director, or an administrator—provide additional ways to build community among students and to foster dialogue across significant differences?
4. How might you as an educator move from *organizing* to *accompanying* students? How might you encourage them, in activities of community engagement, to choose accompanying rather than organizing with community members?

5. This chapter includes several creative approaches to integrative pedagogies that exist outside of traditional learning communities, including ways to make room for community building that allows for *uncongenial diversity*. What innovative approach might your campus adopt to educate for critical hope?

6. In what ways is educating for critical hope an essential, overarching learning outcome for our times?

Notes

1. From the private papers of Ron Faris, Canadian adult educator and author of *The Passionate Educators: Voluntary Associations and the Struggle for Control of Adult Education Broadcasting in Canada* (Faris, 1975).

2. See the foreword to Meiklejohn's *The Experimental College* (1981, pp. ix–xiii) by James Walker Powell, a founding Experimental College staff member and Meiklejohn's assistant.

3. For more information on Evergreen's foci of learning, visit http://evergreen .edu/about/fivefoci.htm

4. The "I am from" poem assignment was developed by Linda Christensen and introduced to higher education by Beverly Daniel Tatum. See *Can We Talk About Race?* (2007, pp. 120–121) for Tatum's version of the poem.

5. Unpublished manuscript (post-1994), *Community, Power, and Diversity: Reflections and Caveats on Learning Communities* (reference number from the archivist at The Evergreen State College, Olympia, WA: Accession 1976–12 h5557 Academic Affairs, Personal Papers 1983–2004).

6. For more information, see the Blue Dot Campaign, David Suzuki Foundation website: bluedot.ca

References

Alverno College Faculty. (1994). *Student assessment-as-learning at Alverno College.* Milwaukee, WI: Alverno College Institute.

Ambrose, S., Bridges, M., DiPietro, M., Lovett, M., & Norman, M. (2010). *How learning works: Seven research-based principles for smart teaching.* San Francisco, CA: Jossey-Bass.

Association of American Colleges & Universities. (2007). *College learning for the new global century: A report from the National Leadership Council for Liberal Education and America's Promise.* Washington, DC: Author.

Boix-Mansilla, V., & Gardner, H. (1998). What are the qualities of understanding? In M. Stone Wiske (Ed.), *Teaching for understanding: Linking research with practice* (pp. 161–196). San Francisco, CA: Jossey-Bass.

Bransford, J. D., Brown, A. L., & Cocking, R. R. (Eds.). (1999). *How people learn: Brain, mind, experience, and school.* Washington, DC: National Academies Press.

Donovan, S., Bransford, J. D., & Pellegrino, J. (Eds.). (1999). *How people learn: Bridging research and practice.* Washington, DC: National Academies Press.

Elder , L., & Paul, R. (2010). *Analytical thinking.* Tomales, CA: Foundation for Critical Thinking.

Faris, R. (1975). *The passionate educators: Voluntary associations and the struggle for control of adult educational broadcasting in Canada, 1919–52.* Toronto, Canada: P. Martin.

Fink, L. D. (2013). *Creating significant learning experiences: An integrated approach to designing college courses* (2nd ed.). San Francisco, CA: Jossey-Bass.

Freire, P. (1970). *Pedagogy of the oppressed* (M. B. Ramos, Trans.). New York, NY: Seabury.

Freire, P. (1994). *Pedagogy of hope: Reliving* Pedagogy of the Oppressed. New York, NY: Continuum.

Gabelnick, F., MacGregor, J., Matthews, R. S., & Smith, B. L. (1990). *Learning communities: Creating connections among students, faculty, and disciplines: New directions for teaching and learning* (No. 41). San Francisco, CA: Jossey-Bass.

Harris, J. (2006). *Rewriting: How to do things with texts.* Logan, UT: Utah State University Press.

Hill, P. (n.d.). *Community, power and diversity: Reflections and caveats on learning communities.* [Unpublished manuscript]. Retrieved from http://archives.evergreen .edu/1976/1976-12/hill_p/h5557home.htm

Hill, P. (1985). *The rationale for learning communities.* Retrieved from http://www .evergreen.edu/washingtoncenter/resources/learningcommunities.html

Hill, P. (1991). Multi-culturalism: The crucial philosophical and organizational issues. *Change, 23*(4), 38–47.

Horton, M., & Freire, P. (1990). *We make the road by walking: Conversations on education and social change.* Philadelphia, PA: Temple University Press.

Huber, M. T., & Hutchings, P. (2004). *Integrative learning: Mapping the terrain.* Washington, DC: Association of American Colleges & Universities.

Lardner, E., & Malnarich, G. (2008a). A new era in learning community work: Why the pedagogy of intentional integration matters. *Change, 40*(4), 30–37.

Lardner, E., & Malnarich, G. (2008b, Winter). Sustaining learning communities: Moving from curricular to educational reform. *Perspectives,* 20–23.

Lardner, E., & Malnarich, G. (2008–2009). Assessing integrative learning: Insights from Washington Center's national project on assessing learning in learning communities. *Journal of Learning Communities Research, 3*(3), 1–20.

Lardner, E., & Malnarich, G. (2009). When faculty assess integrative learning: Faculty inquiry to improve learning community practice. *Change, 41*(5), 28–35.

Lynd, S. (2013). *Accompanying: Pathways to social change.* Oakland, CA: PM Press.

Malnarich, G. (2005). Learning communities and curricular reform: "Academic apprenticeships" for developmental students. In C. A. Kozeracki (Ed.), *Responding to the challenges of developmental education: New directions for community colleges* (No. 129, pp. 51–62). San Francisco, CA: Jossey-Bass.

Marton, F., Hounsell, D., & Entwistle, N. (Eds.). (1984). *The experience of learning*. Edinburgh, Scotland: Scottish Academic Press.

Matthews, R. S., Smith, B. L., & MacGregor, J. (2012). The evolution of learning communities: A retrospective. In K. Buch & K. E. Barron (Eds.), *Discipline-centered learning communities: Creating connections among students, faculty, and curricula: New directions for teaching and learning* (No. 132, pp. 99–111). San Francisco, CA: Jossey-Bass.

Meiklejohn, A. (1981). *The experimental college*. Cabin John, MD, and Washington, DC: Seven Locks Press. (Original work published 1932)

Project Zero, (n.d.). *Visible thinking* Harvard graduate school of education. Retrieved from http:// http://www.pz.harvard.edu/projects/visible-thinking

Schneider, C. G., Gaston, P. L., Adelman, C., & Ewell, P. T. (2014). The Degree Qualifications Profile 2.0: Defining U.S. degrees through demonstration and documentation of college learning. *Liberal Education, 100*(2), 32–35.

Shiva, V. (2002). *Water wars: Privatization, pollution, and profit*. New Delhi, India: India Research Press.

Shulman, L. S. (2004). Toward a pedagogy of substance. In L. S. Shulman (Ed.), *Teaching as community property: Essays on higher education* (pp. 128–138). San Francisco, CA: Jossey-Bass.

Smith, B., MacGregor, J., Matthews, R., & Gabelnick, F. (2004). *Learning communities: Reforming undergraduate education*. San Francisco, CA: Jossey-Bass.

Solnit, R. (2004). *Hope in the dark: Untold histories, wild possibilities*. New York, NY: Nation Books.

Tatum, B. D. (2007). *Can we talk about race? And other conversations in an era of school resegregation*. Boston, MA: Beacon Press.

Wiggins, G., & McTighe, J. (2005). *Understanding by design* (2nd ed.). Alexandria, VA: Association for Supervision and Curriculum Development.

Williams, T. T. (2004). *The open space of democracy*. Great Barrington, MA: The Orion Society.

Yarmie, J. (2014, October 27). The Blue Dot Tour: David Suzuki's last stand. *Manitoban*. Retrieved from http://www.themanitoban.com/2014/10/blue-dot-tour/21222/

SEMINAR MOVES

⑤ (The writer) argues ___.
I agree ___ but think (writer) misses ___.

The point of view presented is ___. If we accept this view the implications are ___. This is why, I (dis)agree . . .

Step 5: Coming to terms/taking a stance
Purpose: To give a fair-minded and generous account of a writer's stance while saying what you think about the "problem" or "issue" (either countering and/or forwarding, extending and/or recasting views).

④ What I wonder about is . . .
Here's something you might want to check . . .

I think you misunderstood. My idea is not ___ but ___.

Step 4: Countering ideas
Purpose: To state puzzles, concerns, and/or differences. Focus is on critiquing ideas, points of view, not criticizing or calling out people.

③ (Writer/speaker) pointed out that ___. I think . . .

___ made a useful point earlier. She said that ___. Does that make sense here?

Step 3: Forwarding others' ideas
Purpose: To make, connect, and extend discussion by referencing or "forwarding" other writers' ideas, classmates' comments, discussion from previous seminars and classes, etc.

② This is what I value about what you've said . . .

I particularly appreciate . . .

Step 2: Acknowledging what you value
Purpose: To be explicit about what you are learning from a new and/or different perspective from your own.

① Does anyone understand what (writer) meant by . . .?

Let me see if I understood what you (or writer) mean . . .

Can you tell me a little more about what you're thinking?

Step 1: Asking clarifying questions
Purpose: To understand a writer's or speaker's ideas, analysis, point of view, etc. Avoid asking "clarifying" questions if you actually have concerns and/or disagree. (See step 4)

FROM THE BUILDING RESILIENT COMMUNITIES (BRC) SYLLABUS

"Class gatherings are privileged occasions to develop your perspective on the program's overarching questions while learning from others; to investigate assumptions, including your own; to seek out opportunities to learn across significant differences; and to develop habits of mind and academic moves underlying Evergreen's expectations for its graduates."

Note. The Seminar Moves integrates terms used in BRC assigned texts, *Rewriting* by Joseph Harris (2006) and *Analytical Thinking* by Linder Elder and Richard Paul (2010). The ladder's visual and value/wonder language is from *Making Thinking Visible Project Zero,* Harvard Graduate School of Education.

BRC COLLABORATIVE LEARNING SELF-ASSESSMENT

Principles for Constructive Engagement	I am doing this	Making progress	Problematic for me	Not thought about it
You don't know what you don't know: Strive for intellectual humility.				
Everyone has an opinion. Opinions are not the same as informed knowledge.				
Let go of personal anecdotal evidence and look at broader societal patterns.				
Notice your own defensive reactions, and attempt to use these reactions as entry points for gaining deeper self-knowledge.				
Recognize how your social positionality (e.g., your own race, class, gender, sexuality, ability-status) informs your reactions to your classmates and those whose work you study in the course.				

Comments:

What I intend to work on in today's seminar:

Note. The five elements or principles for constructive engagement are from "How to Engage Constructively in Courses That Take a Critical Justice Approach," in *Is Everyone Really Equal? An Introduction to Key Concepts in Social Justice Education* (pp. 166–174), by Özlem Sensoy and Robin DiAngelo, 2012, New York, NY: Teachers College Press. The language for the fifth element replaces "instructor" in the original with "classmates."

4

RELATIONAL TEACHING AND LEARNING

The Classroom as Community and the Community as Classroom

David Schoem

Teaching and learning are relational experiences, between the teacher and the students, among the students in the class, and between the teacher and students and the course content. Relational teaching makes visible the humanity of the teacher and each individual student, as well as the humanity of the class content, subject matter, and text.

The relational approach to teaching celebrates the value of finding meaning in life broadly and in one's own individual life and calls on the community of the classroom to search deeply for individual and group meaning. The class is asked to consider how it will construct knowledge and integrate text, theory, practice, and experience. It requires students to connect theory to their personal lives, experience, and understanding of their world and, in turn, to use personal experience to help bring meaning to theory. The deepest classroom learning takes place when we recognize that teachers and students come to class and community as whole persons and not simply with intellects and brainpower. We learn best in community and amid a community of learners.

What I have come to understand is that I am at my best as a teacher, and my students are at their best as engaged learners when I enter as a whole person, just like my students, with not only an active mind but also a loving heart and soulful spirit. My teaching, the students' learning, and our classroom experience are all greatly enhanced by embracing the humanity that is in me and in my students and is alive in the classroom and by developing the rich human relationships of learning that await.

Once we recognize that each one of our students comes to class as a whole person, we understand their eagerness for a classroom experience in which there will be a relationship with the teacher. Clearly, students expect the teacher to advance their cognitive learning, ideas, knowledge, and critical and analytic thinking and writing skills. But, more deeply, many students hope that their teacher, in advancing their learning about content and theory, will also take an authentic interest in them as vibrant, complex individuals and in who they are; what they think and value; and what their challenges, hopes, beliefs, and dreams are. Students also want to see the linkage between their studies, the sometimes-faceless content and data of the discipline, and their own lives in a diverse democracy. They want help in drawing a meaningful connection between the text and their own experiences and making meaning for their own lives from the academic content they are studying. In other words, they want to be deeply engaged as whole selves in their learning.

In contrast, too much of our instruction in higher education is structured to disconnect the self from learning. In large lecture classes, students bring their brains to the classroom but are taught as if their heart and spirit should be left at the door. We encourage students to engage with technology rather than with their teachers and other human educators. In massive open online courses (MOOCs) and similar initiatives, we remove instruction and advising one step further from any personal connection, and we drop any pretext of community or meaningful teacher–student interaction (Kolowich, 2015; Leddy, 2013; Newman & Oh, 2014). Although technology most certainly can enhance instruction, too often we use it to replace teacher–student relationships (Pinker, 2015). We ask students to bring their computers to the classroom, and we hope their brains too, but certainly not their focused attention and presence or their heart and spirit. Students' personal identity, social identities, family, friends, social relations, lived experience, hopes, dreams, and understanding of and searching for meaning in life and the world around them are not considered relevant.

The evidence and exhortation presented in the literature of teaching and learning moves others and me to reach beyond the current ethos of higher education. That ethos is one that values the cost efficiency of impersonal, large weed-out courses and privileges connections with technology above any human interaction. It calls relational teaching "soft," awkwardly distances itself from any notion of "the whole student" or of "community," or invokes the fear and disdain that one might not fully cover all the factual information the discipline demands in one's course. This, of course, overlooks the fact that students learn far more deeply in an open and safe learning community.

This chapter, then, looks at my own experience teaching in a traditional college classroom and also in a residential learning community. In both settings I use the same approach: relationship building; community building; dialogic instruction; and, most important, honoring each individual student as a unique, extraordinary person. The process of relational teaching has several components, and I will address each of these as I discuss both of these teaching settings. These components are as follows:

- Integrity of the whole person
- The classroom as community: Personal and social identity in community
- Community as classroom: Personal and social identity in community
- Engaged learning and integrative pedagogic exercises and approaches

Although these components are integrated and overlapping, for the purposes of this chapter, I attempt to separate them out as distinct entities. I discuss each of these components in both the classroom and the learning community settings after a brief literature review to provide a common definition of *relational teaching*.

A Brief Review of Relational Teaching in the Literature

"What are you teaching this semester?" We all are very familiar with this question from faculty colleagues at the start of every new term, but I've often wondered if this is the correct or only question to be asking. Although I, of course, teach a content area topic, and, obviously, the course content is critically important in my classes, an equally good or companion question would be "*Whom* are you teaching this semester?"

Although for university faculty the practice of teaching content may typically rank as a higher priority than teaching students, the case for relational teaching and the importance of building communities of learners is actually well supported in the literature historically and today. Half a century ago, critics were lamenting the lack of humanity and the loss of community as part of the corporatization and mechanization of higher education. In 1967, Fred Newmann and Donald Oliver wrote in the *Harvard Educational Review*,

> Modern technological society proceeds at an ever increasing rate toward the breakdown of conditions requisite to human dignity. . . . Human relationships take on mechanistic qualities and become determined, not by tradition, human feeling, or spontaneous desires, but impersonal machines or bureaucratic flow charts. (pp. 65–66)

Their voices about the loss of human relationships in schools were echoed by Paul Goodman (1964) in the same era, who stated, "The schools less and less represent *any* human values, but simply adjustments to a mechanical system" (p. 21). Unfortunately, today, the same refrain of disconnection, isolation, mechanization, and loss of community is echoed widely in society. Peter Block (2008) wrote,

> Ironically, we talk today of how small our world has become with the shrinking effect of globalization, instant sharing of information, quick technology, workplaces that operate around the globe. . . . But all this does not create the connection from which we can become grounded and experience the sense of safety that arises from a place where we are emotionally, spiritually, and psychologically a member. (pp. 1–2)

The concept of the "community of scholars" requires that "teaching and learning are a personal relation; it is necessary for both the student and the teacher" (Goodman, 1964, p. 178). John Dewey, of course, had much earlier brought us the insight that "in a school that is a community, education occurs as a 'form of community life'" (as cited in Ancess, 2003, p. 3). Parker Palmer (2007) later built on that idea, urging community and "the community of truth" as the concept that is best suited to guide the "core mission of education—the mission of knowing, teaching, and learning. . . . The hallmark of the community of truth is in its claim that *reality is a web of communal relationships, and we know reality only by being in community with it*" (p. 97).

More recently, Putnam and Feldstein (2003) provided the case for the development of social capital within and across communities. They emphasized the importance for building both bonding social capital and bridging social capital. Their research pointed to the value in the educational setting for helping students in the class bond as a community, but they did not stop there. They also argued for helping students extend themselves and develop the skills of bridging social capital with people from different social identities and perspectives and with other communities through intergroup dialogue and learning in community.

These themes have found support in recent research on higher education (Astin, Astin, & Lindholm, 2011). Astin and colleagues lamented that their data show that the increased emphasis on testing and grades has come at the expense of what they called students' "inner" development—"the sphere of values and beliefs, emotional maturity, moral development, spirituality, and self-understanding" (p. 2). There is also extensive research (Ancess, 2003, pp. 59–60) on the benefit of caring teacher–student relationships in K–12 schools, including influencing student motivation and engagement; making schools more humane, more academically demanding, and more beneficial for low-performing students; and increasing overall student success at school. In a caring community, students increase their capacity for equanimity and for pursuing the big questions of life such as "Who am I? What are my most deeply felt values? Do I have a mission or purpose in my life? Why am I in college? What kind of person do I want to become? What sort of world do I want to help create?" (Astin et al., 2011, p. 1). Furthermore, when students pursue and investigate these big questions, research has shown that they demonstrate tangible academic gains in areas such as grade point average, leadership, well-being, getting along with those of other races and cultures, choosing courses and majors, completing their degree, and considering graduate school (Astin et al., 2011).

It is not surprising that when students "feel safe, supported, and respected, . . . whenever students feel that our classrooms are experienced as communities of belonging, where genuine communion between educators and students is possible, then the activity of meaning-making gets pushed to deeper levels of intensity" (Nash & Murray, 2010, p. 115). David Kirp's (2014) research reinforced the importance of the caring teacher for student learning and educational improvement and argued against an overreliance on the impersonal, whether through competition or through online learning and other technologies. He wrote,

> It's impossible to improve education by doing an end run around inherently complicated and messy human relationships. All youngsters need to believe that they have a stake in the future, a goal worth striving for, if they're going to make it in school. They need a champion, someone who believes in them, and that's where teachers enter the picture. The most effective approaches foster bonds of caring between teachers and their students. (p. SR4)

Part of the struggle to think of education in terms of community, be it the community of scholars, the community of belonging, or the community of truth, is that the value of community has increasingly come to be measured and valued in the limited and exclusive terms of economic prosperity, marginalizing any notion of compassion in the educational arena (Block, 2008). Yet, it is that very loss of and redefining of relationships that negatively affects student learning and faculty collegiality, neglecting the opportunity to learn with both the intellect and the heart (Palmer & Zajonc, 2010). As Wendell Berry reminded us, "The thing being made in a university is humanity. . . . What universities are mandated to make or help to make is human beings in the fullest sense of those words—not just trained workers or knowledgeable citizens but responsible heirs and members of human culture . . . that is, a fully developed human being" (in Palmer & Zajonc, 2010, p. 1).

Cheryl Keen (2002) challenged educators to engage deeply with students by asking, "When was the last time you—staff, administrators, faculty— asked a student, Would you like to have a cup of tea with me and we'll talk about your life?" (p. 41). She continued, saying,

> Students need help beginning to develop the ability to think holistically— to intuit life as a whole. We will make progress if we are conscious of the whole campus as a mentoring environment. We should ask: are there places on campus where it is safe to address one's deepest concerns? Are those known to students? Do our spaces reflect openness? Do we encourage stu- dents to test out their beliefs and values? (pp. 42–43)

Colleges and universities need to be intentional about addressing students' search for meaning and purpose (Thomas & Bahr, 2008), and according to Palmer and Zajonc (2010), it is critical that students have a classroom opportunity to do that searching if we hold out hope that such exploration will occur throughout their life. They wrote,

> By welcoming the *whole* student into our classes, unfamiliar aspects of who they are and what they care about suddenly come into view. What are the heartfelt questions they struggle with? Are they too scared to acknowledge the hopes and aspirations they harbor for their lives and for this world? If they fail to voice them in the safety of a college classroom, will they ever dare to live their aspirations later? (p. 91)

First-Year Seminar Class: Social Justice, Identity, Diversity, and Community (Sociology and University Courses Division)

This seminar class is part of a collection of courses offered on campus to provide students an intellectual experience emphasizing critical thinking in a small class setting. Classes typically have 18 students and meet for 90 min- utes twice per week. This particular seminar brings social scientific perspec- tives to the topic.

Integrity of the Whole Person

I begin the first day of class talking about the course content as well as dis- cussing the importance of community to student learning and the success of the class, and I emphasize that the responsibility for the success of the class rests with each student in addition to me. I then introduce a simple and fun exercise for the students and me to get to know each other's names and begin to feel comfortable with each other. I also ask students to write me a short letter telling me why they enrolled in the class, their expectations, and anything else they are willing to share about themselves. All of these simple tasks are intended to send a message to students about building a safe and welcoming community for learning in the classroom and, individually, with me.

During the second class I invite students to sign up for short individual appointments to meet with me during office hours. I want them to know that I am approachable, accessible, and available to them one-on-one outside of class, as they might desire, in addition to my being present in the classroom.

In addition to meeting students during office hours, I assign analytic journals as part of their writing assignments. These journals include two components, one that is based entirely on students' critical analysis of class readings, and one that asks them to reflect personally on the readings, bringing the theory to their personal experience and back again to theory. Examples of the first component include the following prompts:

> Joseph Graves (2004), on page 5 of his article, argues that race is a social construction and makes the case that "the fact is that no biological races exist in modern humans." Discuss what it means that race is socially constructed and has no biological basis.

> Linda Darling-Hammond (2010) provides data to demonstrate the decline of education in the U.S. compared with OECD nations as well as the growing gap in access to educational opportunity and educational attainment between the wealthy and poor. Review some of the data she presents on both of these issues and discuss.

Examples of the second component include the following prompts:

> Thinking of your own "dominant" social identities, what are some examples of your invisible privileges along the lines of Peggy McIntosh's (1997) article and Allan Johnson's (2006) book on pages 27–33?

> Thinking about this week's articles, reflect upon your experiences with social justice, identity, diversity, and community during the past week at college.

These prompts give students an opportunity to critically analyze readings and the space to find and examine themselves in depth in the articles and content of the course. And, in doing so, it provides them with an opportunity to speak as openly with me, their professor, as they feel comfortable as they reflect personally on these topics. Some students use this as an opportunity to engage deeply with the content on personal, social, and intellectual levels, whereas others move more tentatively into this self-reflective mode. I, of course, respond extensively to their critical analysis of the content, typically urging students to ask more of themselves, raise more complex and nuanced questions and analysis about the readings, and push issues more deeply. With their personal reflections, I typically invite students to think in broader ways about the issues they raise, encourage them to take intellectual risks in perspective taking, and offer support for their introspection and personal reflection. Through their writing, students can take the step to build a deeper relationship with me that leads to more frequent visits to my office hours and much more substantive conversations when we meet one-on-one or in the context of their journal writing and in the open class discussions.

The Classroom as Community: Personal and Social Identity in Community

I also ask students to share with the class about how they are likely to present themselves in class discussions. My goal is for students to become aware and conscious of their own style (quiet, shy, engaging, assertive, boisterous) and the different styles of their classmates. Some of the ways students present themselves are based on individual style, and some are based more on their social identities. I want students to begin the process of trust building in the classroom by recognizing different styles of participation and not misinterpreting styles different from their own or being misinterpreted by others.

I also invite students to develop a set of ground rules for class discussion. Together the students brainstorm a menu of guidelines to help ensure that the class will be one in which they feel safe speaking and listening openly and honestly with one another. In doing this exercise, we have an opportunity to interrogate some of the suggested ground rules to help understand, for instance, how to best be honest and critical yet still sensitive to others and also to be trusting and listening actively, even if we sometimes are uncomfortable with the content of what is being expressed.

As the course develops, my students begin the process of sharing openly with one another about their interpretation and perspective on potentially contentious class topics such as race, class, gender, and inequality. They build a level of trust and comfort to speak honestly and forthrightly, which results from the sense of community that has developed in the classroom. That community connection also translates into their greater willingness to see me, their professor, as someone who is interested in their intellectual growth; their critical thinking skills; their social perspective; and their own self, identity, and future.

For class discussion, I employ a number of dialogic exercises (see Schoem & Hurtado, 2001). The composite of exercises is intended to (a) give students a variety of opportunities to gain skill and experience in discussions that are one-on-one, small group, and large group; (b) provide students with actual experience in dialogic conversations about difficult and contentious topics; and (c) provide students with an opportunity to engage deeply about course content with ample chance to speak and to listen to different perspectives.

One of these dialogic exercises, the concentric circle, involves a simple arrangement of furniture so that each student is facing one other student, forming an inner and outer circle. I prepare a set of questions, focusing on course readings, social identity trigger questions, or a combination of the two, that are ordered in a way to be progressively nuanced, complex, and challenging. Each student in the pair takes a turn separately answering one question, and then they have an opportunity to discuss the question and their different answers together. It is a fast-moving, timed exercise so that each question gets about four minutes of attention total, and then students in the inner circle change seats and move on to face the next person in the outer circle. What emerges is a closely directed series of one-on-one conversations among the class about the class topic. At different points I may call the entire class to attention to lead a short class-wide discussion about a particular question that I want to more closely interrogate.

Another dialogic exercise is the fishbowl exercise, used variously as an open or closed dialogue (Schoem & Saunders, 2001), again to encourage speaking and listening about course topics focusing on course readings or the connection between theory and personal practice. The fishbowl arrangement has a group of about five students sitting in a small circle facing each other surrounded by a larger circle composed of the rest of the students in class. Students in the outside circle cannot speak (but they must actively listen) unless they want to tap someone in the inner circle to take a turn speaking in that group. In the closed fishbowl, I might ask men in the class to sit in the inner circle to talk, for instance, about what it means to them to be a male, having each student speak independently prior to a group discussion among the men. The role of the women on the outer circle is to listen and take notes, until it is time to reverse roles, and the women come into the fishbowl to discuss what it means to each of them to be a female. Students find this particular exercise one of the most enriching and enlightening learning experiences of their semester, as it provides an insider's ear to another group's open and honest discussion and also challenges students to think and speak seriously and critically about their own identity, often for the first time.

Community as Classroom: Personal and Social Identity in Community

There are numerous ways to incorporate learning in and from the community as part of the classroom experience. These range from service-learning projects, community-based learning, community partnership activities, intercultural service activities, internships, political engagement, community-based research, community advocacy, and intergroup dialogue. By placing students in the community with proper educational guidance, we encourage them to push their social comfort zones and existing intellectual paradigms to see themselves and the community and world in deeper ways. Their learning through these engaged approaches is often much more penetrating and sustaining than their simply learning from lecture, books, or discussion. Their experiences and interactions bring the course content to life and challenge their social perspectives and personal values and understandings.

In my class I require students to participate in several community-based learning activities. These range from activities that can be done individually in the community to others that involve other class members. One of the most powerful experiences students have in this class is through their participation in one activity organized by their own social identity and two activities organized by a social identity group different from their own. Students might attend an event on campus or in the community that is organized by groups according to their religion, gender, race, sexual orientation, nationality, ethnicity, ability, or other social identity backgrounds. This requirement not only affirms for students their identity with their own social backgrounds but also allows them to enter, what are for most, worlds that have been closed to them throughout their life. Even though most students speak of a desire to meet and mix with students from other backgrounds, the perceived walls between groups often appear impenetrable to them.

This class assignment gives students permission—it actually requires them—to not only step out of their comfort zone but also to acknowledge that interacting with other groups does not preclude their maintaining a strong affiliation with their own social identities. It reinforces Putnam and Feldstein's (2003) theory of bonding and bridging social capital that for the purpose of building healthy, vibrant communities with strong social capital one can and should learn to both be a part of one's group and have the skills to move easily across social boundaries to interact with people from other groups.

Students also are required to attend together two films that are part of a university–community social and environmental justice film and discussion series at the public library. They watch the films in an audience with community members and then are encouraged to stay and participate with community members in the open discussion that follows.

I also require my students to investigate and track the websites of two dialogue and deliberative democracy organizations throughout the semester. I want them to see that the activities of our classroom regarding civic and dialogic engagement are part of a national and international movement and to give them an opportunity to consider participating in this kind of activity and/or work throughout college and beyond.

Finally, during presidential election years, I require students to attend some event associated with the election. I invite students to choose whatever candidates or issues forum in which they are interested. This is in no way about partisanship, as they can select to attend events of whatever party they choose, though I encourage them to attend events from different political parties to expand their perspective-taking skills. The critical lesson for me as their instructor is that in a time of widespread alienation and disengagement from civic life among this age cohort I want them to see themselves in the practice of democratic deliberation.

It goes without saying that all of these activities are eye opening for students. Most have never participated in any of these activities, and all have not participated in at least a few of them. They see themselves in a new light, with their classmates, as evolving adults and democratic participants, with a new awareness about self, social identity, and community.

Engaged Learning and Integrative Pedagogic Exercises and Approaches

In addition to the various pedagogic exercises and approaches in the classroom and community discussed earlier, I employ several other exercises that involve typical small- and large-group discussions, pairing off in various configurations with different approaches to reporting out by verbal reporting, leading discussion, written notes, and so on according to specific prompts or more general discussion of readings. The following are examples of some other exercises.

The name game. With the class in a circle format, students repeat the first name of their classmates and then add their own name. This can be enhanced by students' attaching an interesting fact or characteristic of each person to his or her name. The idea of the game is to be fast and fun with an emphasis on learning names. It is important that no one feels bad if he or she has difficulty remembering names.

The five-minute poem (courtesy of Beverly Daniel Tatum, 2007, via Linda Christensen at a workshop Tatum and I cofacilitated). Students write and then share a short poem about their family or cultural background using a simple structured format. These poems allow students to introduce themselves in a much deeper manner than the typical naming of one's major or résumé highlights and also teaches students that each one has a rich cultural and personal story and history.

The social identity essay (Schoem, 1991; Schoem, Frankel, Zuniga, & Lewis, 1995). Students write social identity autobiographies, which give them the opportunity to share their own social identity story with classmates. This paper affirms for students their social identity experiences and allows them to reflect on their history of different experiences and encounters. Students are required to include references to about 10 different readings so that their reflections and insights are grounded in the academic literature.

The power exercise (see Schoem & Saunders, 2001). This quick exercise introduces the concept of power and privilege to students, giving them an opportunity to step back and engage with the issue. Students hold a blank sheet of paper in groups of three or four with the instruction of "This piece of paper represents power; do something with it." The students do a wide range of things to the sheet of paper (e.g., yanking it or eating it to control the whole sheet, sharing it equally, or grabbing it and tossing it in the trash), and then as a class discuss the results with faculty guidance. The exercise teaches about the complexity of response to power and raises questions of power as finite or infinite, power as having potential for good or evil, power with, power over, and so on.

Collaborative and project-based assignments. Students are given collaborative verbal or written assignments and guidelines on how to work collaboratively to encourage positive and equitable participation of all.

Residential Learning Community: The Michigan Community Scholars Program

In addition to the traditional classroom setting, the university campus allows for numerous opportunities to create formal and informal learning communities that embrace the whole student by integrating the academic and the cocurricular experience of students. The following is an example of one such intentional learning community that creates a multicultural, dialogic, lived learning experience for students that focuses on the whole individual, inclusive of classroom study and cocurricular experiences in a residential setting (Galura, Pasque, Schoem, & Howard, 2004; Schoem, 2005b). In recent years, the demographic profile of the program has been close to 60% students of color and international students, including almost 30% underrepresented minorities, and about 40% White students, far exceeding the diversity of the campus as a whole. Retention and persistence rates for all students in the program have matched or slightly exceeded university-wide rates, and retention and persistence rates for African American students have far exceeded university-wide rates.

Integrity of the Whole Person

The Michigan Community Scholars Program (MCSP) is built on a foundation of giving attention to the individual student and caring for the whole person within a mission of deep learning and academic success; social justice; community service; diversity; and dialogic, intergroup engagement (Schoem, 2002). At the University of Michigan, the program allows each of the 175 students to stand out as an individual in an otherwise large, sometimes impersonal institution. The program actively works to facilitate student identity development; encourage engagement across different social backgrounds in the development of a multicultural community; and help students find meaning, purpose, and fulfillment in their life and the world (Schoem, 2005a).

One way we accomplish individual attention is to mentor each individual not just in one pathway but also in multiple ones. Our professional staff meets individually with each student so that there is a strong personal connection built between the staff and every student. We actively encourage students to routinely stop by our offices for all kinds of formal and informal reasons and make a point of making every conversation and contact an opportunity for relationship building.

We also have an extensive peer leadership and peer mentoring program. Those participating in the program for a second or third year, representing about one fourth of the total number of students, serve as student leaders. Our peer mentors reach out to first-year college students even prior to their arrival at college and make a point of meeting regularly with their peer protégés to offer guidance and support as they start college. These mentors help socialize students in the values of the program, including dialogue, social justice, diversity, intergroup relations, community service, and academic excellence. The peer leaders, by their example, teach students to explore their personal and social identities, the sense of purpose in their life, their commitment to making a difference in the world, and their skill in crossing social boundaries and engaging with people from different social backgrounds and social and political viewpoints.

Faculty who teach in association with MCSP are carefully selected for their commitment to high-quality teaching and interest in their students. They also teach courses on topics related to the program's mission. These faculty are highly accessible to students, hold office hours in the residence hall, and often participate in and sometimes organize programs for students in MCSP.

The program serves as an academic unit in the residence hall setting, taking advantage of the opportunity for multiple safety nets for students' personal and academic success. Residence hall staff inform the academic staff of personal and mental health and behavioral issues that become evident in students in the residence hall. Faculty, too, bring to staff students' worrisome behavior or performance changes that suggest problems beyond the classroom setting. Because existing relationships between the MCSP staff and the students through mentoring and other individualized contact, they are able to advise students to pursue professional counseling or take advantage of other campus resources to address whatever issues they are confronting. In a similar way, because staff get to know students so well, they are able to point students with specificity toward the many leadership, job, internship, research, and funding opportunities that are available on campus.

The Classroom as Community: Personal and Social Identity in Community

In MCSP, the classroom is literally the living–learning community; that is, the residence hall where students live, study, take classes, dine, and organize and hold meetings and programs together. The program office is located in this same space, and faculty members teach their courses in classrooms located in this same residence hall, where they also hold office hours. It is in this lived space where students learn to live out the values of the program mission, that is, the classroom content, diversity and intergroup relations, social identity development, community building, community service and social justice, and academic excellence.

Having the staff work and faculty teach in the same building where students live reinforces the strong sense of commitment to this learning community. Another critical structure is the fact that the program's student leaders live on the residence hall floors with the first-year students. Ongoing informal discussions of issues related to the program's mission and classes take place day and night in the cafeteria, in the living areas, and in the hallways and lounges. The agency and empowerment students feel about making a difference in the world is palpable, as each student's enthusiasm and purposefulness creates a highly vibrant and contagious collective energy.

In addition to the informal interactions, students are encouraged to participate in structured intergroup dialogues and "hot topics" discussions organized by MCSP's Intergroup Relations Council, where they practice and learn skills of engaging civilly with others around what can be difficult and contentious topics. Students learn to listen carefully and respectfully to one another to try to understand how their well-meaning peers from different social identities and backgrounds and/or with varying social or political viewpoints perceive and make sense of the world. By participating in these dialogues, and then bringing their discussions and learning experiences back to their residential living space and dining hall, students create a unique 24/7 living dialogic community.

With guidance from the program staff, faculty, and student leaders, students organize a multitude of cocurricular programs and service-learning events that introduce ideas, points of view, and in-depth study of a wide range of topics under the broad heading of social justice. There are community service clubs on issues such as youth and education, urban and rural poverty, civil rights, borders and immigration, and public health and environmental sustainability. There is also the Intergroup Relations Council, which focuses on dialogue and campus and program climate issues, and the Programming Board, which has a budget to organize educational, cultural, and social programs in the service of community building.

The unique opportunity of this residential learning program and classroom as community is that all of the learning, study, and programs are immediately translated into lived experiences through relationships, conversations, and activities; at dining tables and on residence hall floors; and so on—students lovingly refer to their community as the "MCSPhamily." Students are encouraged to practice in their lived experience what they learn each day. They do this by taking their classroom topics to dinner and late night conversations on their residential floors for further examination and reflection, by making efforts to build interracial and inclusive friendships and community on their residence floors and in campus activities, by collectively working on community service projects, by treating the residence hall staff with respect, and by refraining from unruly parties or property destruction that can occur in other residence hall settings. The results, although not without stumbles, conflicts, and missteps, provide students with what is often a first opportunity to fully engage deeply with people from many different backgrounds and with many different perspectives in a multicultural community that values openness, dialogue, respect, ideas, critical thinking, and purposefulness to make a difference in the world.

The MCSP students take these special values and relationships as they proceed throughout their college education. They live in houses and apartments with diverse groups of friends; join multicultural organizations; take leadership roles in campus social justice organizations; and stay in touch with their peers, as well as the program staff and faculty, beyond college and into their professional life. Although still in college, the MCSP students make their mark on the campus by holding major student leadership positions and being disproportionately honored with student leadership awards, particularly in areas of diversity, social justice, and community service.

Finally, the program makes an explicit statement at the start of the academic year about the collective responsibility for each student's learning. Students are told not only that they are expected to succeed and excel in their academic studies but also that it is each one's responsibility to make sure that every member of the community has that same successful academic experience.

Community as Classroom: Personal and Social Identity in Community

As a program focusing on community service, the MCSP has the distinct opportunity to take advantage of the engaged, experiential learning that is inherent in community service-learning activities. Through classroom study, structured cocurricular reflection on their community service experiences, relationship building with and mentoring by community members, and supervision by program staff and faculty, students learn an enormous amount about social issues, about power and privilege, about difference, and about themselves.

One exceptional example is the program's ongoing partnership with the Detroit neighborhood organization Neighbors Building Brightmoor (NBB). At Brightmoor, the extraordinary community organizer Riet Schumack routinely speaks to students about the neighborhood and the social, economic, educational, and safety issues facing the community and how the neighbors in the community have chosen to respond. She gives these talks when students come to do service in Brightmoor, and she also has come to MCSP at the college campus on a number of occasions. In particular, she extends herself by mentoring student leaders and teaching them about the relationships and commitments that make NBB's work so successful despite overwhelming odds. She partners students together with individual families to work on large cleanup and building projects.

The student work in Brightmoor has resulted in some notable achievements. One is the development of the Brightmoor Youth Garden and Playground that was completed in partnership between MCSP and NBB to give youth a place to play, garden, and develop a source of fresh, healthy food for local families. As part of this effort, the MCSP students served as mentors to the Brightmoor youth. A second project was organized by two faculty members, Christine Modey and Hannah Smotrich, who had their students interview the families of Brightmoor to learn about their life and to elicit favorite recipes for a published book of these student interviews with photos and original artwork, titled *The Brightmoor Farmway* (Modey & Smotrich, 2012). The faculty received grant money to distribute the full print run of the book free to NBB to be sold for fund-raising purposes.

A second example of using the community as a learning environment is MCSP's Social and Environmental Justice University–Community Film Series, organized in collaboration with the Ann Arbor District Library. Each month in the fall semester, MCSP hosts a film screening on a particular social issue followed by open discussion with the community and university members present. The documentary film directors, university faculty, community members, and college and high school students are invited to be speakers or serve as panelists for the discussions. It is one of the few opportunities for university students to engage in open discussion and dialogue about social issues with people from outside the sheltered university setting.

A third example is MCSP's efforts to have students present at academic conferences. MCSP staff have helped students submit successful proposals for presentations, mentored them in developing their presentations before various higher education audiences, and attended the conferences with the students. MCSP students have presented at the Association of American Colleges & Universities, the National Learning Communities Conference, Michigan Campus Compact, Difficult Dialogues, and the Citizens' Toolbox conferences, to outstanding reviews for the content of the presentations, their professional and thoughtful presence, and their energetic commitment to social justice issues.

MCSP students also are encouraged to participate actively in the campus community and take their leadership experience to other campus organizations. MCSP students have taken leadership roles in dialogue programs on campus, in campus-wide community service units and organizations; in student government; on the student-run campus newspaper; and in social-identity-focused groups on race, ethnicity, gender, religion, disability, and sexual orientation. They have also served as leaders in campus activism around issues of race, sexual orientation, immigration, and other social justice concerns.

In their roles as MCSP student leaders or as part of an MCSP on-campus alumni organization of undergraduates who are not living in the program, former MCSP students mentor current MCSP students in leadership skills and facilitate their getting involved in issues of concern to them. Along the way, they become educated both about the topic of interest and about taking leadership of organizations.

Engaged Learning and Integrative Pedagogic Exercises and Approaches

To begin the process of community building and learning, we take all of our 175 students and student leaders to a low ropes course the first day after they arrive on campus, prior to the start of classes. Students break into small groups to participate in trust-building exercises with their new community members. We then require a day of service for all of our students (frequently to help clear invasive species from a natural areas preservation site in the city) to build on the common ground of commitment to our diverse group of students and to do the bonding and, especially, the bridging social capital work that is so unfamiliar to most of them. Students work in teams led by our student leaders as together they get their hands dirty in the woods, working side by side across their different social backgrounds and identities.

Our students all participate in a common intellectual experience, a one-credit course that introduces them to the values of the program and supports their successful transition from high school to college. The course meets only until the fall midsemester break and is organized into large group sessions (panels, simulation games, lectures, films, and various interactive exercises) and small group discussions led by the MCSP resident adviser student leaders. As part of the course requirements, students are required to attend the office hours of all of their college instructors in the first three weeks of class. It is an assignment that provokes bonding in the community out of an initial common anxiety but results in college habits of engaging with faculty once students find how accessible and welcoming most of their faculty actually are.

All students participate actively in community service-learning activities, typically in teams of MCSP students. They are oriented about entering into a new community and participate in reflection about their experience, with discussion groups, journals, and readings to enhance their understanding and insights. Student enthusiasm for making a difference in the world, and their sense of empowerment through their participation in MCSP committees, community partnerships, courses, and leadership opportunities, are infectious.

Finally, a number of other community activities have become traditions, including MCSP's MLK Day Circle of Unity event, a winter retreat, and an end-of-year celebration. The MLK Day Circle of Unity involves about 300 students, faculty, staff, and community members singing and moving to songs of freedom and social and racial justice together, arm in arm, in the campus commons, or Diag, on what is usually the coldest day of the year. About a third of our students attend an off-campus retreat in winter semester in February to reinvigorate the community with relational events and to spend time thinking strategically and critically about issues facing the MCSP community and the broader university. The end-of-year celebration provides an opportunity to recognize all of the outgoing student leaders and graduating seniors and to collectively pass the torch to the new group of student leaders as students begin to look toward the summer and the next academic year.

All of these activities and approaches comprise the life of the community, and each addresses the goals of honoring the whole of each individual student. They make real the ideal of the program and classroom as a community for modeling the values of the program and using the community as a classroom learning opportunity.

Closing: Personal Reflections

On the basis of my teaching and scholarly work across several disciplines and my administrative experience at the center and margins of higher education, my confidence about the best approach to successful teaching and meaningful student learning has only been reinforced over time. Embracing both academic affairs and student affairs, I have had the opportunity to bring to my work a unified vision in my approach to my wonderful students, and I have seen many thousands flourish, majority and underrepresented students alike, as a result of meaningful, caring relationships with faculty and staff.

Today I am ever more passionate about the central importance and power of relational teaching, engaged learning, integrative pedagogy, and multicultural community building for education and learning and about the inspiring humanity nested within each student, staff member, and faculty member I have had the good fortune to meet.

Reflection Questions

1. What specific steps can you take to incorporate a relational teaching approach into your pedagogy?
2. Whom are you teaching this semester? How would your instructional approach change were you to develop a "teaching the whole student with heart, mind, and spirit" approach?
3. What techniques do you use to build community among the students in your class and to create the traditional collegiate notion of a community of scholars throughout your campus? Do your students have an opportunity to consider "the big questions" and search for meaning and purpose in their life in your classes?
4. How might you facilitate intergroup dialogue, as described in this chapter, in your classroom or learning community? How might it help to foster a sense of community and deeper engagement among your students?
5. How might community-based learning help your students engage more deeply with their classmates, the campus, and the surrounding community?

6. Whether or not your institution has a learning community like the MCSP, how might your campus help students engage with issues of social identity, social justice, community service, and social change in ways that foster their own social and intercultural development, integration of learning from classroom and cocurricular experiences, and connections with the campus and surrounding community?

7. What integrative pedagogical approaches can you use to help students connect theory to their personal experiences and their personal experiences back to theoretical understandings?

8. What approaches, structures, exercises, and techniques do you use to develop an engaged learning experience for your students?

References

Ancess, J. (2003). *Beating the odds: High schools as communities of commitment.* New York, NY: Teachers College Press.

Astin, A., Astin, H., & Lindholm, J. (Eds.). (2011). *Cultivating the spirit: How college can enhance students' inner lives.* San Francisco, CA: John Wiley & Sons.

Block, P. (2008). *Community: The structure of belonging.* San Francisco, CA: Berret-Koehler.

Darling-Hammond, L. (2010). *The flat world and education: How America's commitment to equity will determine our future.* New York, NY: Teachers College/Columbia University.

Galura, J., Pasque, P., Schoem, D., & Howard, J. (Eds.). (2004). *Engaging the whole of service-learning, diversity and learning communities.* Ann Arbor, MI: OCSL Press.

Goodman, P. (1964). *The community of scholars.* New York, NY: Vintage Books.

Graves, J. (2004). *The race myth.* New York, NY: Penguin.

Johnson, A. (2006). *Privilege, power, and difference* (2nd ed.). New York, NY: McGraw-Hill.

Keen, C. (2002). Spiritual assumptions undergird educational priorities: A personal narrative. In V. Kazanjian, Jr. & P. Laurence (Eds.), *Education as transformation* (pp. 37–44). New York, NY: Peter Lang.

Kirp, D. (2014, August 16). Teaching is not a business. *New York Times.* Retrieved from http://www.nytimes.com/2014/08/17/opinion/sunday/teaching-is-not-a-business.html?_r=0

Kolowich, S. (2015, January 15). Doubts about MOOCs continue to rise, survey finds. *Chronicle of Higher Education.* Retrieved from http://chronicle.com/article/Doubts-About-MOOCs-Continue-to/144007/

Leddy, T. (2013, June 14). Are MOOCs good for students? *Boston Review.* Retrieved from http://bostonreview.net/us/are-moocs-good-students

McIntosh, P. (1997). White privilege: Unpacking the invisible knapsack. In B. Schneider (Ed.), *Race: An anthology in the first person* (pp. 118–126). New York, NY: Three Rivers Press.

Modey, C., & Smotrich, H. (2012). *The Brightmoor farmway.* Ann Arbor, MI: Neighbors Building Brightmoor.

Nash, R., & Murray, M. (2010). *Helping college students find purpose: The campus guide to meaning-making.* San Francisco, CA: John Wiley & Sons.

Newman, J., & Oh, S. (2014, June 13). 8 things you should know about MOOCs. *Chronicle of Higher Education.* Retrieved from http://chronicle.com/article/8-Things-You-Should-Know-About/146901/

Newmann, F., & Oliver, D. (1967). Education and community. *Harvard Educational Review, 37*(1), 61–106.

Palmer, P. (2007). *The courage to teach: Exploring the inner landscape of a teacher's life.* San Francisco, CA: Jossey-Bass.

Palmer, P., & Zajonc, A. (2010). *The heart of higher education: A call to renewal.* San Francisco, CA: Jossey-Bass.

Pinker, S. (2015, January 30). Can students have too much tech? *New York Times,* p. A21.

Putnam, R., & Feldstein, L. (2003). *Better together: Restoring the American community.* New York, NY: Simon & Schuster.

Schoem, D. (Ed.). (1991). *Inside separate worlds: Life stories of young Blacks, Jews, and Latinos.* Ann Arbor, MI: University of Michigan Press.

Schoem, D. (2002). Transforming undergraduate education: Moving beyond distinct undergraduate initiatives. *Change: The Magazine of Higher Learning, 34*(6), 50–55.

Schoem, D. (2005a). *College knowledge: 101 tips.* Ann Arbor, MI: University of Michigan Press.

Schoem, D. (2005b). Modeling a diverse and democratic America: The Michigan Community Scholars Program. *About Campus, 10*(5), 18–23.

Schoem, D., Frankel, L., Zuniga, X., & Lewis, E. (Eds.). (1995). *Multicultural teaching in the university.* New York, NY: Praeger Press.

Schoem, D., & Hurtado, S. (Eds.). (2001). *Intergroup dialogue: Deliberative democracy in school, college, community and workplace.* Ann Arbor, MI: University of Michigan Press.

Schoem, D., & Saunders, S. (2001). Adapting intergroup dialogue processes for use in a variety of settings. In D. Schoem & S. Hurtado (Eds.), *Intergroup dialogue: Deliberative democracy in school, college, community and workplace* (pp. 328–344). Ann Arbor, MI: University of Michigan Press.

Tatum, B. D. (2007). *Can we talk about race?* Boston, MA: Beacon Press.

Thomas, N., & Bahr, A. M. (2008). Higher education's opportunities and challenges. In M. R. Diamond (Ed.), *Encountering faith in the classroom: Turning difficult discussions into constructive engagement* (pp. 3–29). Sterling, VA: Stylus.

5

TOWARD A NEW PEDAGOGY TO HELP CREATE A SUSTAINABLE FUTURE

James Crowfoot

This chapter tells the story of discoveries using engaged learning and integrative pedagogies that transformed a multidisciplinary seminar on the challenges of unsustainability begun in 1999 for first-year college students. This story also illuminates possible ways students and teachers can enable each other's learning. The discoveries within this seminar were (a) dialogues for learning from students' diverse ultimate values and beliefs, as well as their backgrounds, relating to sustainability; (b) psycho-spiritual experiential practices in the out-of-doors to enable deepened emotional and cognitive relating with nature—human and more than human; and (c) group practices of "gratitude," "honoring our pain," and "seeing with new eyes" to foster students' "active hope" in the face of uncertainty, crisis, and fear (Macy & Johnstone, 2012). The impetus for these unexpected innovations in this seminar and their implementation resulted from the experiences and willingness of its members (students and me, their teacher) to learn and practice new ways of knowing through engaged learning and integrative pedagogy. Together with other elements of this seminar, these changes enabled students to begin emotionally and cognitively integrating their own ultimate values and beliefs with information from the sciences and the humanities relevant to the multiple challenges, complexities, and urgency of unsustainability—what Harden Tibbs (1999) termed the *crisis of crises*.

The parts of this chapter provide the reader information on the seminar's (a) context, (b) a description of the seminar, and (c) three discoveries within it that were implemented to provide students opportunities for engaged and integrative learning in response to the challenges of unsustainability.

Context for the Seminar

This section will introduce you to the challenging topic of unsustainability, the backgrounds of entering college students on this topic, my beginning to teach this topic to these students, and my own background and commitment to doing introductory teaching on this complex and contested topic.

Unsustainability: Bad News and Glimmers of Better News

The topic of this seminar is the crisis of unsustainability, along with emerging responses and alternative scenarios for humans' and Earth's future. The roots of this global emergency are multiple increasing human impacts on the Earth system as documented by the 24 "Great Acceleration Graphs," originally published in 2004 covering the years from 1750 to 2000 and recently updated to 2010 and published as I was completing this chapter (Steffen et al., 2004; Steffen, Richardson, et al., 2015). These graphs track relations between changes in 12 socioeconomic trends and "12 Earth System indicators that track change in major features of the system's structure and functioning" (Steffen, Broadgate, Deutsch, Gaffney, & Ludwig, 2015, p. 3). As just reported,

> The dominant feature of the socio-economic trends is that the economic graphs clearly show that economic activity of the human enterprise continues to grow at a rapid rate. . . . The Earth System indicators, in general, continued their long-term, post-industrial rise, although a few, such as atmospheric methane concentration and stratospheric ozone loss, show a slowing or apparent stabilization over the past decade. The post-1950 acceleration in the Earth System indicators remains clear. Only beyond the mid-20th century is there clear evidence for fundamental shifts in the state and functioning of the Earth System that are beyond the range of variability of the Holocene and driven by human activities. (Steffen, Broadgate, et al., 2015, p. 1)

In the late 1980s, the United Nations' (UN's) World Commission on Environment and Development (WCED) anticipated and began to document the unprecedented changes described here, and in its final report, *Our Common Future*, it defined *sustainable development* as "development that meets the needs of the present without compromising the ability of future generations to meet their own needs" (WCED, 1987). The United Nations General Assembly in its 96th plenary meeting, on December 11, 1987, explicitly stated that this "should become a central guiding principle for the United Nations, governments, and private institutions, organizations and enterprises" (United Nations, 1987). It stated that it did this out of its concern for the accelerating deterioration of the human environment and natural resources and the consequences of that deterioration for economic and social development, particularly for poverty-stricken people of the world. At this time all the leaders of the world, along with many other leaders and elites in higher education, business, and politics, were put on notice about the seriousness of these unprecedented and accelerating human and planetary conditions.[1]

Since the 1987 UN report, there has been increasing attention at all levels of the world to mitigating (and sometimes ignoring or resisting mitigation of) the impacts of unsustainability. Together, mitigation efforts have neither reversed nor stopped the patterns that constitute unsustainability.

Most hopeful in my judgment are the positive results of the Millennium Development Goals undertaken by the UN in 2000 with the explicit support and involvement of almost all world leaders to improve by 2015 the conditions of the world's poorest people and secondarily the sustainability of the natural environment (United Nations, Department of Economic and Social Affairs, 2006–2014). Some goals have been fully met and some only partially. Nevertheless, these achievements demonstrate that a coordinated worldwide effort can be effective. This is a major step toward fulfilling the UN General Assembly's 1987 wake-up call to organizations throughout the world. To continue this momentum, better planning was done to develop new goals in which member nations had more opportunity to participate.

The UN General Assembly representing all the countries of the world adopted these 17 new Sustainable Development Goals on September 25, 2015. These goals aspire to "end poverty, fight inequality and injustice and tackle climate change" by 2030 (United Nations Development Program, 2016). It is hoped this will continue and accelerate the progress that began in 2000 with the initiation of the Millennium Development Goals (United Nations Development Program, 2016).[2]

Meanwhile, in late 2015, in Paris, world leaders from 197 countries negotiated an agreement to reduce greenhouse gases to slow climate disruption and change. This agreement, officially referred to as a "convention," requires action from every country, rich or poor (Davenport, 2015). Subsequently, at the UN in New York on Earth Day in April 2016, leaders of 175 nations signed the Paris climate agreement ("175 Nations," 2016). By October 5, 2016, 125 countries had officially ratified it, and on November 6, 2016, the agreement "entered into force" when the threshold was reached of "at least 55 nations party to the agreement and accounting in total for at least an estimated 55% of the total greenhouse gas admissions had deposited their instruments of ratification, acceptance of approval" with the UN (United Nations Framework Convention on Climate Change, 2016).

We know from an early 2015 scientific report on the state of the Earth system's boundaries in relation to humans' threatening impacts that the two most important such threats in the judgment of these scientists' analyses are already beyond safe boundaries and thus are progressively destabilizing the climate and irreversibly degrading the marine, freshwater, and land habitats of our planet (Steffen, Richardson, et al., 2015). This report, along with the most recent report from the scientists on the Intergovernmental Panel on Climate Change (IPCC, 2014), definitively shows human impacts are disrupting and destabilizing our climate (Steffen, Richardson, et al., 2015).

The 2014 Worldwatch Institute's *State of the World Report* focuses all of its articles on answering the question "Is sustainability still possible?" The fact that this publication seriously and substantively addresses this question is further evidence of how the time is long past for every person's education to include learning about unsustainability and sustainability (Engelman, 2014).

Entering College Students' Lack of Knowledge About Unsustainability

In the United States, virtually no high schools offer a course on the challenges of unsustainability, much less require one. Furthermore, most students in the United States graduate from high school without a course on environmental science; relatively few high schools even offer such a course as an advanced placement elective. In 1999, when I began offering my seminar "Environment, Sustainability, and Social Change," typically I would have only a couple of students who had heard about unsustainability, and I would usually have 1 or 2 enrollees out of the 20 or 22 students who had completed a high school course on environmental science. I observed this number slowly increasing to 3 or 4 students. Since beginning to offer this seminar, I have had only 2 U.S. students enroll having completed a high school course that focused on issues of social injustice that are integral to the social aspects of unsustainability. This is out of a total of about 350 students who have taken my seminar over the 16 years that I have taught it. The few students who enter the seminar knowing unsustainability exists and a bit about it learned this from another family member, an exceptional teacher, or some youth activity in their community or on occasion a high school club. If they enter knowing about unsustainability and sustainability, they think of it as only an environmental matter and not a social (including economic, political, and cultural) matter. By contrast, most of the few international students taking my seminar have learned about unsustainability environmentally and socially before enrolling, and most have taken environmental courses that include the topic of sustainability as part of their secondary education in Western Europe, India, or Hong Kong.

How the Seminar Began and Developed

This seminar began in 1999 because of the interest and work of two under-graduates supported by others who worked with me to develop its initial form and influenced me to teach it as a first-year seminar.[3] As a retired faculty member with strong interest in and some background on the challenges of unsustainability, I wanted entering undergraduates to be able to learn about this topic because of its potentially major influence on their life. At the time, no such course focused on unsustainability was available to entering under-grads at the University of Michigan, and even now there are very few options for first-year students to take courses focused on unsustainability.

From its beginning in the fall of 1999 until 2005, the seminar was titled "Environment, Sustainability, and Social Change," and it was often cotaught with Susan Santone, a community partner with expertise on the environmental and social aspects of sustainability.[4] The seminar's process for its 20 enrolled students emphasized multidisciplinary collaborative learning within a seminar format. The content consisted of assigned and optional readings and discussions about the existence of unsustainability, the sever-ity of this condition, and what local communities and organizations in the United States were beginning to do to become more sustainable. It covered a variety of topics, including land use, agriculture and food, energy, water, housing, consumption, waste reduction, and recycling. In the final part of the seminar, students were required to do small group research projects on topics students chose in relationship to sustainability. It also included two field trips to local sustainability projects, one a local farm and the other a small intentional housing community. Students' evaluations of these early seminars were very positive given the overall topic, collaborative learning, and opportunity for small projects focused on multiple, relevant topics chosen by students.

This initial phase of the seminar's development was documented and analyzed based on evaluations by both students and faculty. These results were published in 2004.[5] The discoveries and innovations that occurred in the subsequent development of this seminar are the subject of this chapter. These changes were substantial enough that they led to the renaming of the seminar to "Environment, Religions, Spirituality, and Sustainability" and, in the process, to the proposed changes being reviewed and again approved. The changes described in this chapter and particularly the additions of three different types of engaged learning and related topics eventually resulted in the seminar allowing students to experience second- and third-order changes that enabled "doing better things" (as opposed to doing things better) and "seeing things differently" in ways that were transformative for students (Sterling, 2010–2011, p. 25).

My Background, Role, and Commitments

As indicated earlier, I undertook leadership in collaboration with students. I did this as an emeritus faculty member whose only teaching was to be this seminar. This gave me much more time and energy to devote to its development, continual change, and teaching than would have been possible during my preretirement appointments. It also gave me as much time as needed to work with entering college students experiencing this seminar.

I had not previously taught entering undergraduates but was attracted to their education during a period when I was president of a liberal arts college. I had observed entering students' high levels of enthusiasm, energy, and hopes that college would be different from high school.[6] My academic background in physical science and physics, social science and social psychology, and humanities and religion, along with my long involvement in teaching, scholarship, and administration in a multidisciplinary college of natural resources and environment, prepared me to deepen my focus and engagement in both learning about and teaching others about the emerging challenges of unsustainability.

As I continued teaching this seminar, I continued my own learning with my students, and together this has led to ongoing changes in the seminar and in me. Some of the changes came from suggestions and insights of students, some from the rapidly increasing scholarship and grassroots actions focused on the crisis of unsustainability, and some from my own study, learning, and sustainability practices.[7]

As I have been engaged in developing and teaching the seminar and seeking deeper understanding of unsustainability and sustainability intellectually and practically, I have become aware of and seek to embrace as fully as possible the following three injunctions:

1. *Albert Einstein:* "Problems cannot be solved at the same level of consciousness that created them" (BrainyQuote.com, 2017).
2. *Parker Palmer:* "We teach who we are" (Palmer, 1998, p. 1). *Heesoon Bai, which she attributed to her colleague A. Cohen:* "We teach who we are, and that's the problem" (Bai, 2012, p. 312).
3. *Bai's commitment based on both Palmer's and Cohen's injunctions:* "To take to heart means daily engaging in my own self-healing and self-cultivation . . . so that when I go into my class I can speak from a place of mind-body-heart-spirit integrity-in-the making, and offer my own self and life as a resource, including my own mistakes, limitations and struggles for my students' learning" (Bai, 2012, p. 325).

Description of the Seminar

What is described in this section briefly covers the contents of the seminar and some of how this content is integrated and identifies the different ways of knowing that take place in the seminar. Each semester I teach the seminar it is different as I weave the topics together based on the backgrounds and interests of the enrolled students and the group's development, as well as current events pertaining to unsustainability and sustainability. Consider the following list of topics and related methods as my palette of different colored yarns from which I seek to creatively weave the different iterations of the seminar.

Ultimate Values and Belief Systems of Students

The ultimate values and belief systems of students enrolled in the seminar are a major element of students' contributions. This topic includes students' religious or nonreligious core values and beliefs in relation to nonhuman nature, human social relations, and diverse cultures. This includes these students' individual definitions of *religion* and *spirituality*, because increasing numbers of young people state that they are spiritual but not religious. This is done using the process of dialogue, and as one of the three seminar innovations being focused on in this chapter, it will be covered in its final section.

Introductory Environmental Science and Unsustainability

This topic always occupies a major amount of the reading and classroom time in the first half of the seminar. To do this learning, students begin reading and discussing an introduction to environmental science (Uhl, 2013).[8] The first part of this text focuses on the 13.7-billion-year history of the universe, with an emphasis on the planet Earth and its evolutionary development. Throughout this topic, Uhl emphasized humans' integral relationship to the Earth's evolutionary dynamics. He continued this emphasis in the second part of the book, where he described the extensive evidence of progressive human damage to nature locally and globally. As he did this, he provided ample examples and related questions to engage students in relating his scientific findings to their own experiences of nature. In the final section of the book, Uhl described contemporary cultural values and practices that result in humans, through their anthropocentrism, causing environmental unsustainability by means of economism, including economic and social inequities and related cultural practices of mass consumption. He instructed and challenged his readers to discover the need for fundamental changes in their own values and beliefs and human consciousness that are required to reduce and reverse environmental and social exploitation and realize sustainable environmental, social, and cultural practices.

Christopher Uhl, in addition to presenting multidisciplinary scientific information and attendant ways of knowing, included his own experiences and encouraged students to identify and reflect on their related experiences. Although advocating strongly for the need and usefulness of scientific knowledge, he also recognized the necessity of including subjective ways of knowing. He rejected "scientism," as it asserts science as the best and only legitimate way of knowing, and accepted the need to integrate scientific knowledge with the subjective experiences of nature that can bring with them a relationship with and respect and love for nature—human and more than human.

Almost all the seminar's students respond enthusiastically to this book and related opportunities for discussing it in different ways and for pursuing the questions that Uhl asked and modeled pursuing as he shared his own experiences related to the topics he covered.[9] Some students spontaneously share what they are learning and reading on these topics with family members, roommates, and friends and even on occasion give this book as gifts to others who became interested as a result of their sharing their own learning. Students' highly positive responses to this approach to learning environmental science are enhanced by the next seminar topic.

Deepening Students' Relationships With Nature

This topic of the seminar occurs in the early warmer weather period of the fall seminar, paralleling their learning about introductory environmental science and unsustainability. This topic is pursued largely out-of-doors in a nearby natural area. Experiential learning allows students to integrate emotional, spiritual, and cognitive ways of learning as they expand and deepen their relationship with nature—human and more than human. As one of the three seminar innovations on which this chapter focuses, its inclusion in the seminar and its content will be described in greater detail in the final section of this chapter.

Native Americans' Worldviews, Values, and Practices in Relation to Sustainability

As the seminar's students begin their outdoor experiential learning of ways of being in and with nature, they are guided by Don Alverto Taxo's (2005) indigenous teachings. This necessitates and legitimates inquiry about Native Americans' past and their contemporary experiences in relation to European Americans who colonized the Americas. This introduces students to one pattern of the multiple social injustices (e.g., sexism, racism) among humans that is, along with the exploitation of the natural environment (i.e., more than human nature), an essential though often minimized or even ignored element of unsustainability. From the writings of indigenous people, students learn tribal perceptions of "industrial" ways of knowing as contrasted to indigenous ways of knowing based in "natural law" (Armstrong, 1996; LaDuke, 1997; Nelson, 2008). Students also learn about the centrality of communities that are environmentally, socially, and culturally sustainable and their maintenance through redistribution of material goods (e.g., potlatch), ritual celebrations, and lifelong learning practices. Students learn they are related to indigenous peoples in that they have many more generations of hunter-gatherer human ancestors than ancestors who have lived in settled agricultural and industrial civilizations. They also learn that many indigenous cultures have been and continue to be degraded and destroyed and that some have sustained themselves through thousands of years, including through periods of colonization and other destructive experiences.[10]

Students are learning new and paradoxical information (e.g., people labeled *savages* and *pagans* were living sustainably, and so-called primitive people have much of value to teach us) from indigenous cultures, which our dominant Euro-American culture has oppressed and degraded and sometimes eliminated. The students are cautioned to not romanticize the very hard way of life of hunter-gatherers, who had much shorter life expectancies than people living in our industrialized culture and who existed in very diverse tribes. Students also learn that the large numbers and diversity of these Native American tribes require we be cautious in making generalizations about Native Americans (Treuer, 2013). In this context, students learn about the relationships between cultural diversity, including linguistic diversity, and the biological diversity of the different regions inhabited by these tribes.

Because of the long and continuing struggles of indigenous people, whose committed values and behaviors promote sustainability and are rooted in deep relationships to nature—human and more than human— that incorporate thousands of years of experience, they are for all of the planet's people the proverbial "canaries in the coal mines." This is true in at least three fundamental ways: They are protecting lands and waters yet to be degraded and destroyed; they are living archives of invaluable life ways that are sustainable; and, last, the history of industrialized cultures' relationships to these peoples potentially can show us some of the violence of "settler" and industrialized cultures that we have internalized and practice not only toward indigenous peoples but also toward our own women and children, as well as other racial and impoverished groups. Thus, we can ill afford now to further harm, denigrate, exploit, and ignore our past atrocities and present injustices toward these our ancestors. Waking up to this is morally just. Also, if we can do this, in the process we will recognize the folly of what we have done and are doing to these indigenous people, all of nature, and ourselves as we destroy our own life support systems. Furthermore, if we can recognize industrialized cultures' terrible mistakes, we need what indigenous cultures have to teach us materially, spiritually, intellectually, and practically (Chandra, 2014; Jacobs, 2013; LaDuke, 1997; Whiteley, 2013). Since this seminar was initiated, more research and practice are focusing on potentials for integrating environmental pedagogies by indigenous teachers and conventional Western teachers (Kulnieks, Longboat, & Young, 2013).

Social and Economic Injustice

Intergroup inequities contribute significantly to unsustainability. Sometimes I have pursued this topic by focusing on gender relationships and other times by focusing on relationships between underrepresented minorities and White people. These patterns of inequity involve the domination of one group relative to another group or groups, resulting in exploitation and oppression whose roots are in physical, economic, emotional, or other forms of violence, including violence exercised through environmental conditions. For students to learn from this topic requires both knowledge of research results describing and analyzing these forms of violence and their consequences and personal experience–based knowledge of being in a dominating group and being in a subordinated group that all students bring with them in the seminar. This is based on where and how they have lived, including the racial and economic composition of their neighborhoods and schools and the pattern of privilege and discrimination relative to equity in these experiences. In teaching about gender and racial relationships, the seminar also focuses on students' experiences of these relationships since coming to the university and the potentials that are available during college for learning and practicing antiracist and antisexist ways of relating individually and collectively (Chesler, Lewis, & Crowfoot, 2005).

To focus on students' individual and collective experiences—as dominator and/or victim in regard to environmental benefits and costs—requires use of a distinctive and powerful social process and pedagogical method of dialogue that is used in this seminar and will be further described in the final section of this chapter. Also dialogue and discussion can be used to facilitate the essential learning about diverse and equitable multicultural relationships, social structures, and environmentally just living and working conditions that can be major contributors to sustainability (McCanty et al., 2011a, 2011b). Simulations and role plays are other methods that can be used to access experience-based knowledge of both inequitable and equitable conditions and the needed changes to transform the environmental, socio-economic, and cultural aspects of unsustainability.[11]

A major subtopic is measurement of the ecological footprint for the household or other living arrangement where each student resided in the year before coming to college. After being introduced to ecological footprint science (Bastianoni, 2012; Global Footprint Network, 2017; Uhl, 2013), students are able to make self-assessments of their family's home and lifestyle in relation to its impacts on the natural environment. Over the course of several semesters of this seminar, students have analyzed and reported that if every household in the world had similar environmental footprints, the aggregation of these footprints would require three to nine planet Earths. For most students, this is a major shock, particularly when they compare the results for their household to those of the average household in the United States and the average household ecological footprint in other countries. As they move beyond their shock and reflect on how they are living in college in comparison to how they lived in their senior year in high school, they begin to learn what would be necessary to reduce a household's ecological footprint. In pursuing this topic further, they also become familiar with the ecological footprints of different countries in the developed world, rapidly developing world, and poorer and poorest countries of the world. In study-ing this topic, they also gain knowledge about countries that have reduced their ecological footprints. This also leads to learning about the impact of economic inequity within countries and the fact that the greater the level of this internal country inequity, the lower the quality of life is for everyone in the country—rich and poor alike (Wilkinson & Pickett, 2014).

Integrating Environmental, Socioeconomic, and Cultural Aspects of Unsustainability and Sustainability

Theories and related research integrating various aspects of unsustainability are the topic areas of the seminar. One such theory that I have used exten-sively in the seminar is Riane Eisler's as developed in her books (1987, 2000, 2003, 2007). She is a cultural historian and systems analyst who has devel-oped a "multilinear theory" emphasizing "that underlying human cultural history are two basic models or 'attractors' for social and ideological organiza-tion: the *domination* model and the *partnership* model" (Eisler, 2004). Her theory, research, and practice provide a rich, multifaceted integration that provides theoretical and practical applications useful in the pursuit of sus-tainability. Her work initially focused on authority, power, and interpersonal and intergroup gender relationships in prehistory and later extended into history, including the modern period. In particular, she studied how these relationships have negatively affected and continue to affect women and children and other intergroup relations, as well as related social processes and structures, including social and environmental decision-making, distribution of power, and divisions of labor (Eisler, 1987).

This pioneering research led her to identify patterns of domination and subordination contrasted with patterns of partnership and the effects they have on the quality of life in different societies. Her later work and that of others have found evidence for these same contrasting patterns and dynamics in many different cultures. While applying her theory and research to social change, she focused more on social relationships but also recognized its applicability to the natural environment and socioenvironmental change (Eisler, 2000). At the same time, her social emphasis has the advantage of illuminating roots of unsustainability in our culture's gender relationships, child-rearing practices, and schooling practices that are typically ignored in many analyses.

Another theory that I have found very useful for the seminar is the work of scholars of education who focus on both the natural environment and social relations. The central publication in this area of scholarship is *Eco-Justice Education: Toward Diverse, Democratic, and Sustainable Communities* (Martusewicz, Edmundson, & Lupinacci, 2013). Although the book was written for use in social foundation courses that are an integral part of teacher education, it is very applicable to teaching about unsustainability—environmentally, socially (including economically and politically), and culturally. It provides a balanced integration of each of these distinctive elements of unsustainability, including many examples and the authors' own experiences.

Ecojustice education critically examines a worldview organized by a logic of domination and explains to teachers and students means of transforming the constituent social and environmental relationships, including such relationships within their own local communities. This theory includes attention to how beliefs and the language with which they are expressed pass on social and cultural systems of modern industrial societies. To do this, the theory identifies and describes *root metaphors* that include, for example, *anthropocentrism, individualism, progress, consumerism,* and *ethnocentrism* and describes local community processes and outcomes that include the impacts of these root metaphors and others as well. Doing this illuminates and leads learners to become conscious about taken-for-granted patterns of thinking and behavior that are abusive and exploitative through relationships among humans, as well as between humans and other than human nature (Lowenstein, Martusewicz, & Voelker, 2010).

The authors of both of these described theories and research also have outstanding action projects based on their theories. Eisler's focus is on developing a "caring economy" and "eliminating violence in intimate relationships" and developing schools and teaching practices that reflect partnership relating (Caring Economy Campaign, 2017; Eisler, 2000; Spiritual Alliance to Stop Intimate Violence, n.d.). Martusewicz and others' work on ecojustice education is implemented in the Great Lakes region through the Southeast Michigan Stewardship Coalition's work on projects helping teachers to learn the skills for advancing ecojustice and supporting a network of private and public schools, including middle and high schools pursuing ecojustice projects implemented by students, teachers, and members in their respective communities (Lowenstein et al., 2010; Southeast Michigan Stewardship Coalition, 2017). Each of these major change projects contributes directly to sustainability and provides rich ideas for further individual, organizational, and community change projects to foster sustainability.

Attending to Students' Fears, Uncertainties, and Hopelessness

Almost everyone when he or she initially learns about the reality of unsustainability is shocked and then becomes disbelieving and fearful when he or she learns that there is no quick fix. Sometimes this feeling, along with anger, is exacerbated on observing that many, many people including powerful public and private leaders are in denial that a major problem exists and is getting worse. Students are comforted by the awareness that people who are very knowledgeable about this "crisis of crises" and who seek to make changes often experience these feelings and their impacts. Discovery of ways of inviting expression of these feelings and regaining balance through supportive social processes is one of the discoveries being implemented in the seminar and will be covered in the next and final section of this chapter.

Scenarios for Alternative Futures in Response to the Forces for Unsustainability and Sustainability

This topic area of the seminar consists of scenarios for alternative futures. A simple understanding of alternative futures was provided by Macy and Johnstone (2012, pp. 13–33) in the form of three stories: "business as usual," "the great unraveling," and "the great turning." This simple characterization of alternative possible futures can be introduced early in the seminar. This is helpful as students begin to grapple with the differences between what they are learning about unsustainability and their own assumptions about the future. These assumptions were based on narratives they have been taught and accepted about continuing progress, technological innovations, economic growth, and natural resources.

The other version of future scenarios that I have used toward the end of the seminar are ones developed over the past 15 years by an international network of futurists and other related experts on the environment, social and economic relations, and cultural change. These scenarios are part of the Great Transition Initiative and consist of three possible future scenarios of human civilization, each with two variants. These scenarios and their variants are "Conventional World With Market Forces and/or Policy Reforms," "Barbarization With Fortress World or Breakdown," and "Great Transition With Eco-Communities or New Paradigm" (Great Transition Initiative, 2017). Recently this project's director, Paul Raskin, made an appraisal of where present patterns and projected possible scenarios are leading (Raskin, 2014). This project also provides a substantive foundational analysis of the dynamics of human social changes from our hunter-gatherer past to the present (Raskin et al., 2002). The Great Transition Initiative's scenario work is useful in helping students acquire a broad view of different stages of human evolution and history and some dynamics of the involved changes as a foundation for their own perspective toward the future and particularly the future they want to be a part of and contribute to bringing about.

Seminar's Three Discoveries of Needed New Topics and Related Integrative Learning

To accomplish understanding unsustainability and sustainability that transforms students individually and collectively, I discovered that new content and learning processes are needed. Students need to reflect critically about their own deepest values and behaviors contributing to unsustainability, as well as discover new values and practices that help to achieve sustainability. To do this requires focusing on students' experiences growing up and what they have come to believe. In addition, because of students' past estrangement from other than human nature, they need new opportunities to be outdoors in nature and discover new means of relating cognitively, emotionally, and spiritually. Discovering how unsustainable modern society is and one's own part in this dysfunction is challenging, sometimes frightening, and even overwhelming. To enable grounded hope and not denial, cynicism, and flight requires peer social support and exposure to people and social processes that model such hope. This section describes my discovery of three innovations that are required for foundational transformative learning catalyzing changes in consciousness and behavior. This is required to begin to achieve more sustainable relationships among humans and between humans and other than human nature.

Adding Students' Ultimate Values and Beliefs Along With Dialogues

In the early years of the seminar, explicit attention to students' ultimate values and beliefs took place only briefly toward the end of the semester. This happened in the context of learning about the Earth Charter, a well-developed and internationally recognized civil society statement of the vision and ethics necessary to achieve sustainability (Earth Charter Initiative, 2017).[12] From the seminar's discussions of the Earth Charter, I perceived that students were open to and desirous of having more time earlier in the seminar to begin to reflect on their own ultimate values and beliefs and those of other members of the seminar in relation to the challenges of unsustainability. It was also becoming clear to me that the seminar's students needed the opportunity to reflect on and articulate their ultimate values and beliefs, given the family into which they were born or adopted. Also, they needed to be able to express in relation to unsustainability and sustainability their core values and beliefs as they had been developed and possibly questioned prior to coming to college. This would require reflecting on the influences of their schooling, adolescent peer groups, adult mentors, heroines and heroes, and other cultural influences, including media.

At about the same time as what I described in the prior paragraph, I took an opportunity to participate in a yearlong faculty development activity on the influence of religions and other related ultimate belief systems and values on individual faculty members' scholarship and teaching, particularly in public universities.[13] Through this experience I discovered that these value and belief systems experienced by individual faculty, including me, had substantial influence, even though this was rarely explicitly acknowledged in our scholarship and/or teaching. Also through this seminar and to my surprise, I became aware of extensive research that was ongoing in U.S. higher education that focused on both students' and faculty members' interests and views about spirituality and religion. At the time, I was learning this through newsletters from the project group at the University of California, Los Angeles, that was doing the research, which subsequently was published in two books (Astin, Astin, & Lindholm, 2010; Lindholm, Astin, & Astin, 2012).

This research showed clear and strong student expectations and hopes that in colleges or universities they would have the opportunity to reflect critically on their ultimate values and belief systems as an integral part of their search for meaning and for their own life direction or path. These findings also showed evidence of students' desire to learn about the belief systems of their peers, including particularly from people very different from themselves. They hope for opportunities to befriend and collaborate with diverse peers and staff members and faculty. The research on faculty showed that some faculty favored and attempted to respond to these student expectations but that many faculty did not because they considered doing so irrelevant and/or illegitimate to what they considered their educational role.

Also through my own experience as a Quaker and initially the research and writing of Gary Gardner of the Worldwatch Institute, I learned that the world religions were becoming interested in unsustainability—environmentally, socially, and economically—and discovering what in their traditions could, if focused on, contribute directly and explicitly to sustainability (Gardner, 2002, 2006). Subsequently, I learned of the work of Bron Taylor (2010), who termed what Gardner was focusing on as *green religion* in contrast with his focus on *dark green religion*. These emergent religious beliefs and practices consider nature as ultimate and sacred and seek in their practices to preserve and conserve nature.

These influences led me to conclude that given the changes in basic values, beliefs, and consciousness that are required to foster sustainability, the seminar needed to give explicit attention to its students' ultimate beliefs and values and their implications for unsustainability and sustainability. Based on this conclusion, the question for me was "How to do this?"

First, it became clear that it was essential to communicate this added aspect of the seminar to prospective enrollees and faculty colleagues and at the same time clearly and explicitly invite and welcome all religious and non-religious students, including atheists, agnostics, and individuals with other ultimate belief systems. This required gaining approval to retitle the seminar as "Environment, Religions, Spirituality, and Sustainability" and change its brief description. In doing this I recognized that this is not what most students are used to based on their K–12 schooling or what is typical in much of higher education.

Second, I recognized that readings, videos, and small group projects could be added to extend and deepen students' knowledge of their own ultimate value and belief system in relation to unsustainability and sustainability and to familiarize students with values and belief systems very different from their own.

Third, I realized that discussion was not going to be adequate for including this new topic in the seminar and that the pedagogical process of dialogue was needed.[14] This would be the process by which individual students and the seminar as a whole could use each other's personal experiences and observations to learn from the diversity within the seminar about different ultimate value and belief systems and their relevance to unsustainability and sustainability.

Some of the guidelines for dialogues include the following: Individuals should speak only for themselves (i.e., use "I" statements), listen actively, suspend judgment and seek to understand, step back (share speaking time to enable all voices to be heard), be willing to experience discomfort, not freeze people in time, expect and accept nonclosure, and keep confidentiality. Also, in dialogues, participants challenge each other's preconceived ideas, explore thoughts and feelings, validate each other's experiences and feelings, identify and articulate areas of difference and conflict from their own perspective, build relationships and honor silence, express paradox and ambiguity, broaden their own perspective, and discover collective meaning. By way of contrast, whereas discussions often focus on saying the right thing and debates on winning the argument, dialogues focus on seeking to understand.

In the early uses of dialogues in the seminar, I invited an experienced faculty dialogue facilitator from the Intergroup Relations Program to facilitate the seminar's dialogues until I learned how to do this (Maxwell, Nagda, & Thompson, 2012). In addition to observing the guest dialogue facilitator, my own prior training and practice as a facilitator helped me to facilitate the seminar's dialogues.

Over time as the seminar put greater emphasis on social and economic inequities rooted in patriarchy and sexism, heterosexism, and racism and classism as major elements of unsustainability, dialogues were sometimes used. This was done for students to more deeply discover the relevance and applicability of selected learning resources (e.g., readings, interviews, and films). In this way, deeply and often unrecognized exploitative assumptions that had been normalized in the course of growing up could be more directly explored. Also, "social correctness" could be identified and explored in relation to more deeply held assumptions.

Overall integrating students' core values and ultimate beliefs with the academic content of the seminar by means of dialogues has garnered highly positive results. On entering the seminar, students were enthusiastic about the prospect of doing this, though appropriately cautious and sometimes apprehensive, given this was a new way of learning for most of them. Often at the conclusion of the seminar, use of this learning process was one of the most positively evaluated aspects of the seminar.

More specifically, students' responses to these dialogues included the following: "I no longer feel that I am the only person who has had _____ experience," "I really appreciate being listened to and not judged because my beliefs are so different," "I had never before talked to a person who is _____, much less learned what they believe and what their holidays are about," "I don't feel as negative and judgmental about the _____ as I did when I entered the seminar," and "I found much more in common than I expected to with people whose religious and nonreligious beliefs and practices are so different than mine."

More generally, students reported the dialogues as a process of mutual support and inquiry where they experienced safety and being listened to as they shared experiences, values, and beliefs that they feared would result in criticism or rejection (e.g., being very religious or being an atheist or not knowing what is ultimate or sacred to them, being rich or poor, living in segregated neighborships, and going to racially homogeneous schools). Also, students reported being surprised and relieved to find out that divorces, mixed marriages, geographical relocations, and illnesses and disabilities had as deeply affected other students' values and beliefs as they had their own. Students discovered that some of their peers wanted to be more religious and others less and why. Also, some students expressed their desire to be spiritual and not religious and others to be primarily religious.

These dialogues enabled students to learn how established religions and other ultimate belief systems furthered unsustainability and also how aspects of some religions and political ideologies, if practiced, had the potential to contribute to sustainability. Students shared their varying levels of concern about religions and religious, as well as political, commitments causing violent conflicts, violations of human rights, and environmental degradation. Many students discovered they were more comfortable than they had anticipated in hearing about ultimate belief systems different from their own because they had gotten to know and respect through seminar collaborations people with values and beliefs very different from their own.

Most important in relation to learning about ultimate values and beliefs is inquiry and consideration of the following question: "Is it possible to move toward a moral consensus on actions to implement sustainability—environmentally, socioeconomically, and culturally—and if so, how?" The urgency of impending negative and irreversible changes in each of these areas and their interdependence makes this a "real-world" question and not one only for philosophers, ethicists, and other academics. This is an existential question for everyone who is conscious about the crisis of crises that human civilization is now experiencing (Moore & Nelson, 2013).

Adding Deepening Students' Relationships With Nature by Experiential Means of Psycho-Spiritual Relating

During the early years of this seminar when it was titled "Environment, Sustainability, and Social Change," almost all class sessions were held indoors, where we discussed, debated, and engaged in problem-solving and other learning activities developed from the natural-science- and social-science-based reading and video materials related to environmental science and sustainability. These were the major learning resources of the seminar. Also, the seminar included a few field trips to local sustainability projects (e.g., an organic-community-supported agriculture farm and an intentional residential community seeking to implement sustainable projects). I didn't expect to do experiential education in and with nature.

One fall, on impulse to supplement one of our indoor class sessions based on introductory readings about watersheds, I decided to have an outdoor class session in the University of Michigan's arboretum, which was within walking distance of our classroom. The river running through this natural area is the defining feature of our local watershed, and on its banks was an attractive map of the watershed. We agreed to meet together at the closest entrance of the arboretum. When we were there, I suggested that we walk silently to the river to give our full attention to being in nature. Although the discussion on the riverbank about the Huron River Watershed went well, other things also attracted my attention. I learned that most students did not know the arboretum existed and that it was so close by and so beautiful. I further observed the students' enjoyment of being outside in this area and their curiosity about it and desire to explore it further. Later, in discussion with the students, I learned that walking in silence as a group was challenging to them and in doing it they became more aware than usual of the nature surrounding them and its attractiveness. At the time I had no sense that this would lead to a major change in this seminar.

After this class, one student shared with me that her mother, a college professor, regularly took her introductory class outside to experience nature by means of the teaching of an indigenous person from Ecuador.[15] I was immediately interested and arranged to talk with this other teacher. Through her I learned about another local person who had studied with and assisted Don Alverto Taxo in writing a short English-language book describing his own worldview; ways of interacting with nature; and his reasons for seeking to communicate with people in developed countries who needed, in addition to their rational ways of knowing, another very different way of relating to and with nature (Taxo, 2005, 2017).[16]

I began using this book as a guide for relating with the five elements: air, fire, water, earth, and a fifth unifying element (*Ushai* in Taxo's culture). Doing this over time became my own daily nature-based practice.[17] It was neither easy nor difficult but rather required intention and emotional and spiritual awareness of nature—human and more than human. Relating with the five elements required overcoming resistance to deliberately taking time regularly to relate with nature by greeting an element, feeling the element, and thanking the element. In retrospect, I think I was both deepening of my own long-standing relationship with nature based on my use of Taxo's teaching and encountering all I had been taught growing up in U.S. culture about nature being inanimate and that humans were superior and did not communicate much less talk with nature.

My sense is that my receptivity to my seminar students' experiences during the silent group walk in the arboretum, the follow-up conversations I initiated because of the suggestion of one student, and my finding and responding to Taxo's teaching was connected to my own earlier life journey or path to discover and nurture my own relationship with nature. In perceiving and doing these things, I was continuing a long-standing series of nature-based experiences that were and are invaluable to me. From beginning to practice Taxo's teachings, I found intentional times in nature relating to the elements helped me day to day to be more regularly and deeply aware of nature and thankful for this time and experiences in and with nature.

While I was "discovering" Taxo's teachings and learning from them personally, I learned much more about my students' deficits in relating to nature from talking about what for many of them were inadequate childhood experiences in nature and later for most of them their almost total lack of such experiences in their K–12 schooling. Also, I observed over the time that I taught this seminar that fewer enrolling students had in their growing up significant experiences in nature. Consequently, more and more of the seminar's students had weaker ties with nature. To check my own observations, I sought out and learned that what I was hearing and observing with my students had already been discovered, validated, and written about (Sturm, Metz, & Oxford, 2013) by others like Richard Louv (2005, 2011). What I was slowly realizing is that others too were asking, "How can young people protect and restore nature if it is just an object to be used rather than something you respect and love based on having a vital nourishing relationship with nonhuman nature?" A related question is this: "How can young people accord more than human nature the high-importance it deserves unless they have learned to experience themselves as integral elements of nature who are totally dependent on nature?"

This was the basis of my decision to hold more outdoor classes focused on helping students develop a deeper relationship in and with nature by means of activities fostering emotional and spiritual relating involving both inner knowing and external relating. As I made this decision, I hoped that it also would help the seminar be much more effective in enabling students to understand unsustainability and their own mostly unconscious involvement in it. I hoped that they would discover what they had been missing and that our culture and its teachers had badly misinformed them about their needs for relating closely with nature and about their superiority to more than human nature.

I hoped developing a cognitive, affective, and spiritual relationship with nature would bring students engaged learning experiences of great personal and collective value. On the basis of my own experiences, I thought it possible that some students would be attracted to and experience an "I-Thou" as contrasted to an "I-It" relationship with nature based on the experiences and terms used by the philosopher Martin Buber (1970). My strong hunch was that when students discovered they could relate to nature "emotionally at a level sometimes beyond words," as some students described their experiences, this would be an immense source of support to them to become involved in seeking greater sustainability. Also, I thought these new relationships would be a source of hope and related courage and determination in the face of their discovering—many for the first time and to their great shock—the ever-increasing impacts of unsustainability. One effect of these experiences would be for students to care about nature and increase the likelihood that they would contribute to conserving, preserving, and restoring nature.

To implement this decision, I designated six of our classes to times to model for the students and coach them to develop their own intentional experiencing being in and with nature. These class sessions took place outdoors in the university's arboretum. At the same time, I also designated "intentional time in nature" as part of the students' weekly homework in the first nine weeks of the seminar. I always remind students that these experiential activities are voluntary, and if for any reason they want or need to not do them, then honor themselves and do not participate. I ask them to let me know they have done this so I can be aware of what they are experiencing and make needed adjustments for them. In addition, I periodically request written feedback from students on what the seminar's experiential activities are like for them, about questions they have, and on any difficulties they are experiencing. In addition, I hold regular office hours and circulate a sign-up sheet to encourage their use of these times. Also, when I have questions or concerns about a student's individual work, experiences, or attendance, I request him or her to come talk with me individually.

As part of this relating to nature, I also coach students to engage in indoor intentional times relating to nature. After all, the elements—air, water, earth (i.e., food, plants, insects, etc.), and fire (warming and cooling)—are present where the students live, study, and experience most of their classes. I suggest students consider having a plant in their room, and sometimes I bring a flowering plant to our seminar room when we meet indoors. I suggest they devote intentional times with and in nature when taking a shower and eating, which are so directly part of the elements water and earth, respectively.

To complement these "being" times in nature, the seminar also requires students to fulfill a 2- to 3-hour volunteer outdoor service to nature activity. This requirement is completed by writing a two-page report on their experience and how it relates to other learning activities in the seminar. These volunteer "doing times in nature" are of two types: ecological restoration and gardening or farming that is intentionally sustainable. As students are engaged in these outdoor "doing" activities, they experience how they can directly care for nature through volunteer experience and, as they do these tasks, take the opportunity to experience some of the awareness and connectedness that they have learned to experience through their "being" in nature activities. Through these activities students also have the opportunity to interact with nonstudents who seek out volunteer work that allows them to be outside and at the same time directly care for nature. Through these experiences students are exposed, often for the first time, to ecological restoration and/or farming or gardening, which are opportunities they can access throughout their college years and very likely wherever they live after college.

Along with allocating significant class and homework time to intentional nature relating, I require students to develop a nature journal to document and describe their direct experiences with nature and their reflections on these experiences, including barriers they encounter and their discoveries about themselves and about more than human nature and the multiple connections and dynamics between them. This journal is also a place where every two weeks they reflect back on their learning and how their connection with nature was changing or was not changing. Also, this journaling requires students to integrate

- experiences in nature with what they are learning from their readings and discussions on environmental science topics,
- nature-focused experiences with their dialogues on ecojustice and social justice, and
- learning about each other's ultimate values and belief systems in comparison to values and beliefs needed by individuals and groups to contribute to sustainability.

Every two weeks for the first six weeks of the seminar, I collect and read each of these journals and provide students my feedback, including affirmations, suggestions, and questions to which I seek answers by e-mail or in conversation with me.

Implementing this new part of the seminar required me to go beyond my own nature practice and develop intentional nature time activities that would help students learn how to relate with nature. These activities were drawn from diverse sources, including the visionary and innovative teachings and practices of Taxo (2005), Cohen (2007), Scull (2003), and Cornell (1987, 1998, 2014). As I have been pursuing this integrative pedagogy, I have sought out and received additional education and experiential training in the practices and skills called for by Taxo, Cohen, and Cornell. I continue to widen my own education and practices through exposure to other teachers who are helping people deepen their psycho-spiritual relating with nature (Abram, 1996, 2017; Pfeiffer, 2013; Skolimowski, 1994; Swanson, 2001).[18] Also, in doing this learning, I discovered one other faculty member in my university who is teaching mindfulness in contemplative studies in a program on jazz. Her teaching includes outdoor courses in nature and reflection helping students learn contemplative practices in nature (Nature and Healing, 2017; Travers, 2007). Over time, more and more students in my seminar subsequently sought out these courses and reported very positive experiences continuing the learning in and with nature begun in my seminar.

When I added outdoor seminar sessions focused on intentional being in relationship with nature—one's own inner nature and the outer nonhuman or, as I prefer, "more than human" nature—they became central to the seminar. To integrate the intentional being-in-nature times and their emphases on inner and outer knowing with the rest of the seminar, I transitioned to beginning each of our seminars' indoor or outdoor sessions with a "centering time" that is usually five to eight minutes in length and is generally a guided meditation—with eyes open or closed depending on students' comfort levels. These times focus on present nature wherever we are or remembered nature from some prior experienced time in nature or some imagined experience in and with nature. Almost all students like this as a transition from whatever they were doing prior to class to the multiple ways of knowing that characterize this seminar. This seminar is generally very different from the students' other classes, and the centerings are times to be quiet, slow down, and be in touch with their inner selves in relation to nature and with each other as we do these centerings in the full group. Sometimes after centering, a few students volunteer to share what they experienced.

Students report welcoming these times in our seminar and finding in them something they like and long for. I have been pleasantly surprised that some students report creating their own centering times outside of class and especially in times in which they are highly stressed or lacking motivation or feeling directionless or even lost.

Both from my own personal experience and from that of the students with whom I have interacted, I have become conscious that we have had many more generations of indigenous ancestors than ancestors who lived in agricultural and modern societies. Thus, we carry an amazing readiness individually and collectively for much closer emotional and spiritual, as well as conscious, behavioral relationships with nature than is now prevalent in most modern societies. Despite having been socialized into anthropocentrism and speciesism, we have the capacity under the right conditions to again learn to relate deeply and intimately with nature and come into new relationships of mutuality and respect with nature—both with the other than or more than human aspects and with our fellow humans.

Adding Attention to Students' Fears and Hopelessness by Fostering "Active Hope"

Over the time I have taught this seminar, the topic of unsustainability has been more and more often front-page news and more present in other publications. This news, as well as the relevant academic material, continues to be clearer and clearer about the present and potential negative consequences of unsustainability—environmentally, socioeconomically, and culturally. At the same time, debates over these matters, with their extremes of total denial and imminent catastrophe, are more and more publicly accessible. Not surprising for many people, including individuals who begin to become aware of these threatening conditions, there is often fear and even despair, along with other feelings like anger and hopelessness.

Like many if not most people who focus on these challenges and the attendant crises, I too experience such feelings and find it important to not ignore them or go into denial that these conditions and growing uncertainties are real. It is better to express the feelings that come up with learning, teaching, and living with these circumstances. These reactions to the conditions of unsustainability have become an explicit topic in this seminar, along with how to remain engaged and hopeful while not ignoring the unprecedented character of what is taking place and the major uncertainties about the consequences.

This challenge was one that antinuclear experts and activists experienced in the late 1950s and 1960s. At that time Joanna Macy pioneered "despair and empowerment" processes to help these individuals and their peer groups to face what they were feeling and to effectively as individuals and groups engage in self-nurturing. On the basis of this work, Macy, working over many years, developed "the work that reconnects" that she and Molly Brown first put into book form in 1998 and have recently updated and revised (Macy & Brown, 2014). Throughout this time Macy was educating and training a committed group who in turn have been sharing this work. This long work addressing the conditions of unsustainability and activists seeking inner knowing to enable their teaching and activism is the foundation for the "active hope" process. This is the process Macy and Johnstone (2012) have developed and written about and are now teaching, along with others. I personally value and benefit from this process and have taken some training in it to enable my work to adapt it to the seminar.

Briefly, the active hope process is a group process that involves regular "coming from gratitude," "honoring our pain for the world," "seeing with new eyes," and "going forth" to act on our personally focused initiative to contribute to sustainability. This is a process of individual and collective balancing of positives and opportunities with negatives and uncertainties and seeing in new ways what is happening while not being captured by fear or hopelessness.

In the seminar, we begin elements of this process at the beginning to legitimate that difficult feelings will arise and will be part of our learning. Also, developing group trust and support is essential for students to have a place to share their questions as they begin to realize what they have not known about the unprecedented and very important changes that are taking place, from global climate disruption to loss of habitat and biodiversity to water shortages and destroyed fisheries. The list goes on.

Conclusion

As we enter a new geological epoch, the Anthropocene, it is a time for accelerated learning about planet Earth and its interactions with the now dominating species of which we are a part. It is also a time of great opportunity for discovering and realizing new human potentials and new human intergroup relationships, along with deepened relationships with nature of which we are an integral part. I hope that all children and youth have increased opportunities to participate in this engaged, experiential learning about how to mitigate and adapt to radically new conditions globally and locally that they and all of Earth's living systems are increasingly experiencing.

Reflection Questions

1. To what extent and in what ways has your formal and/or informal education prepared you to understand unsustainability—environmentally and socially (including economic, political, and cultural aspects)—and to relate this crisis to your teaching and research?
2. In what ways has your spiritual or religious (i.e., your ultimate beliefs and values) journey intersected with your teaching and/or research?
3. This chapter suggests that undergraduate students long for guides or teachers who will help them integrate their deeply held values and beliefs with course material and with significant social challenges. Have you

seen or experienced that longing in the students you teach? Have you witnessed in faculty discussions of possible and/or needed curriculum changes the assumption suggested by this chapter?

4. What significant social, economic, environmental, or political challenges does your course material intersect with? How might addressing students' ultimate beliefs and values (whether expressed religiously or in different terms) allow you to explore the material differently?

5. Understanding each other's deeply held beliefs and values—religious, political, social, spiritual, or otherwise—through dialogue strengthens engagement and helps students see course material, each other, and themselves differently. How might you use dialogue in your classes to deepen students' engagement with the material and allow them to integrate their emotional, intellectual, and spiritual ways of knowing?

6. What is your understanding of multiple ways of knowing? How does this influence your own inquiry and learning practices? How does this influence your teaching and research in regard to both content and process? How might you expand and deepen your own ways of knowing?

7. How does your own understanding of humans' relationships with more than human nature (i.e., the natural environment) influence what you teach and/or how you teach your students? How do your own experiences in outdoor nature presently influence your teaching? How might this change if you were to deepen your own relatedness with more than human nature (i.e., the natural environment)?

Acknowledgments

For support in writing this chapter, I am grateful to the Michigan Community Scholars Program and also to Community Resources Limited. David Schoem and Mark Chesler supported me patiently through this period of thinking and writing, without which I am not sure I would have completed this project. I deeply appreciate all of the students in this seminar with whom it has been my privilege to continue learning and sharing what I had to offer. Also, I am grateful for the influences of my longtime colleagues and for their sharing their ideas, commitments, research, and teaching that have inspired and enlightened me. These colleagues include the late Bill Stapp, Bunyan Bryant, Rachel Kaplan, the late Donald Michael, and of course Mark Chesler and David Schoem. My wife Ruth Carey's teaching, thinking, and wisdom have helped me so much, as has her patience with me for the time I took to write this chapter and do the seminar development and teaching on which this chapter is based. Her caring support and honest feedback to me on my path personally and professionally has been and is an immense gift to me. Thank you, Ruth and colleagues. Of course, none of these individuals are responsible for what I have written in this chapter. I am glad for whatever written here that is of value to readers, and I take responsibility for the perspectives I have expressed and for errors that inevitably are present in an experience-based work such as this one.

Notes

1. This warning was reissued and further refined in a series of subsequent UN conferences. Noteworthy among them are the 1992 "Earth Summit in Rio"; the 1994 International Conference on Population and Development; and the 2012 Conference on Sustainable Development, Rio+20.

2. In addition, the UN's Environment Programme continues to monitor global environmental conditions and will launch its sixth *Global Environment Outlook* in mid-2017. The UN's *Human Development Reports* are giving attention to changing social conditions—improvements and worsening conditions. Also, the Millennium Ecosystem Assessment (2005), based on participation and work of physical, natural, and social scientists from 95 countries, has provided a comprehensive assessment. Globally the work and reports of the Intergovernmental Panel on Climate Change (2014) continue to gather more and more attention from leaders and citizens because of the increasing attention they are receiving in the mass media.

3. The two students who most wanted this seminar to be taught were Kate DeGroot LaBare and Paul Siersma, who helped plan its initial version and participated with me in teaching it in the fall of 1999. We first met in a onetime class organized in relation to the university's first high-profile semester-long lecture series on the challenges of unsustainability that took place in the winter of 1999. Many of the students in this class wanted very much for entering university students to have the opportunity they had not had to learn about the unprecedented and urgent changes resulting in the unsustainability of human civilization as we know it. Paul and Kate acted on the desires of their peers and participated with me in teaching such a course the first time it was offered in the fall semester of 1999.

4. After its first year when the seminar was taught in the university's Residential College, it was offered as a seminar of the Michigan Community Scholars Program, a living–learning program supported by the College of Literature, Science, and the Arts (LSA) and University Housing. Any undergraduate at the university was eligible to enroll in this seminar. When this college and the School of Natural Resources and Environment jointly founded the Program in the Environment in 2002, this seminar became part of this new major and minor. The seminar met this program's requirement for an introductory course and LSA's interdisciplinary distribution requirement. The seminar has continued these affiliations from 2000 to the present.

5. These published results were two book chapters, "Collaborative Learning About Unsustainability: An Interdisciplinary Seminar to Help Achieve Sustainability" (Crowfoot & Santone, 2004) and "Collaborative Learning About Sustainability: Major Projects to Empower Ongoing Learning and Action" (Santone & Crowfoot, 2004).

6. Also, I observed their capacity for inquiry and learning and their desire to be challenged. They had yet to be inducted into college-level disciplinary specialization and attendant abstraction, reductionism, and resulting distancing from holistic learning and often from complex contemporary problems and opportunities.

7. These include my practice of psycho-spiritual being in nature, meditation, and sporadically yoga. Also, living for the past 16 years in an intentional community seeking to become more ecologically and socially sustainable has influenced me. Over this period I have sought to deepen my knowledge of community sustainability—environmentally, socially, and culturally.

8. Christopher Uhl is an ecologist with research experience in the Amazon and sustainability leadership responsibility along with students for the initiated Penn State University's sustainability program.

9. Christopher Uhl regularly teaches a large class using the same text as used in my seminar. To do this he trains selected undergraduates who have previously completed his class to be leaders of small learning groups and sections to assist him when he next teaches the large class. He trains these student leaders using his book *Teaching as if Life Matters: The Promise of a New Education Culture* (Uhl, 2011). From my perspective the content and processes of my seminar described in this chapter could be taught to a much larger student group if Uhl's pedagogy was adapted to my seminar's content and processes. Doing this would have the twofold advantage of more students being able to enroll for the content and processes I have pioneered and there being a more advanced opportunity for learning the content of this seminar for the students who become small-group leaders in the teaching of the large-group version of what I have been teaching using a seminar format.

10. For almost all students, this learning about indigenous peoples and particularly Native Americans has not been part of their prior educational experience. They are very interested in being introduced to this period of human history and its relevance to sustainability and shocked to learn about how Native Americans have been treated since European settlement of the United States and continue to be treated in contrast to Canada's "truth and reconciliation" process and Canada's related policies for its First Nation citizens.

11. An important aspect for learning in relation to this fifth topic is exemplified by real-world examples, such as in the field of urban and regional planning, where there is tension between those who emphasized increasing social equity and social justice and those who emphasize increasing environmental sustainability (Campbell, 2013). Pursuit of this example also includes the insights of Julian Agyeman, who is the "originator of the concept 'just environmental sustainability,'" which he described as the full integration of social justice and environmental sustainability. On the basis of this understanding, Agyeman redefined *sustainability* as "the need

to ensure a better quality of life for all, now and into the future in a just and equitable manner, whilst living within the limits of supporting ecosystems" (Agyeman, 2012; Brehm, 2014). Very recent research on this topic has shown a small number of examples of city-based plans and related projects that are including social equity projects as necessary elements of sustainability efforts (Svara, Watt, & Takai, 2014). Although it is hopeful that these examples exist, the fact that they are small in number makes the case for long overdue changes in U.S. cities.

12. Along with the Earth Charter, sometimes (depending on available class time) consideration was given to the World Parliament of Religions' (1993) "Declaration Toward a Global Ethic" that was drafted initially by Hans Kung and was referred to as an interfaith system of values and ethics similar to that of the Earth Charter though incorporating more explicitly religious concerns. More recently, another formulation on ethics for everyday life with relevance for sustainability has also been added (Kellert, 2012).

13. This faculty development process was planned and implemented among faculty and staff in the Michigan Community Scholars Program. It included the use of outside resource persons and readings and presentations by members of the group who had committed to this yearlong process. All of this was enabled by a grant from the Ford Foundation to the University of Michigan that focused on examining the role of religions in public universities.

14. Fortunately, at the time I had access to the Innovative Programs on Intergroup Relations at the University of Michigan, which was using this dialogue process for students to learn about intergroup differences, including race and racism, gender and sexism and heterosexism, and income and wealth, to learn about classism. Subsequently, this program used this method to promote dialogue among people committed to different religions (Dessel, 2010). Also, at the time I was considering the possibility of including dialogues within the seminar, and I was helped by my own reading about dialogues as a distinctive social process contrasted with lectures and discussions (Dessel, Rogge, & Garlington, 2006; Zúñiga, Nagda, Chesler, & Cytron-Walker, 2007).

15. This student was Carina Easley-Appleyard, who subsequently majored in the university's Program in the Environment. Her mother is Linda Easley, a professor at Sienna Heights College in Adrian, Michigan. I am grateful to both of them for helping me discover something important that I had been seeking.

16. The late Helen Slomovitz was the local person who had studied with Don Alverto Taxo and in collaboration with him translated some of his core teachings into English. I deeply appreciate my conversation with her about our respective relationships with nature, my seminar, and what I was learning from students about their desire for more experiences in nature. She then gave me a copy of this book with the hope it would assist me with what I was seeking. Her sharing her own experience of learning from Taxo and the importance of his teachings was and is invaluable to me and enabled me to share these teachings with many students.

17. Being outdoors as a child playing in a sandbox under a huge maple tree provided me a place of solitude and safety. Also, later, gardening was a family activity

with which I was expected to help. I enjoyed the time outside growing plants. In my early 30s, I realized a childhood dream of owning a place "up north," which was accomplished by becoming a co-owner of a cabin without electricity or running water in Northern Ontario in the Algoma Region. It was in the midst of the Canadian Shield–defined lakes, bogs, and forests and in subsequent years became dear to my heart and a retreat to which I returned again and again with my family for times of renewal. Later, in my early 40s, I remembered long-suppressed trauma of my childhood. As I was seeking healing in a nearby mature woods in the middle of Ann Arbor, being with and in nature was an intense, powerful, emotional presence that like nothing else brought me hope and solace and the resilience required to help me, along with other assistance, make the journey from victim to survivor. During this period I reflected regularly on these nature-based experiences and wrote about them in a private journal.

18. Selecting, modifying, and developing intentional nature activities for my seminar made me wonder about the existence of research that would help me, and others seeking to teach and mentor young and older adults, relate to nature. After an extensive search, I found an excellent, recent, peer-reviewed article on this topic that stated, "Little empirical attention in the scientific literature has been given to context-specific strategies, practices, and actions which may be effective in helping individuals of groups cultivate CWN [connection with nature]" (Zylstra, Knight, Esler, & Le Grange, 2014, p. 130). These researchers went on to state, "Since CWN [connection with nature] comprises cognitive, affective, experiential, and possibly spiritual aspects, an effective suite of practices should target each of these fields of human consciousness. It is difficult to partition or classify activities according to these areas since a given activity may appeal to multiple faculties, depending on personal and situational contexts" (p. 130). On the basis of the success I have had in teaching and mentoring students to expand and deepen their relationships with nature, I expect in the future there will be more research done to guide teacher practitioners such as myself.

References

175 Nations Sign Historic Paris Climate Deal on Earth Day. (2016, April 22). *USA Today*. Retrieved from http://www.usatoday.com/story/news/world/2016/04/22/paris-climate-agreement-signing-united-nations-new-york/83381218/

Abram, D. (1996). *The spell of the sensuous: Perception and language in a more-than-human world.* New York, NY: Vintage Books.

Abram, D. (2017, Winter). On wild ethics. *Tikkun*, pp. 13–14.

Agyeman, J. (2012). *Just sustainabilities.* Retrieved from http://julianagyeman.com/2012/09/just-sustainabilities/

Armstrong, J. (1996). Sharing one skin: Okanagan community. In J. S. Mander & E. Goldsmith (Eds.), *The case against the global economy: And for a turn toward the local* (pp. 460–470). San Francisco, CA: Sierra Club Books.

Astin, A. W., Astin, H. S., & Lindholm, J. A. (2010). *Cultivating the spirit: How college can enhance students' inner lives.* San Francisco, CA: Jossey-Bass.

Bai, H. (2012). Reclaiming our moral agency through healing: A call to moral, social, environmental activists. *Journal of Moral Education, 41*(3), 311–328.

Bastianoni, S. (Ed.). (2012, May). The state of the art in ecological footprint theory and applications. *Ecological Indicators, 16,* 1–166.

BrainyQuote.com. (2017). *Albert Einstein quotation.* Retrieved from https://www .brainyquote.com/quotes/quotes/a/alberteins130982.html

Brehm, J. (2014, October 14). *Demystifying social equity: Where research meets the road.* Sustainable City Network: For Leaders in Government, Education & Healthcare. Retrieved from http://www.sustainablecitynetwork.com/topic_ channels/community/article_220451f8-49a1-11e4-b083-0017a43b2370.html

Buber, M. (1970). *I and thou.* New York, NY: Charles Scribner's Sons.

Campbell, S. D. (2013). Sustainable development and social justice: Conflicting urgencies and the search for common ground in urban and regional planning. *Michigan Journal of Sustainability, 1,* 75–91.

Caring Economy Campaign. (2017). *About the CEC.* Retrieved from http:// caringeconomy.org/about/

Chandra, D. V. (2014). Re-examining the importance of indigenous perspectives in the Western environmental education for sustainability. *Journal of Teacher Education for Sustainability, 16*(1), 117–127.

Chesler, M., Lewis, A., & Crowfoot, J. (2005). *Challenging racism in higher education.* Lanham, MD: Rowman & Littlefield.

Cohen, M. P. (2007). *Reconnecting with nature.* Lakeville, MN: EcoPress.

Cornell, J. B. (1987). *Listening to nature: How to deepen your awareness of nature.* Nevada City, CA: Dawn Publications.

Cornell, J. B. (1998). *Sharing nature with children: 20th anniversary edition.* Nevada City, CA: Dawn Publications.

Cornell, J. B. (2014). *The sky and earth touched me.* Nevada City, CA: Crystal Clarity.

Crowfoot, J., & Santone, S. (2004). Collaborative learning about unsustainability: An interdisciplinary seminar to help achieve sustainability. In J. A. Galura, P. A. Pasque, D. Schoem, & J. Howard (Eds.), *Engaging the whole of service-learning, diversity, and learning communities* (pp. 85–97). Ann Arbor, MI: OCSL Press.

Davenport, C. (2015, December 12). Nations approve landmark climate accord in Paris. *New York Times.* Retrieved from http://www.nytimes.com/2015/12/13/ world/europe/climate-change-accord-paris.html?_r=0

Dessel, A. (2010). Exploring religious identity through intergroup dialogue. *Diversity and Democracy, 13*(2), 33–34.

Dessel, A., Rogge, M. E., & Garlington, S. B. (2006). Using intergroup dialogues to promote social justice and change. *Social Work, 51*(4), 303–315.

Earth Charter Initiative. (2017). *The Earth Charter.* Retrieved from http://www .earthcharter.org

Eisler, R. (1987). *The chalice and the blade: Our history, our future.* New York, NY: HarperCollins.

Eisler, R. (2000). *Tomorrow's children: A blueprint for partnership education in the 21st century.* Cambridge, MA: Westview Books.

Eisler, R. (2003). *The power of partnership: Seven relationships that will change your life.* Novato, CA: New World Library.

Eisler, R. (2004). A multilinear theory of cultural evolution, genes, culture and technology. In D. Loye (Ed.), *The great adventure: Toward a fully human theory of evolution* (pp. 67–98). Albany, NY: State University of New York Press.

Eisler, R. (2007). *The real wealth of nations: Creating a caring economics.* San Francisco, CA: Berrett-Kohler.

Engelman, R. (2014). Beyond sustainababble. In Worldwatch Institute (Ed.), *State of the world 2013: Is sustainability still possible?* (pp. 3–16). Washington, DC: Island Press.

Gardner, G. T. (2002). *Invoking the spirit: Religion and spirituality in the quest for a sustainable world* (Worldwatch Paper 164). Washington, DC: Worldwatch Institute.

Gardner, G. T. (2006). *Inspiring progress: Religions' contributions to sustainable development.* New York, NY: W. W. Norton.

Global Footprint Network. (2017). Retrieved from http://www.footprintnetwork.org/en/index.php/GFN/

Great Transition Initiative. (2017). *Global scenarios.* Retrieved from http://www.greattransition.org

Intergovernmental Panel on Climate Change. (2014). *Climate change 2014: Synthesis report. Contribution of Working Groups I, II, and III to the fifth assessment report of the Intergovernmental Panel on Climate Change* (Core Writing Team, R. K. Pachauri & L. A. Meyer, Eds.). Geneva, Switzerland: Author. Retrieved from http://www.ipcc.ch/

Jacobs (Four Arrows), J. T. (2013). *Teaching truly: A curriculum to indigenize mainstream education.* New York, NY: Peter Lang.

Kellert, S. R. (2012). *Birthright: People and nature in the modern world.* New Haven, CT: Yale University Press.

Kulnieks, A., Longboat, D. R., & Young, K. (Eds.). (2013). *Contemporary studies in environmental and indigenous pedagogies.* Rotterdam, the Netherlands: Sense.

LaDuke, W. (1997). Voices from white earth: Gaa-waabaabiganikaag. In H. Hannum (Ed.), *People, land, and community* (pp. 23–37). New Haven, CT: Yale University Press.

Lindholm, J. A., Astin, A. W., & Astin, H. S. (2012). *The quest for meaning and wholeness: Spiritual and religious connections in the lives of college faculty.* New York, NY: Wiley.

Louv, R. (2005). *Last child in the woods: Saving our children from nature-deficit disorder.* Chapel Hill, NC: Algonquin Books.

Louv, R. (2011). *The nature principle: Reconnection with life in a virtual age.* Chapel Hill, NC: Algonquin Books.

Lowenstein, E., Martusewicz, R., & Voelker, L. (2010, Fall). Developing teachers' capacity for ecojustice education and community-based learning. *Teacher Education Quarterly, 37,* 99–118.

Macy, J., & Brown, M. Y. (2014). *Coming back to life: Practices to reconnect our lives, our world* (2nd ed.). Gabriola Island, BC: New Society Publishers.

Macy, J., & Johnstone, J. (2012). *Active hope: How to face the mess we're in without going crazy.* Novato, CA: New World Library.

Martusewicz, R. A., Edmundson, J., & Lupinacci, J. (2013). *EcoJustice education: Toward diverse, democratic, and sustainable communities* (2nd ed.). New York, NY: Routledge.

Maxwell, K. E., Nagda, B. R., & Thompson, M. C. (2012). *Facilitating intergroup dialogues: Bridging differences, catalyzing change.* Sterling, VA: Stylus.

McCanty, J. M., Amster, R., Anthony, C., Benally, S., Dellinger, D., & Rooks, B. (2011a). Race, environment and sustainability: Part 1. *Sustainability, 4*(5), 238–241.

McCanty, J. M., Amster, R., Anthony, C., Benally, S., Dellinger, D., & Rooks, B. (2011b). Race, environment and sustainability: Part 2. *Sustainability, 4*(6), 288–292.

Millennium Ecosystem Assessment. (2005). *Ecosystems and human well-being: Synthesis.* Retrieved from http://www.millenniumassessment.org/documents/document.356.aspx.pdf

Moore, K. D., & Nelson, M. P. (2013). Moving toward a global moral consensus on environmental action. In Worldwatch Institute (Ed.), *State of the world: Is sustainability still possible?* (pp. 225–233). Washington, DC: Island Press.

Nature and Healing. (2017). *Work of Martha W. Travers.* Retrieved from http://www.natureandhealing.org/

Nelson, M. K. (Ed.). (2008). *Original instructions: Indigenous teachings for a sustainable future.* Rochester, VT: Bear and Company.

Palmer, P. (1998). *The courage to teach: Exploring the inner landscape of a teacher's life.* San Francisco, CA: Jossey-Bass.

Pfeiffer, B. (2013). *Wild earth, wild soul: A manual for an ecstatic culture.* Hants, UK: Moon Books.

Raskin, P. (2014, August). *A great transition? Where we stand.* Keynote address at the biennial conference of the Society for Ecological Economics, Reykjavik, Iceland. Retrieved from http://www.greattransition.org/publication/a-great-transition-where-we-stand

Raskin, P., Banuri, T., Gallopin, G., Gutman, P., Hammond, A., Kates, R., & Swart, R. (2002). *Great transition: The promise and lure of the times ahead: A report of the Global Scenario Group.* Boston, MA: Stockholm Environment Institute and Tellus Institute. Retrieved from http://www.greattransition.org/documents/Great_Transition.pdf

Santone, S., & Crowfoot, J. (2004). Collaborative learning about sustainability: Major projects to empower ongoing learning and action. In J. A. Galura, P. S.

Pasque, D. Schoem, & J. Howard (Eds.), *Engaging the whole of service-learning, diversity and learning communities* (pp. 153–161). Ann Arbor, MI: OCSI Press.

Scull, J. (2003). Applied ecopsychology: The unusual language of Michael J. Cohen. *Trumpeter, 19*(2), 59–68.

Skolimowski, H. (1994). *EcoYoga*. London, UK: Gaia Books.

Southeast Michigan Stewardship Coalition. (2017). Retrieved from http://semiscoalition.org

Spiritual Alliance to Stop Intimate Violence. (n.d.). *Co-founders*. Retrieved from http://saiv.org/co-founders/

Steffen, W., Broadgate, W., Deutsch, L., Gaffney, O., & Ludwig, C. (2015, January 16). The trajectory of the Anthropocene: The great acceleration. *The Anthropocene Review*, 1–18. doi:10.1177/2053019614564785

Steffen, W., Richardson, K., Rockstrom, J., Cornell, S. E., Fetzer, I., Bennett, E. M., . . . Sörlin, S. (2015, February 13). Planetary boundaries: Guiding human development on a changing planet. *Science, 347*, 736. doi:10.1126/science.1259855

Steffen, W., Sanderson, W., Tyson, P. D., Jäger, J., Matson, P. A., Moore, B., III, . . . Wasson, R. J. (2004). *Global change and the Earth system: A planet under pressure.* New York, NY: Springer-Verlag.

Sterling, S. (2010–2011). Transformative learning and sustainability: Sketching the conceptual ground. *Learning and Teaching in Higher Education, 5*, 17–33. Retrieved from http://www2.glos.ac.uk/offload/tli/lets/lathe/issue5/lathe_5_s%20sterling.pdf

Sturm, D. C., Metz, A., & Oxford, R. L. (2013). Toward an ecological self amid an empathy deficit: Higher education, psychology, and mindful connection with nature. In J. Line, R. L. Oxford, & E. J. Brantmeier (Eds.), *Re-visioning higher education: Embodied pathways to wisdom and social transformation* (pp. 231–248). Charlotte, NC: Information Age.

Svara, J. W., Watt, T., & Takai, C. (2014). *Advancing social equity goals to achieve sustainability: Local governments, social equity, and sustainable communities.* Retrieved from http://icma.org/en/icma/knowledge_network/documents/kn/Document/306328

Swanson, J. L. (2001). *Communing with nature: A guidebook for enhancing your relationship with the living earth.* Corvallis, OR: Illahee Press.

Taxo, D. A. (2005). *Friendship with the elements: Opening the channels of communication.* Ann Arbor, MI: Little Light Press.

Taxo, D. A. (2017). *Don Alverto Taxo*. Retrieved from http://www.ushai.com/about.php

Taylor, B. (2010). *Dark green religion: Nature spirituality and the planetary future.* Berkeley, CA: University of California Press.

Tibbs, H. (1999). Sustainability. *Deeper News, 10*(1), 1–76.

Travers, M. W. (2007). Elemental play: Encouraging children to connect with earth, wind, water, and fire. In E. Goodenough (Ed.), *Where do the children play: A study guide to the film*. Ann Arbor: University of Michigan Press.

Treuer, A. (2013). *Atlas of Indian nations*. Washington, DC: National Geographic Society.

Uhl, C. (with Stuchul, D. L.). (2011). *Teaching as if life matters: The promise of a new education culture*. Baltimore, MD: John Hopkins University Press.

Uhl, C. (2013). *Developing ecological consciousness: The end of separation*. Lanham, MD: Rowman & Littlefield.

United Nations. (1987, December). *General Assembly 42/187: Report of the World Commission on Environment and Development*. 96th plenary meeting. Retrieved from http://www.un.org/documents/ga/res/42/ares42-187.htm

United Nations, Department of Economic and Social Affairs. (2006–2014). *Millennium Development Goals reports*. Retrieved from http://www.un.org/millenniumgoals/reports.shtml

United Nations Development Program. (2016). *Sustainable Development Goals*. Retrieved from http://www.undp.org/content/undp/en/home/sdgoverview/post-2015-development-agenda.html

United Nations Framework Convention on Climate Change. (2016). *Paris Agreement: Status of ratification*. Retrieved from http://unfccc.int/paris_agreement/items/9485.php

Whiteley, P. (2013, November 25). The fire burns yet: Native American peoples are still here and still caring for their land. Can conquerors say the same? *Aeon Magazine*. Retrieved from https://aeon.co/essays/the-love-of-land-still-burns-bright-for-native-americans

Wilkinson, R., & Pickett, K. (2014). *A convenient truth: A better society for us and the planet* (Fabian Reports 638). London, UK: Fabian Society. Retrieved from http://www.fabians.org.uk/publications/a-convenient-truth/

World Commission on Environment and Development. (1987). *Our common future*. New York, NY: Oxford University Press.

World Parliament of Religions. (1993, September). *Declaration toward a global ethic*. Presented at 1993 Parliament of the World's Religions, A Global Ethic Now!, Chicago, IL. Retrieved from http://www.global-ethic-now.de/gen-eng/0a_was-ist-weltethos/0a-03-capitel-3/0a-03-00-die-erklaerung.php

Zúñiga, X., Nagda, B. A., Chesler, M., & Cytron-Walker, A. (Eds.). (2007). Intergroup dialogues in higher education: Meaningful learning about social justice [Special issue]. *ASHE Higher Education Report, 32*(4).

Zylstra, M. H., Knight, A. T., Esler, K. J., & Le Grange, L. L. (2014). Connectedness as a core conservation concern: An interdisciplinary review of theory and a call for practice. *Springer Science Reviews, 2*(1–2), 119–143. doi:10.1007/s40362-014-0021-3

6

EXPERIENTIAL AND DIALOGIC PEDAGOGY IN A RELIGIOUS AND ETHNIC CONFLICT COURSE

Adrienne B. Dessel

xperiential teaching methods—one type of engaged learning—are used to engage students around a wide variety of course topics, such as feminism, globalization, and international relations (Raymond & Sorensen, 2008; Robinson-Keilig, Hamill, Gwin-Visant, & Dashner, 2014; Roholt & Fisher, 2013). These methods often incorporate feminist pedagogical principles of equalizing the faculty–student hierarchy by incorporating students' life experiences and facilitating critical consciousness around power inequality (Robinson-Keilig et al., 2014). Experiential learning methods are student centered, in contrast to teacher centered, in that they engage students in activities and facilitate learning through reflection that places students at the center of this learning (Estes, 2004). This approach engages the whole student, integrating the cognitive content that is presented in conjunction with the student's lived experience.

Dialogic methods of teaching are based in experiential learning philosophy and also seek to balance social power in the classroom to create a more democratic learning environment (Zúñiga, Nagda, Chesler, & Cytron-Walker, 2007). This approach builds on practices of democratic education that support students in applying their own knowledge and life experiences, in combination with course content, to engage with real-world problems (Banks, 2004). These methods also incorporate social justice education practices of attending to the group process within the classroom (Adams, 2007). Dialogic methods create a space where emotions can be acknowledged in the classroom, again, for the purpose of engaging the whole student in his or her own learning process (Adams, 2007; Zúñiga et al., 2007). Finally, in all of these approaches, dialogic pedagogy fosters warm, empathic, nondirective teacher–student relationships, qualities that are highly correlated with positive student learning outcomes (Cornelius-White, 2007).

The experiential and dialogic pedagogies of engaged learning are particularly important when teaching about controversial issues such as religious and ethnic conflict. Teaching about and navigating intergroup conflict is challenging for faculty in the academy (Pasque, Chesler, Charbeneau, & Carlson, 2013), although little has been written specifically about religious and ethnic identity conflicts in the classroom (Bing & Talmadge, 2008; Dessel, Maxwell, Massé, & Ramus, 2010). Students are highly engaged and identified with their own religious and ethnic identities and still developmentally working through what these identities mean to them in the context of their family and burgeoning independence (Barry & Nelson, 2005; Bowman & Small, 2012). Conflict in the classroom may be ignored or not handled productively, and faculty who are unprepared to negotiate it may avoid, minimize, or distract from these tensions (Anderson, 1999; Pasque et al., 2013). Yet, students appreciate when faculty directly handle incidents of ethnic bias and conflict (Boysen, 2012). It is critical that faculty engage students in a cooperative learning agreement of shared responsibility for learning and promote a safe and respectful environment in which to explore conflicting ideas (Anderson, 1999).

Teaching About Intergroup Religious and Ethnic Conflict

The academy has had an ambivalent relationship with religion. Stand-alone religion departments at public universities have dwindled (Edwards, 2006), and some view religious studies courses as unconstitutional (American Academy of Religion, 2009). However, the number of students choosing to major in religious studies is growing (American Academy of Religion, 2009), and religion plays an important developmental role in the life of college students (Barry & Nelson, 2005; Bowman & Small, 2012). A large percentage of college students identify with a religious affiliation, primarily Christianity (Higher Education Research Institute, 2004). A study of 112,000 freshmen at 236 colleges found that although 79% of these students said they believe in God, fewer students attended religious services, and only 20% reported discussing religion frequently (Higher Education Research Institute, 2004). There may be few opportunities for college students to comfortably explore religion topics, especially related to religious conflict, and students may be unsure of where and how to discuss their views about religion or how to integrate it with course content they encounter during their academic careers.

Religious conflict is present in academic settings and college campuses. This conflict can focus around issues of sexual orientation (Love, Bock, Jannarone, & Richardson, 2005; Masci, 2010), denominational differences (Small & Bowman, 2011), religious diversity (Kazanjian, 2007), and conservative ideologies versus liberal ideologies (Britt, 2006; Moran, Lang, & Oliver, 2007). Religious oppression is experienced on campuses across the country (Jaschik, 2006; Lewin, 2007). Religion has been called a "hot topic," and academics and student affairs professionals struggle to determine the appropriate role of organized religion in nonsectarian campus life (Mayrl & Oeur, 2009).

Undoubtedly, campus religious conflict is a reflection of broader debates about religion in social and civic life. Yet, identifying religion as the sole or even main cause of social and cultural conflict is problematic and misses the complexity involved in perceived religious conflict (Caprioli & Boyer, 2001; Hunsberger & Jackson, 2005). Although the media represents religion as the cause of many conflicts, this is an oversimplified perspective. Many other factors come into play, such as gender, prejudice, and power and resources (Chew, 2007; Fabick, 2007; Winter & Cava, 2006), but the media typically ignores these. Instead, from a global viewpoint, religious conflict is portrayed as a worldwide phenomenon, and armed conflicts are often attributed solely to religious persecution (Henne, Hudgins, & Shah, 2012; International Center for Religion and Diplomacy, 2009). The same religious groups are often depicted in the media as both oppressing and being oppressed to varying degrees. Such reporting includes, for example, the following:

- In Bangladesh, Muslims persecuted Hindus (Ganguly, 2007).
- In Bosnia, Orthodox Christians killed Muslims and Catholics (Butler, 1993).
- In India, Hindus oppress Muslims and Christians (Henne et al., 2012).
- In Iran, Muslims kill Christians, Jews, and Baha'is (Hassan, 2008).
- In Israel, Gaza, and the West Bank, Jews oppress and kill Christians and Muslims (Jiryis, 2012; Lee, 2014).
- In Russia, Orthodox Christians oppress Jews, Muslims, and those of other religious minorities (Henne et al., 2012).
- In Sri Lanka, Buddhists oppress Hindus, Muslims, and Christians (Henne, 2012).
- In Thailand, Buddhists killed Muslim and Christian minorities (Chuah, 2010).

- In Sudan and Nigeria, Muslims kill Christians and indigenous religious people (Barnard, 2013).
- In the United States, Christians oppress Jews, Muslims, and people of other religions (Blumenfeld, 2006).

Thus, it becomes clear that no one religious group is either always dominant or always oppressed, and the direction of the oppression or violence shifts and is contextual. To better understand and reduce so-called religious and related ethnic and cultural conflicts, researchers need to examine religious tensions and understand them through an interdisciplinary lens that permits their interconnections with other forms of oppression so that the causes of conflict can be more clearly understood.

Religion supports the development of both individual identity and group identity and thus is a natural locus for social identity conflict (Seul, 1999; Ysseldyk, Matheson, & Anisman, 2010). Religious group identity serves individual needs of self-affirmation, security, belonging, and survival (Seul, 1999; Ysseldyk et al., 2010). Religion provides symbolic and social boundaries that mobilize individual and group identity conflict, and along with the belief in a "truth," it is a powerful motivator because it cannot be disproven (Wellman & Tokuno, 2004). Scholars of religious conflict challenge the notion that it is religion alone that causes, or contributes to, much of the world's violent conflicts. Factors such as resource scarcity (Winter & Cava, 2006), psychological processes (Canetti, Hobfall, Pedahzur, & Zaidise, 2010), and, critically, gender (Keynan, 2000; Klein, 2000) combine with religion to fuel global intergroup conflict.

Some faculty embrace conflict that arises when teaching religious and ethnic topics and use different approaches to teaching about the challenges of navigating different political beliefs about religious and interethnic conflict (Ambrosio, 2004; Neal, 2013; Sharp & Clark-Soles, 2012). These pedagogies may include nonviolent communication methods to teach about religion and conflict (Agnew, 2012) and student simulations (Ambrosio, 2004). Glennon (2004) used experiential pedagogy to promote learning about social justice in a religious ethics course. Educators use critical pedagogy to promote learning by students who may fall along the religiosity spectrum, for example, conservative religious students in liberal academic settings (Trelstad, 2008). Pedagogy should support students in making connections between their worlds inside and outside of the classroom (Winkelmes, 2004). Experiential, critical, and dialogic pedagogy are all designed to promote this type of integrative pedagogy.

This chapter outlines the use of experiential and dialogic methods in a course I have taught for the past four years on religious, ethnic, and cultural conflict. The course development is described, along with the use of experiential and dialogic pedagogy that is designed to promote critical thinking about religious, interethnic, and intercultural conflict. Finally, reflections on teaching the course are offered. Religious conflict is clearly deeply entwined with ethnicity, politics, and gender (Caprioli & Boyer, 2001; Chew, 2007; Rabie, 1994). However, to say religion is the primary cause of these conflicts would be an oversimplification (Hunsberger & Jackson, 2005). This course problematizes the notion that any of these social identities are the cause of protracted violent conflict and also seeks to tease out the role of religion in intergroup conflict.

The course uses a dialogic method adapted from intergroup dialogue courses taught in the Program on Intergroup Relations (Maxwell, Nagda, & Thompson, 2011). Traditional intergroup dialogue courses are often peer facilitated, use a highly structured pedagogy, and engage equal numbers of students who represent two different social identities with historical conflict (Dessel, Massé, & Walker, 2013). This chapter offers ways in which the method can be adapted to more traditional classroom settings. Critical pedagogy underlies this method, which is based in Freirian pedagogy and aims to examine bias, positionality, and power (Britt, 2006; Freire, 1970). In this course there are multiple perspectives and ways of knowing and a constant questioning of assumptions (Palmer & Zajonc, 2010). Through this pedagogy students gain an opportunity to learn about each other's positionality and views, examine assumptions and biases about the role of religion in intergroup conflict, and become exposed to a wide range of theories and practices designed to reduce violent intergroup conflict.

Description of the Course

This course is part of a series of courses offered by the Program on Intergroup Relations at the University of Michigan. The program's mission is social justice through education, and this course offers students the opportunity to broaden their thinking about intergroup conflict into the international arena.

Development of the Course

The course development was based on an expansion of an earlier course that examined the Palestinian–Israeli conflict. A close study of a previous version of this course, which many view as a religious one, led to a number of observations that inform the current course content. First, there are many factors that contribute to this conflict other than religion (Stephan,

Hertz-Lazarowitz, Zelniker, & Stephan, 2004). Primary among them are resource scarcity (Winter & Cava, 2006) and psychological trauma (Volkan, 2009), along with segregation and the creation of enemy images (Fabick, 2007). As noted previously, religion is pervasive and embedded in culture and ethnicity and is also often held accountable for many ethnic and geopolitical conflicts. Religious identity can be both helpful and problematic and thus is a complex factor when analyzing group conflict. Students can be challenged to critically examine the role of religion in global ethnic conflict. The course examines interdisciplinary theories in order to understand this particular conflict, and other related conflicts are compared and contrasted to further understand the roots of these global intergroup conflicts.

Second, there are many examples of coexistence and conflict resolution work that are being implemented in religious and ethnic conflicts across the world. However, these efforts are unacknowledged and underreported, and, importantly, underfunded. If these efforts are to grow, then we need to teach them to our students. Most students are unaware of the fields of peace studies or peace journalism, for example (Shaw, Lynch, & Hackett, 2011). They should be introduced to the nature of conflict resolution and peace work and supported in critically analyzing the information they receive through the media about so-called religious conflicts.

Focus and Organization of the Course

These two themes, focus and organization, undergird the development of the course, "Intergroup Conflict and Coexistence: Religion, Ethnicity, and Culture," which is designed around three different foci. First, the course aims to examine religious (and ethnic and cultural) conflict from an interdisciplinary perspective. This is key to introduce students to interdisciplinary fields of study and theories regarding religious and cultural conflict. Students receive a broad base of resources from which to draw in analyzing conflicts that they find most compelling. Alongside this is a focus on critical thinking, which uses Socratic questioning to promote examination of assumptions, understanding of the process of inferences, and recognition of multiple relevant perspectives (Golding, 2011; Paul, Elder, & Bartell, 1997). For example, attention is called the social identities of the assigned authors, and their identities are discussed. Neuroscience and the study of brain activity inform us that prompting new ways of thinking and making connections enhances students' learning (Sousa, 2001).

Second, the course highlights current coalition building and coexistence work that is being done related to various religious conflicts across the globe. Third, the course engages students in the question about whether conflict is always negative, their experiences and views on conflict, and the idea of productive conflict. An overarching goal of the course is to integrate an understanding of the intersection of individual, psychological, and interpersonal processes with global conflict and conflict resolution work.

The course was first offered in winter 2009, with seven students who registered for independent study credit. Student demand led to approval for a permanent course number, and the second- and third-year enrollment was 20 to 30 students. In the past two years that the course has been offered, up to 60 students registered or were on a wait list, and the course has remained capped at 30 to offer a seminar experience.

The course competencies and goals are as follows:

- Learn about and understand interdisciplinary theories of intergroup conflict.
- Learn about and understand interdisciplinary theories of conflict resolution and coexistence.
- Recognize the connection between personal and individual conflict resolution style and larger societal conflict and coexistence.
- Become familiar with a range of case studies on interethnic and interreligious conflict and conflict resolution practices in various international communities.
- Understand how conflict has been used as a positive force for personal and social change.
- Be prepared to engage in social change practices and coexistence work in regard to ethnic, religious, and cultural conflicts.

The course is organized into two sections, with the first half of the semester covering interdisciplinary theories of conflict and the second half covering theories of coexistence. The first three classes provide an overview of religion, ethnicity, and culture as social identity groups and an introduction to the idea of social constructionism (Burr, 1995; Markus, 2008; Marsella, 2005; Ysseldyk et al., 2010). Theories from psychology, anthropology, political science, communication, religion, neuropsychology, gender, and media analysis are the focus during the first half of the course. At about the middle of the semester, three case studies are examined during two classes each: the Palestinian–Israeli conflict, the Northern Ireland conflict, and the conflict in Rwanda. These case examples offer students an opportunity to apply the theories they are learning to these specific conflicts. Then, theories and examples of peace and coexistence work are studied, including international intergroup dialogue work (Democratic Dialogue, 2013).

Course Activities and Assignments

The course begins with the use of icebreakers, personal sharing, and seating in small groups of five to six students to promote safety and the development of relationships. The creation of a safe space for learning attends to students' emotional and intellectual needs and can enhance students' overall educational experience (Hyde & Ruth, 2002; Mendez, Hernandez, Clayton, Elsey, & Lahrman, 2013). One example of an icebreaker is the name story, where students go around the room and share their name and the meaning of their name or who gave it to them. Students appreciate sharing this information, and they learn a great deal about each other from this deceptively simple but profound exercise, which creates a connection between culture and identity.

Experiential activities are included in each class agenda to connect emotional and intellectual learning (Adams, Bell, & Griffin, 2007) (see Table 6.1). For example, in the second class, students complete a conflict-style inventory and share the results with each other in small groups. This activity helps them examine their own family and social experiences with conflict. Many students talk about roommate conflicts, and the intensity of these struggles helps them begin to focus on the interpersonal dynamics of conflicts that can translate to escalation on a national and international scale.

They are then asked to connect this activity, using guided reflection questions, to the readings on culture to examine how culture influences conflict style. They complete a Social Group Membership Profile (Hardiman, Jackson, & Griffin, 2007), which is used in our intergroup dialogue courses, to explore and share with each other their religious, ethnic, and cultural identities. A "Nature–Nurture" Take a Stand activity (adapted from Bell, Love, & Roberts, 2007) is used to promote reflection and discussion. The words *nature* and *nurture* are posted on either end of the classroom, the instructor reads out loud different examples of interpersonal and intergroup conflict, and students are asked to stand at either end or on the continuum to indicate whether they attribute each conflict to nature (biology) or nurture (socialization). Students often connect with the gender aspects of these questions, noting the assumptions and prejudices they bring with them surrounding gender and conflict, such as that men are biologically prone to be more violent. This "nature versus nurture" argument in the classroom, as in the literature, is an ongoing discussion throughout the semester that helps students link their life outside the classroom to the theories being discussed (Boyer et al., 2009; Tessler, Nachtwey, & Grant, 1999).

At this point in the course, students have completed their first assignment, which asks them to choose a particular religion, ethnicity, or culture that represents their own identity or heritage; provide a brief description of that cultural group and then locate original work by an author within

TABLE 6.1

Experiential Activities to Promote Dialogue

Dialogic Goal	Experiential Classroom Activity
Give attention to physical space that promotes dialogic interaction	• Arrangement of chairs in a circle • Arrangement of tables and chairs into small groups of five to six • Instructor circulating among the groups
Create a safe space for sharing views on controversial subjects such as religion, ethnicity, and culture	• Use of dialogic guidelines that are shared and added to by the class • Use of icebreakers (name story, common ground, concentric circles) • Use of dyadic and small-group exchanges
Use self and personal experiences	• Instructor sharing about personal identity and examples to the extent she or he feels comfortable • Use of life interview exercise, culture box
Help students be comfortable talking about religious or ethnic social identity	• Use of Social Group Membership Profile • Recognition that the conversation is different depending on the social identity balance in the room (often gender is the only balanced identity in the room) • Instructor helping students understand the roles of identity in social life, including in-class dynamics
Talk about power as instructor and power as student	• Use of power analysis related to social identity • Use of power analysis activities (privilege walk, power document, etc.)
Recognize the socialization process	• Use of time line exercise • Use of cycle of socialization visual
Negotiate conflict productively	• Use of dialogue, debate, or discussion handout • Awareness of triggers (handout) • Use of role plays (on a note card, write down an example of one of these you've experienced or heard about recently and role-play using The Third Side activities) • Use of conflict-style inventory • Use of activities from The Third Side, Psychologists for Social Responsibility, and the Program on Negotiation at Harvard Law School

this religious, ethnic, or cultural group; and write a brief description of the person and his or her work and how religion, ethnicity, or culture is represented in his or her work. Then they do the same for a religion, ethnicity, or culture that is in conflict with the one they chose and an author from that group. The purpose of this assignment is twofold. First, it prompts students to locate and learn about someone who represents a group in conflict with one of their own identified groups, and they often report that this was a new experience for them, as they typically read authors that are more in line with their own religion or culture.

Second, the information in their papers allows me to pair them up with other students in the class who may represent opposing group identities, and within the safety of the class that has been created, they begin to practice the sharing and perspective-taking activities involved in coexistence work. These activities are drawn from Psychologists for Social Responsibility (www.psysr .org), The Third Side (www.thirdside.org; Weiss, 2003), and the Program on Negotiation at Harvard Law School (Weiss & Rees, 2005). Each class also includes small-group discussions with reading prompts that weave in the concepts with the activities. Videos are also shown that highlight important concepts from the readings. For example, one week the students view a clip of Marshall Rosenberg talking about how he used nonviolent communication practices with two warring tribal chiefs; they read two articles on culture, communication, conflict, and nonviolent communication practices; and then they practice some of the techniques in pairs across their own identity divides (based on their first paper). Although some religions have both violent and peaceful teachings, Christian students are particularly challenged when they recognize the conflicts fostered by some of their own religion's tenets. Muslim students often struggle to distance themselves from the media portrayals of their religion. These college students are at a crossroads in regard to their own religious identities (Barry & Nelson, 2005).

Another "Take a Stand" activity (Dessel & Corvidae, 2017) aims to illuminate the students' views on religion and religious conflict and involves an "agree" and "disagree" side of the classroom, with phrases that are read out loud and students choosing where to stand. Phrases such as "Religion plays a big part in my life" and "It is people's interpretation of religious texts that leads to oppression" are read. This experiential exercise often shows the wide diversity in a room that is often explicitly assumed by many students to be all of one perspective (religiously and politically liberal) and gives many students the chance to share their thoughts about a topic that is often off limits in less engaged classrooms. This is often a turning point for the class to delve deeper into the divides that may exist within the people and groups represented in the classroom. For example, students who hold more conservative religious beliefs about American political policies or war get to share these views in class, acknowledge that they may hold a minority viewpoint, and have other students welcome them into conversations about global violence.

We spend three classes on gender, a factor that cannot be overlooked in international religious conflict (Caprioli & Boyer, 2001; Chew, 2007; Connell, 2000; De La Ray & McKay, 2006; Hunt, 2007; Potter, 2005). Students participate in a Gender Boxes activity (adapted from gender.care2share .wikispaces.net/file/view/Activity+4+Man+Box.pdf) that asks them to identify binary gender qualities in themselves and then connect these to readings on global gender violence that is religiously or ethnically based. The students have a piece of paper that has categories of "man" and "woman," and they list qualities they associate with each of these categories, and they then review the qualities with which they themselves identify. In this way, they bring their own gender identities into the discussion of the role gender plays in international intergroup conflict. One student talked about her recognition that her boyfriend held sexist views about equal pay for women, and she connected this to women's representation in political leadership.

A second assignment asks students to choose a particular religious or ethnic conflict and follow how it is reported by two different news sources for a period of eight days and report on the quantity and quality of conflict and coexistence work reported. Students often describe new awareness about the type of information they consume, the unconscious assumptions they make based on this information, and the lack of public attention and support for conflict resolution work.

Two films are shown: *Coexist* by Adam Mazo (2010), about the Rwandan conflict, and *Refusing to Be Enemies: The Zeitouna Story* by Laurie White (2007), about the Palestinian–Israeli conflict. Both filmmakers and participants from the Zeitouna women's dialogue group are invited to come and talk with the students about the topics. For the Northern Ireland case study, the class watches video clips of youth who participate in peace camps. This case study is perhaps the most illustrative of the complexity of the role of religion, as the two warring groups, Catholics and Protestants, are strikingly similar in many ways and both located within Christianity.

The course ends with a review of resources for conflict resolution work, including intergroup dialogue work (Chakraverti, 2009; Dessel & Rogge, 2008) and readings on using conflict constructively. Students also do brief in-class presentations about peace studies's graduate and nonprofit programs. A final paper asks students to again choose a specific religious, ethnic, or cultural conflict (which can be unrelated to their own identities this time) and reflect on the theories they have learned. They are asked to answer the following questions:

- What is your understanding of your own experience with and attitudes about conflict and conflict resolution? Please discuss this in relationship to your understanding of a specific intercultural or religious conflict that you have chosen that interests you.
- Discuss your understanding of the *theories and manifestations of conflict* that were explored in this course. Which make sense to you, and which may not? How do these theories help you understand the specific conflict you chose?
- Discuss your understanding of the *theories and practice of coexistence* that were explored in this course. Which ones seem most promising? Which ones would you want to learn more about? Which do not make sense to you, if any?

Instructor Reflections

This course was developed from an acknowledgment of the power of religion and the tension between religion's positive and negative influence. Being an atheist for my whole life, with a scientific and psychological bent to my own way of knowing and understanding the world, I embrace the opportunity to work with students in exploring the criticisms of religion as a primary cause of global conflict. With this approach, I problematize with students the notion that religious beliefs necessarily lead to religious conflict, raising my own questions about this issue. I encourage them to explore how religion functions as both a personal identity and a social identity, seeking out other theories that explain religious conflicts and then creating an environment in which students can connect their personal views and experiences with intellectual theories in an integrative manner.

Throughout all of my teaching, I strive to connect with my students on a personal level, so that we develop mutual trust and a classroom environment where they connect with each other as well. I participate in the small-group discussions in the classroom, often sharing my own experiences related to the religious and ethnic aspects of the Arab–Israeli conflict, which is one of our case studies. In this way, I model self-disclosure in the interest of fostering learning. The students then share their own narratives with each other and develop relationships in the class that allow them to explore difficult topics. I invite them to bring their personal life experiences to bear on the course topics, and in this way I am teaching to the whole student—heart, mind, and spirit. For example, students who were raised Catholic gain a new perspective on their religion when examining the Northern Ireland conflict. A number of students who identify with nationalities or ethnicities such as Korean, Chinese, or Hungarian have taken the opportunity to apply the course materials to an understanding of their own family and cultural conflicts. Many students enter the class with an apprehension of conflict and come away with a stronger understanding of the skills and theory needed to negotiate conflict in their own life and in society.

Thus, I have found that students are open to reevaluating the nature of religious conflict and the information that they receive about such conflicts. Religious views are often understood as "protected free speech" (Melendez & LaSala, 2006). My students have stated that one's religion is "sacred" or "untouchable" in terms of challenging its tenets. However, as strong as students' religious identities may be, it is unclear as to whether and how college influences these religious beliefs and behaviors. Although students may retain their religious identity and orientations, they also appear to question religious teachings and reevaluate their beliefs (Mayrl & Oeur, 2009).

Over the course of the semester, students appreciate the opportunity to examine perspectives different from their own, they are highly engaged in the small-group analysis of the readings and activities, and they talk about new learning in regard to how to approach conflict. Course evaluations indicate students need support in establishing safety and relationships within the classroom to share their views honestly. They struggle with the current proliferation of serious intergroup conflict worldwide related to religion, ethnicity, and other group identities such as gender and political affiliation. They question whether peace and coexistence is possible and whether biology or culture is a determinant of human behavior. We talk about the idea of being "consumers" of violent media, and we begin to explore the vast amounts of conflict resolution work that are rarely publicized and researched (Smith, 2007). Although not all students embrace the idea that peace and coexistence is possible, we work and learn together about the potential for improved and peaceful human interactions.

Instructor Tips

Why is there a need for dialogic and experiential pedagogy in classrooms?

1. Difficult conversations occur in the classroom around religion and religious identity.
2. There is often imbalanced identity representation in the classroom and therefore an imbalance of social power.
3. Conflict styles are different. Students may lack experience successfully negotiating conflict or may want to avoid conflict, and they need to learn skills to negotiate conflict.

Reflection Questions

1. What are the hardest topics related to religion and conflict for you to teach about?
2. When have you been more successful? Less successful?
3. This chapter notes that for peace-making strategies to gain a foothold in global conversations about conflict resolution, we must teach them to our students. Considering your own field, what paradigm-shifting practices might you teach to students that would help effect long-term social change?
4. Interdisciplinarity can help students see a subject from a variety of angles and to think about how different fields' perspectives can be integrated into a single activity or approach. How does or could your teaching include interdisciplinary approaches that would encourage students to see an important social issue in a more complex way?
5. This chapter presents numerous strategies for fostering dialogue in classroom settings. What strategies related to dialogue could help you, as a teacher, build a classroom community where difficult topics can be discussed?
6. In addition to dialogue, what other experiential strategies might be useful for helping students engage with course material that asks them to reexamine their deeply held beliefs and values?
7. How do you position yourself in the classroom when discussing important issues central to identity—religion, ethnicity, gender, and so on? Are you a full participant? A guide? What are the advantages and disadvantages to these approaches?

Acknowledgement

With great appreciation to the undergraduate students in my "Intergroup Conflict and Coexistence: Religion, Ethnicity, and Culture" (UC/Soc 375/ Psych 312) course from 2009 to 2016 at the University of Michigan.

References

Adams, M. (2007). Pedagogical frameworks for social justice education. In M. Adams, L. A. Bell, & P. Griffin (Eds.), *Teaching for diversity and social justice* (pp. 15–33). New York, NY: Routledge.

Adams, M., Bell, L. A., & Griffin, P. (2007). *Teaching for diversity and social justice.* New York, NY: Routledge.

Agnew, E. (2012). Needs and nonviolent communication in the religious studies classroom. *Teaching Theology and Religion, 15*(3), 210–224.

Ambrosio, T. (2004). Bringing ethnic conflict into the classroom: A student-centered simulation of multiethnic politics. *Political Science and Politics, 37*(2), 285–289.

American Academy of Religion. (2009). The religious studies major and liberal education. *Liberal Education, 95*(2), 48–55.

Anderson, J. A. (1999). Faculty responsibility for promoting conflict-free college classrooms. *New Directions for Teaching and Learning, 77,* 69–76.

Banks, J. A. (Ed.). (2004). *Diversity and citizenship education: Global perspectives.* San Francisco, CA: Jossey-Bass.

Barnard, T. (2013). *The role of religion in African conflicts: The cases of Nigeria and Sudan.* Retrieved from http://sun.academia.edu/TjaartBarnard

Barry, C., & Nelson, L. (2005). The role of religion in the transition to adulthood for young emerging adults. *Journal of Youth and Adolescence, 34*(3), 245–255.

Bell, L., Love, B., & Roberts, R. (2007). Racism and White privilege curriculum design. In M. Adams, L. Bell, & P. Griffin (Eds.), *Teaching for diversity and social justice* (2nd ed., pp. 123–144). New York, NY: Taylor & Francis.

Bing, V., & Talmadge, R. (2008). Speaking of religion: Facilitating difficult dialogues. *Diversity and Democracy, 11*(1), 12–13.

Blumenfeld, W. (2006). Christian privilege and the promotion of "secular" and not-so-"secular" mainline Christianity in public schooling and in the larger society. *Equity and Excellence in Education, 39,* 195–210.

Bowman, N., & Small, J. (2012). Exploring a hidden form of minority status: College students' religious affiliation and well-being. *Journal of College Student Development, 53*(4), 491–509.

Boyer, M., Urlacher, B., Hudson, N., Niv-Solomon, A., Janik, L., Butler, M., & Brown, S. (2009). Gender and negotiation: Some experimental findings from an international negotiation simulation. *International Studies Quarterly, 53,* 23–47.

Boysen, G. A. (2012). Teachers' responses to bias in the classroom: How response type and situational factors affect student perceptions. *Journal of Applied Social Psychology, 42*(2), 506–534.

Britt, B. (2006). Secularism, criticism, and religious studies pedagogy. *Teaching Theology and Religion, 9*(4), 203–210.

Burr, V. (1995). *An introduction to social constructionism.* New York, NY: Routledge.

Butler, T. (1993). Yugoslavia mon amour. *The Wilson Quarterly, 17*(1), 118–125.

Canetti, D., Hobfall, S., Pedahzur, A., & Zaidise, E. (2010). Much ado about religion: Religiosity, resource loss, and support for political violence. *Journal of Peace Research, 47*(5), 575–587.

Caprioli, M., & Boyer, M. (2001). Gender, violence, and international crisis. *Journal of Conflict Resolution, 45*(4), 503–518.

Chakraverti, M. (2009). Deliberate dialogue. In J. deRivera (Ed.), *Handbook on building cultures of peace* (pp. 259–272). New York, NY: Springer Science.

Chew, H. (2007, June 16). Women and war: Reclaiming a feminist perspective. *Left Turn: Notes From the Global Intifada.* Retrieved from http://www.incite-national .org/sites/default/files/incite_files/resource_docs/3429_women-war.pdf

Chuah, O. (2010). Conflicts and peace initiatives between minority Muslims and Thai Buddhists in the southern Thailand. *Journal of Religion, Conflict, and Peace, 3*(2). Retrieved from http://www.religionconflictpeace.org/volume-3-issue-2-spring-2010/conflicts-and-peace-initiatives-between-minority-muslims-and-thai

Connell, R. (2000). Arms and the man: Using the new research on masculinity to understand violence and promote peace in the contemporary world. In I. Breines, R. Connell, & I. Eide (Eds.), *Male roles, masculinities and violence: A culture of peace perspective* (pp. 21–33). Paris, France: UNESCO.

Cornelius-White, J. (2007). Learner-centered teacher–student relationships are effective: A meta-analysis. *Review of Educational Research, 77*(1), 113–143.

De La Ray, C., & McKay, S. (2006). Peacebuilding as a gendered process. *Journal of Social Issues, 62*(1), 141–153.

Democratic Dialogue. (2013). Retrieved from http://www.democraticdialoguenetwork .org/

Dessel, A., & Corvidae, T. (2017). Experiential activities for engaging intersectionality in social justice pedagogy. In K. Case (Ed.), *Intersectional pedagogy: Complicating identity and social justice* (pp. 214–231). New York, NY: Routledge.

Dessel, A., Massé, J., & Walker, L. (2013). Intergroup dialogue pedagogy: Teaching about intersectional and under-examined privilege in heterosexual, Christian, and Jewish identities. In K. Case (Ed.), *Deconstructing privilege: Teaching and learning as allies in the classroom* (pp. 133–148). New York, NY: Routledge.

Dessel, A., Maxwell, K. E., Massé, J., & Ramus, E. (2010). Exploring religious identity through intergroup dialogue. *Diversity and Democracy, 13*(2), 13–14.

Dessel, A., & Rogge, M. (2008). Evaluation of intergroup dialogue: A review of the empirical literature. *Conflict Resolution Quarterly, 26*(2), 199–238.

Edwards, M. (2006). *Religion on our campuses: A professor's guide to communities, conflicts, and promising conversations.* New York, NY: Palgrave Macmillan.

Estes, C. A. (2004). Promoting student-centered learning in experiential education. *Journal of Experiential Education, 27*(2), 141–160.

Fabick, S. (2007). Two psychologically based conflict resolution programs: Enemy images and US and THEM. *Journal for Social Action in Counseling and Psychology, 1*(2), 72–81.

Freire, P. (1970). *Pedagogy of the oppressed* (M. B. Ramos, Trans.). New York, NY: Seabury.

Ganguly, S. (2007). The roots of religious violence in India, Pakistan, and Bangladesh. In L. Cady & S. Simon (Eds.), *Religion and conflict in South and Southeast Asia: Disrupting violence* (pp. 70–84). New York, NY: Routledge.

Glennon, F. (2004). Experiential learning and social justice action: An experiment in the scholarship of teaching and learning. *Teaching Theology and Religion, 7*(1), 30–37.

Golding, C. (2011). Educating for critical thinking: Thought-encouraging questions in a community of inquiry. *Higher Education Research and Development, 30*(3), 357–370.

Hardiman, R., Jackson, B., & Griffin, P. (2007). Conceptual foundations for social justice education. In M. Adams, L. Bell, & P. Griffin (Eds.), *Teaching for diversity and social justice* (2nd ed., pp. 35–66). New York, NY: Taylor & Francis.

Hassan, H. (2008). *Iran: Ethnic and religious minorities.* CRS Report for Congress. Retrieved from http://www.fas.org/sgp/crs/mideast/RL34021.pdf

Henne, P., Hudgins, S., & Shah, T. S. (2012). *Religious freedom and violent religious extremism: A sourcebook of modern cases and analysis.* Washington, DC: Berkley Center for Religion, Peace, and World Affairs, Georgetown University.

Higher Education Research Institute. (2004). *The spiritual life of college students: A national study of college students' search for meaning and purpose.* Los Angeles, CA: Author.

Hunsberger, B., & Jackson, L. (2005). Religion, meaning, and prejudice. *Journal of Social Issues, 61*(4), 807–826.

Hunt, S. (2007). Let women rule. *Foreign Affairs, 86*(3), 1–6.

Hyde, C., & Ruth, B. J. (2002). Multicultural content and class participation: Do students self-censor? *Journal of Social Work Education, 38*(2), 241–257.

International Center for Religion and Diplomacy. (2009). *The first decade: 1999–2009.* Retrieved from http://icrd.org/wp-content/uploads/2011/09/ICRD-The-First-Decade.pdf

Jaschik, S. (2006, December 27). Signs of the cross (and its removal). *Inside Higher Ed.* Retrieved from http://insidehighered.com/news/2006/12/27/cross

Jiryis, F. (2012). *The myth of Israel's favorable treatment of Palestinian Christians.* Retrieved from http://mondoweiss.net/2012/03/the-myth-of-israels-favorable-treatment-of-palestinian-christians.htm

Kazanjian, V. (2007). Beyond tolerance: An interview on religious pluralism with Victor Kazanjian. *Spirituality in Higher Education, 3*(4), 1–6.

Keynan, H. (2000). Male roles and the making of the Somali tragedy. In I. Breines, R. Connell, & I. Eide (Eds.), *Male roles, masculinities and violence: A culture of peace perspective* (pp. 189–199). Paris, France: UNESCO.

Klein, U. (2000). "Our best boys": The making of masculinity in Israeli society. In I. Breines, R. Connell, & I. Eide (Eds.), *Male roles, masculinities and violence: A culture of peace perspective* (pp. 163–179). Paris, France: UNESCO.

Lee, M. (2014). *Palestinian Christian: Western Christians don't understand Gaza/Israeli conflict.* Retrieved from http://m.christianpost.com/news/palestinian-christian-western-christians-dont-understand-gaza-israeli-conflict--123272/

Lewin, T. (2007, August 7). Universities install footbaths to benefit Muslims, and not everyone is pleased. *New York Times.* Retrieved from http://www.nytimes.com/2007/08/07/education/07muslim.html

Love, P., Bock, M., Jannarone, A., & Richardson, P. (2005). Identity interaction: Exploring the spiritual experiences of lesbian and gay college students. *Journal of College Student Development, 46*(2), 193–209.

Markus, H. (2008). Pride, prejudice, and ambivalence: Toward a unified theory of race and ethnicity. *American Psychologist, 63,* 651–665.

Marsella, A. (2005). Culture and conflict: Understanding, negotiating, and reconciling conflicting constructions of reality. *International Journal of Intercultural Relations, 29,* 651–673.

Masci, D. (2010). *High court rules against campus Christian group.* The Pew Forum on Religion and Public Life. Retrieved from http://www.pewforum.org/High-Court-Rules-Against-Campus-Christian-Group.aspx

Maxwell, K. E., Nagda, B., & Thompson, M. (Eds.). (2011). *Facilitating intergroup dialogues: Bridging differences, catalyzing change.* Sterling, VA: Stylus.

Mayrl, D., & Oeur, F. (2009). Religion and higher education: Current knowledge and directions for future research. *Journal for the Scientific Study of Religion, 48*(2), 260–275.

Mazo, A. (Director). (2010). *Coexist* [Motion picture]. Retrieved from http://upstanderproject.org/coexist/

Melendez, M. P., & LaSala, M. C. (2006). Who's oppressing whom? Homosexuality, Christianity, and social work. *Social Work, 51,* 371–377.

Mendez, S., Hernandez, N., Clayton, G., Elsey, S., & Lahrman, H. (2013). Walking the walk: Student expectations of faculty in the classroom. *Understanding and Dismantling Privilege, 4*(1), 61–76.

Moran, C., Lang, D., & Oliver, J. (2007). Cultural incongruity and social status ambiguity: The experiences of Evangelical Christian student leaders at two midwestern public universities. *Journal of College Student Development, 48*(1), 23–38.

Neal, L. (2013). From classroom to controversy: Conflict in the teaching of religion. *Teaching Theology and Religion, 16*(1), 66–75.

Palmer, P., & Zajonc, A. (2010). *The heart of higher education: A call to renewal.* San Francisco, CA: Jossey-Bass.

Pasque, P. A., Chesler, M. A., Charbeneau, J., & Carlson, C. (2013). Pedagogical approaches to student racial conflict in the classroom. *Journal of Diversity in Higher Education, 6*(1), 1–16. doi:10.1037/a0031695

Paul, R., Elder, L., & Bartell, T. (1997). *California teacher preparation for instruction in critical thinking: Research findings and policy recommendations.* Sacramento, CA: Foundation for Critical Thinking.

Potter, A. (2005). *We the women: Why conflict mediation is not just a job for men.* Geneva, Switzerland: Centre for Humanitarian Dialogue. Retrieved from http://www.hdcentre.org/uploads/tx_news/164Wethewomen.pdf

Rabie, M. (1994). *Conflict resolution and ethnicity.* Westport, CT: Praeger.

Raymond, C., & Sorensen, K. (2008). The use of a Middle East crisis simulation in an international relations course. *Political Science and Politics, 41*(1), 179–182.

Robinson-Keilig, R. A., Hamill, C., Gwin-Visant, A., & Dashner, M. (2014). Feminist pedagogy in action: Photovoice as an experiential class project. *Psychology of Women Quarterly, 38*(2), 292–297. doi:10.1177/0361684314525580

Roholt, R. V., & Fisher, C. (2013). Expect the unexpected: International short-term study course pedagogies and practices. *Journal of Social Work Education, 49,* 48–65. doi:10.1080/10437797.2013.755416

Seul, J. (1999). "Ours is the way of God": Religion, identity, and intergroup conflict. *Journal of Peace Research, 36*(5), 553–569.

Sharp, C., & Clark-Soles, J. (2012). Helping students navigate faith challenges in the biblical studies classroom. *Teaching Theology and Religion, 15*(4), 357–371.

Shaw, I., Lynch, J., & Hackett, R. (Eds.). (2011). *Expanding peace journalism: Comparative and critical approaches.* Sydney, Australia: Sydney University Press.

Small, J., & Bowman, N. (2011). Religious commitment, skepticism, and struggle among U.S. college students: The impact of majority/minority religious affiliation and institutional type. *Journal for the Scientific Study of Religion, 50*(1), 154–174.

Smith, D. (2007). A map of peace and conflict studies in U.S. undergraduate colleges and universities. *Conflict Resolution Quarterly, 25*(1), 145–151.

Sousa, D. A. (2001). *How the brain learns: A classroom teacher's guide* (2nd ed.). Thousand Oaks, CA: Corwin Press.

Stephan, C. W., Hertz-Lazarowitz, R., Zelniker, T., & Stephan, W. G. (2004). Introduction to improving Arab–Jewish relations in Israel: Theory and practice in coexistence educational programs. *Journal of Social Issues, 60*(2), 237–252.

Tessler, M., Nachtwey, J., & Grant, A. (1999). Further tests of the women and peace hypothesis: Evidence from cross-national survey research in the Middle East. *International Studies Quarterly, 43*, 519–531.

Trelstad, M. (2008). The ethics of effective teaching: Challenges from the religious right and critical pedagogy. *Teaching Theology and Religion, 11*(4), 191–202.

Volkan, V. (2009). Large-group identity: "Us and them" polarizations in the international arena. *Psychoanalysis, Culture, and Society, 14*(1), 4–15.

Weiss, J. (2003). *The Third Side: A pedagogical accompaniment, college version.* Retrieved from http://www.thirdside.org/college_cur.pdf

Weiss, J., & Rees, S. (2005). *"You didn't just say that!" Quotes, quips, and proverbs when dealing in the world of conflict and negotiation.* Cambridge, MA: Program on Negotiation at Harvard Law School.

Wellman, J., & Tokuno, K. (2004). Is religious violence inevitable? *Journal for the Scientific Study of Religion, 43*(3), 291–296.

White, L. (Director). (2007). *Refusing to be enemies: The Zeitouna Story* [Motion picture]. Retrieved from http://refusingtobeenemies.org

Winkelmes, M. (2004). The classroom as a place of formation: Purposefully creating a transformative environment for today's diverse seminary population. *Teaching Theology and Religion, 7*(4), 213–222.

Winter, D., & Cava, M. (2006). The psych-ecology of armed conflict. *Journal of Social Issues, 62*(1), 19–40.

Ysseldyk, R., Matheson, K., & Anisman, H. (2010). Religiosity as identity: Toward an understanding of religion from a social identity perspective. *Personality and Social Psychology Review, 14*(1), 60–71.

Zúñiga, X., Nagda, B. A., Chesler, M., & Cytron-Walker, A. (Eds.). (2007). Intergroup dialogues in higher education: Meaningful learning about social justice [Special issue]. *ASHE Higher Education Report, 32*(4).

7

SERVICE-LEARNING AND INTEGRATIVE PEDAGOGY FOR ENGAGING THE WHOLE STUDENT

Joseph A. Galura

My academic career has been nontraditional. For more than 20 years, I was a service-learning educator, based in a partnership between student affairs and sociology, but marked by appointments in interdisciplinary university courses, education, American culture, and social work. In these positions, I primarily developed, implemented, and taught service-learning courses. My current appointment is in social work, with a focus on integrative learning, especially using e-portfolios as a tool to help students make sense of their undergraduate minor in community action and social change, which requires at least one service-learning course.

In the first section of this chapter, I reflect on my experiences as a service-learning educator, experiences that provide the context for the integrative teaching strategies I discuss in the next section for engaging the whole student—mind, heart, and spirit.

Part One: Reflections of a Service-Learning Educator

The literature about *service-learning* abounds with definitions of that term but considers Robert Sigmon's (1994) typology of service-learning as seminal because it examines the relationship between the service and the learning in a straightforward manner. Sometimes I use it as a pretest with students in my courses: Which one of the following spellings (with explanation) do you think is correct?

1. *service-LEARNING:* Learning goals are primary; service outcomes are secondary.
2. *SERVICE-learning:* Service outcomes are primary; learning goals are secondary.
3. *service learning:* Service and learning goals are completely separate.
4. *SERVICE-LEARNING:* Service and learning goals are of equal weight, and each enhances the other for all participants.

Although the "right" answer is item 4, and I will use this spelling for the remainder of this article, there are benefits and challenges associated with each type as applied to a SERVICE-LEARNING course. During my career as a SERVICE-LEARNING educator, I have constructed and taught all four versions, sometimes unintentionally.

service-LEARNING

I wrote about teaching this type of course in "We Made the Road by Talking: Teaching Education 310, 'Service-LEARNING [emphasis added] With Multicultural Elders' at the University of Michigan" (Raudenbush & Galura, 2000). At that time, the late Stella Raudenbush, my coteacher, was writing *Wisdom Teachings: Lessons Learned From Gatherings of Elders* with McClellan Hall (Hall & Raudenbush, 2005) while I was hoping to gather data about Filipino immigration to Metro Detroit (i.e., the Detroit metropolitan area). We dedicated virtually all our course preparation to generating the reading list and were both very pleased with our syllabus.

However, this is an example of a course where the learning goals were primary and the service outcomes were secondary. The syllabus was very explicit in its review of the literature on multiculturalism and the importance of elders in various communities but virtually silent on when during the week and where in the community our students were expected to serve. As Stella and I concluded,

> We are embarrassed to say that despite our professional standings as service-LEARNING [emphasis added] educators, service was the aspect of the course given last consideration. It was clear to us that students needed to be taught specific skills. . . . It was less clear how students should be meaningfully involved in the community. . . . Our advice to instructors is to specify, as much as possible, the weekly hours students are expected to serve in the community, and to make this information available to students before they enroll. Simply hoping that there will be a match between the enrolled student's availability and the community need places all parties involved in a compromising position. (Raudenbush & Galura, 2000, pp. 160, 162)

SERVICE-learning

Sometimes I promoted my courses using the tagline "academic credit for community service." In retrospect, it is not hard to see how students might view the course's service outcomes as primary and the learning goals as secondary, if considered at all. This challenge is compounded when the course is a first-year seminar. First-year students have recently graduated from high schools where virtually all of them participated in some community service, which was often extracurricular. At the University of Michigan, for example, first-year students were surveyed, and 95% had performed community service in high school but only 56% reported community service as a course requirement (Matney, 2013).

I have been "dinged" on student course evaluations when I did not address this mismatch directly. In a first-year seminar on urban education, students were assigned books about tutoring, as well as the history of Detroit, and articles about understanding one's multiple social identities and communicating across differences in race, class, and gender. This was all in addition to their service, a weekly four-hour block, prearranged, where students tutored at elementary schools in Detroit. Although the links between the readings and the service were obvious to me, one student opined on the course evaluation that the entire time in class should be dedicated only to specific tutoring techniques "AND NOTHING ELSE!!!"

In retrospect, I now realize that it is the faculty's task to broaden and deepen students' perspectives by emphasizing how the service and the learning are connected. Bloom's taxonomy of educational objectives (Bloom & Krathwohl, 1956) is a helpful tool I use with students to process with them the differences among simply repeating "knowledge"; applying it in a variety of situations in the classroom, community, or personal life; and synthesizing these multiple inputs to create a new, integrated whole.

service learning

One of my job duties has been to develop field placements. After discovering one of my colleagues was doing a lecture series at a local hospital about how to raise strong and confident daughters, I had a terrific idea: Would she be interested in developing feminist mentorships? I could recruit female college students that she would train to mentor the teenage daughters of the parents who were already attending her lecture series. There was immediate interest from all parties, especially the female college students, or feminist mentors (which they eventually shortened to *femtors*), who, remembering their own adolescence, enthusiastically agreed to enroll in this innovative service learning course.

But it was indeed a service learning course, because, unfortunately, the service and the learning goals were somewhat separate. Most universities run on calendars that do not readily map onto how much of the rest of the world operates. Although the femtors had very positive engagement in the community, I did not have the time or the knowledge base necessary to develop a placement-specific syllabus for them. As a consequence, they were grouped in a section where the readings and discussions were about tutoring in elementary schools, specifically, how to address the (racial) achievement gap in science and mathematics. The femtors found the discussion interesting but difficult to relate to their field experience.

SERVICE-LEARNING

I like to think that in the majority of my courses, the service and learning goals are of equal weight and that each enhances the other for everyone involved. If I were to single out two examples that best fit this type, the communication workshops I organized in prison settings would be one. There were two types of workshops: creative writing and debate. Both workshops were responses to specific requests from the deputy warden, with whom I had placed students for 10 years. In fact, the deputy warden was relaying to me a need for programming expressed by the inmates themselves. Knowing the need, I could then target for recruitment of student groups who had the appropriate skill set (creative writing majors, high school debaters, even the university's debate team). It also helped that the syllabus was already about contemporary issues in criminal justice. "Teaching Creative Writing in Prisons" received the Faculty/Staff Award from Michigan Campus Compact as

> an extraordinary example of a SERVICE-LEARNING [emphasis added] course that provides both meaningful service to, in this case, prisoners, and meaningful learning for University students. It was far and away the most creative, innovative, and successful SERVICE-LEARNING [emphasis added] effort on campus this year. (Howard, 1997)

The other example is the Lives of Urban Children and Youth (LUCY) Initiative, honored by the Ginsberg Center for Community Service and Learning as the Outstanding University Program. Here is the course description:

> The LUCY Initiative was conceived as a two-year curricular and co-curricular pathway for first- and second-year students interested in examining the lives of urban children and youth as a topic of serious academic inquiry. SERVICE-LEARNING [emphasis added] is the instructional methodology, with a special interest on university–community partnerships. Specifically, the idea was that students would be able to serve at the

same agency for up to two years. The intent here is that extended involvement in the community would both broaden and deepen the students'
learning objectives, while increasing the quality of service delivered to our
community partners. (Galura et al., 2004, p. 52)

In both examples, I attempted to design the service and learning goals to
be of equal weight and mutually reinforcing. From the perspective of college
students, as they learn more about the prison system or the life of urban children and youth, they become better equipped to provide service, in this case,
teaching creative writing or tutoring in elementary schools. The inmates or
urban children and youth benefit from the service, taking away from the
experience specific skills and competencies related to communication, verbal or written, or to the standard elementary curriculum. One supervising
teacher remarked, "I hope [your students] are getting as much out of this as
mine. We find them to be very helpful." The deputy warden confided to me
that he observed a decrease in violence among workshop participants, which
he attributed to their increased communications skills. "They are much more
likely to express their complaints verbally or in writing," he said. "In fact, I
have never received so many beautifully written memos."

Although both award winning, these examples underscore the importance of individual faculty making an ongoing commitment to identified
communities and partnering with specific agencies and organizations to create effective engaged learning opportunities. More recent literature about
SERVICE-LEARNING observes a historic emphasis on student learning,
often upstaging any discussion of community benefit. Boyte (2009) called
for "repairing the breach" between campus and community, recasting service
as "public work" with an emphasis on "the capacities, talents and energies in
all involved in addressing public challenges" (p. 7). This is meant to address
the "two classes" implicit in service—those who give and those who receive—
at least in theory. However, returning to Sigmon's (1994) four types, "public
work" raises a troubling question: Given the inherent inequality in access to
resources between a major university and virtually any community agency, is
it ever really possible for the goals of each respective partner to carry "equal
weight," as Sigmon suggested they must?

Part Two: Integrative Pedagogy for Engaging the Whole Student

Assuming that I am teaching a SERVICE-LEARNING course, integrative pedagogy for me has three broad and overlapping keywords: *pedagogy*,
boundaries, and *invitation*. My educational objectives and strategies roughly
correspond, respectively, to teaching the mind, the heart, and the spirit.

Although, I also recognize that in practice these distinctions may be continuous rather than discrete, perhaps more present in my explanation than in my classroom.

Pedagogy: Engaging the Mind

In a SERVICE-LEARNING class, the discussion that follows exists as talking points, which I present in the abstract to students, then enact with them in dialogue on various levels rather than as formal lectures. Usually my starting point is Paulo Freire (1970), notably his observation that *banking education* describes students as empty receptacles waiting to be filled by the teacher's gift of knowledge.

Freire's metaphor makes little sense in a SERVICE-LEARNING course: How can students be expected to be actively engaged in service and knowledge generation in the community but be cast as passive learners in the classroom? Once this contradiction is named, the students and I generate a set of classroom norms, such as honesty, respect, listening, and support. I also have students articulate their learning objectives for the semester, which tend to emphasize the field experience. We revisit the norms and objectives at different points throughout the term.

Dewey (1929) provided a second talking point: "We do not learn by doing. . . . We learn by doing . . . and then realizing [or reflecting on] what came of what we did" (p. 367). As noted previously, this is an important point because students often arrive in SERVICE-LEARNING classes having done community service, which is not connected to the intentional learning of academic content. For faculty, Chesler, Galura, Ford, and Charbeneau (2006), among others, provided compelling motivation to require students to analyze and apply the literature. They argued that given no conceptual framework, student engagement in the community may well reinforce preexisting stereotypes.

Returning to Freire (1970), I have found it helpful to discuss his definition of *praxis* with students. The idea here is that an iterative process of action and reflection leads to social change. For students and faculty, this raises the following series of critical questions:

- As a class, do our service and learning correspond to Freire's model of action and reflection?
- To what extent is Freire's critique of education applicable in an American Research I university in the twenty-first century?
- What does Freire mean by *social change*, and can any class even begin to approximate it during a single semester?

Palmer (1987) made the point that epistemology (how we know what we know) is the groundwork for pedagogy (how we teach what we know). A SERVICE-LEARNING course is an opportunity for students to cross pedagogical and epistemological borders by actively learning and teaching in the classroom and in the community, with the potential that their engagement produces new knowledge.

An example of this is the Filipino American Oral History Project of Michigan, which Emily Lawsin and I established (Galura & Lawsin, 2002). In our class, students learned about the history of Filipino immigration to the United States, along with oral history methods. In the community, students conducted interviews with Filipino Americans older than 40 years living in Metro Detroit. They also taught a weekly Filipino American history and identity class at the Philippine American Community Center of Michigan to an intergenerational group of students, ranging in age from 7 years to older than 70 years. To prepare to teach, the college students interviewed members of their own families, uncovering their own stories of immigration with the intent of including these narratives in their discourse with others about history and identity.

This iterative process of action and reflection casts students as knowledge producers, contributing original research to a field that scholars have only begun to document. These findings are then shared with the community, sparking interest in Filipino Americans not only to know their history but also to tell and retell it themselves, using their own words.

Boundaries: Engaging the Heart

One of my very first students wrote, "How did I like [the mini-lecture on closure]? I didn't. My stomach knotted up, and I started feeling sick." This should not be surprising. In a SERVICE-LEARNING course, students often develop deep emotional bonds to the people in the community they engage with over the course of a semester. I tell students that we have a contract to provide service, which has a beginning, a middle, and an end. In the case of the student quoted, closure was especially important because her placement was at a prison and the Department of Corrections has rigid rules about when, how, and by whom inmates may be contacted.

In emotional situations, displacement can be a helpful teaching tool. How have students at other universities concluded their SERVICE-LEARNING experiences? I have assigned books by Dunlap (2000) and Chin, Rabow, and Estrada (2011) so that my class can read about other students in similar courses at Connecticut College and UCLA, respectively; discuss the lessons learned; and then plan accordingly. The goal here is "no closure disasters," such as students not showing up on the last day to say good-bye or making false promises to stay in touch. But probably more important than any specific closure strategy is the practice of modeling clear boundaries, which create safe spaces for teaching the heart throughout the term.

Students have told me that it is helpful for them that my classes follow similar scripts. I usually open with a video from YouTube to introduce the topic for the day. Two resources that I have found useful are Lynskey's (2011) *33 Revolutions per Minute: A History of Protest Songs, From Billie Holiday to Green Day*, particularly in social work when teaching about social movements, and Smith's (2001) *Dancing in the Street: Motown and the Cultural Politics of Detroit*, when I taught the LUCY courses with placements in Detroit. I close the class with a slide of Abraham Lincoln and a brief summary of the day's content, because Gopnik (2009) noted that a 50-word conclusion, usually stated in one- or two-syllable words, was the secret of Lincoln's oratorical success.

I use the Lincoln summaries to validate student-led discussions (students are required to pick one article from the syllabus to lead a 15-minute discussion about in class, which they plan with me during my office hours). Howard (2014) observed that although his students like participating in discussion, they often ask what they should be taking away from the experience. One student concluded, "I really liked the stability of your class and appreciated your PowerPoints. It was nice reviewing concepts often and connecting them to what we were currently learning."

Cocreating a supportive learning environment begins on the first day. I mention a quote attributed to Gandhi, "There is more to life than simply increasing its speed," then explain that my technology policy prohibits use of electronic devices, especially laptops and cell phones, by students during class. I show a slide of a bumper sticker: "Honk if you love Jesus. Text while driving if you want to meet him." At least in theory, my aim for students is to fully engage others in the present moment, safely and without outside distractions, especially digital multitasking. I also give each student a blank 100-page composition book for note taking.

About halfway through the semester, I draw from my training as a social worker and distinguish the different types of group experiences students may encounter in their field experiences. This was particularly relevant when I placed students at agencies doing substance abuse treatment. The types of groups are as follows:

- *Didactic:* This type of group disseminates information to clients, usually about their medical condition.
- *Support:* This group offers nonprofessionally led informal discussion with self-directed participants, often based on the 12 steps of Alcoholics

Anonymous: "Men and women who share their experience, strength and hope with each other so that they may solve their common problem" (AA Grapevine, Inc., n.d.).

- *Treatment:* These types of groups are professionally led therapy groups with formal rules of interaction, with structured activities addressing clients' specific diagnoses.

I suggest connections between students' communities and classroom experiences. Do didactic groups relate to Freire's (1970) banking education, where the all-knowing teacher deposits "ready to wear" information into student receptacles? Is there a need for lecture and, if so, under what circumstances? I also posit that support groups relate to aspects of Freire, particularly his idea that the power dynamic in the student–teacher relationships can be transformed when teacher–student and student–teacher work in solidarity—or join with one another to build a supportive classroom community.

One aspect of that community building is to be clear about what is outside the walls. Integrative pedagogy may be rare in a university setting, and I have had students mistake their feelings about community building for being in therapy. Indeed, some have even resisted loved ones' recommendations that they seek professional help because they felt so supported and affirmed by the classroom environment. So I state and restate the boundary clearly: "This is an educational group, not a therapy group. You are a student with learning objectives, not a client with a specified diagnosis. And probably most important, even though I have worked as a therapist, I am not your therapist. If you present issues that require professional attention, I am ethically bound to make the appropriate referral." For me, this boundary setting is essential. I developed and implemented this framework because at one point I was seeing clients as a clinical social worker while developing sections of SERVICE-LEARNING courses with placements at chemical dependency treatment facilities. These placements attracted students in various stages of recovery.

Since my appointment in social work, I have grafted the topic of self-care into this conversation tree. If I am teaching an introductory course, I mention the literature. For example, a recent issue of *Social Work Today* (Jackson, 2014) is dedicated to "self-care—the overlooked core competency" (p. 14). If I am teaching a capstone course with seniors, who are often contemplating what an ongoing commitment to make the world a better place through their work with individuals and communities may look like for them, I pose a series of questions for class discussion that align with the trajectory of this chapter, as well as this book:

- What are you doing now that indicates a healthy approach to diet, exercise, sleep, and rest?
- What are your sources for education about social justice issues? How will this education continue after graduation?
- Where, how, and with whom do you recharge your emotional batteries?
- What are your core values, and how will you continue to nurture them?

Invitation: Engaging the Spirit

For students, this boundary setting and the related safe spaces that are cocreated for engagement in the community, in the classroom, among their peers, and with me are the necessary foundation for teaching the spirit. On one hand, my strategy for teaching the spirit is deceptively simple: Invite the students to bring their diverse faiths and traditions into classroom discussion. On the other hand, in the context of a SERVICE-LEARNING course, this invitation must be coordinated with the related and overlapping strategies around boundaries and pedagogy.

In a SERVICE-LEARNING course, it is reasonable to assume that some students are motivated to deliver service to the community based on their faith traditions. At the University of Michigan, there have been repeated surveys of incoming first-year students (Matney, 2007) that indicate that one third reported "service to my religious community." This is the second-highest ranking category of precollege community service. Given this finding, my task becomes crafting assignments that give permission for students to bring their spiritual values into the classroom and language to relate these values to each other, their work in the community, and the academic texts. I have found two assignments to be especially useful.

One is for students to introduce themselves to the class using a Power-Point slide. The introduction needs to reference the readings. Recently, these have been the core values in the National Association of Social Workers' (2008) *Code of Ethics* (service, social justice, dignity and worth of the person, importance of human relationships, integrity, competence) and Canda's (2009) reflection on them (the core of spirituality is compassion, which he defined as serving others with heart). Sacred texts have often been quoted on slides, in English but also in Hebrew, Arabic, and Anishinaabe (Ojibwe). One student envisioned himself as Nachshon, willing to step into the unknown, the first among his people to step away from the oppression of the pursuing Egyptian army when the Red Sea parts.

In a first-year seminar on urban education, I asked students to compose a "Where I'm From" poem, which asks explicitly for religious images and other markers of social identity. I later encouraged students to read their poems aloud in class and modeled the activity by performing my version. I was surprised by how lyrically students expressed links between their faith tradition and ethnicity:

I am from Poland and kielbasa and kolaches.
I am from the crucifix. And strong morals.
I am from the belief of Immaculate Conception, Sunday visits to church
and the daughter of a proud Irish Catholic father who still has yet to learn
a line of the Bible.
I'm from Royal Oak, the Ireland of America.
I am from Catholicism. True believers till the day of our death.
I'm from Potensia and Italy, Gnocchi and Marasala.

I'm from prayer before bed and Bibles with pictures, the Black version.

I am from Judaism, the trains of the Holocaust, the ghettos of Shanghai
and the hills of West Virginia.

I am from Hinduism, with a variety of many different gods and goddesses.
I am from traveling to India and always being with family members.
I am from many deities that each provides something specific that is needed
to be happy.

I am from suitcases, from Egypt Air and jetlag.
From stay clean: alcohol-free and abstinent. And blood is thicker than
water.
I am from half-read Quran and half-fasted Ramadan.

The "Where I'm From" activity is not my creation. Beverly Daniel Tatum (2007) in *Can We Talk About Race? And Other Conversations in an Era of School Resegregation* described "The ABC's of Creating a Climate of Engagement: Affirming Identity, Building Community, and Cultivating Leadership" and suggested this poetry exercise to help create that climate. Describing the poem, Tatum wrote,

Using the stem "I am from" for each stanza, we asked students to describe familiar items found around their homes, sights, sounds, and smells from their neighborhoods, names of foods and dishes enjoyed at family gatherings, familiar family sayings, and names of relatives or other people who are a link to their past. The act of writing the poems helped to make each student's culture visible, not only to others but to herself. (p. 120)

I found it interesting that without my prompting, students were articulating their various intersectionalities—they saw themselves as Irish Catholic or Pakistani Muslim or Indian Hindu or Punjabi Sikh—but with past and current engagement in the community at least partially rooted in these self-defined religious traditions. Or to use Tatum's language, that is how they made their culture visible, both to themselves and to their classmates. At the end of the term, one student concluded,

> As one of my peers said at the end of [class], "I want to always remember this moment, right now, in this classroom, and take it with me wherever I go." I was very touched by this fellow student's comment and struck by her sincerity and the truth of her words. I have learned more from this class about myself . . . than I have during any other class I have taken at [the University of Michigan] thus far. When I step out into the real world, I hope to always carry and remember the words of my peers from UC 151.

This student's conclusion is important on a number of levels. First, it is made possible by my practice of integrative pedagogy. Hidden motives for community service, in this case religious tradition connecting students to their respective ethnic communities, were invited into the open. Second, once these motives were in the open, students made a remarkable discovery. In many cases, University of Michigan students arrive on campus from communities segregated by race or ethnicity or social class—the particular students in this seminar had few, if any, meaningful interactions with people from social backgrounds that were different from their own. This was an empirical point forcefully made by historian Thomas Sugrue (2012) in his expert testimony during the Supreme Court's rulings on the University of Michigan's affirmative action policies. However, in this seminar, students from diverse religious traditions and ethnic communities were united in service, tutoring children in two Detroit schools—an experience that at least two students never wanted to forget.

Thus, inviting students to share in the classroom their spiritual traditions regarding service also allows them to locate their values relative to a particular body of academic or professional literature, as well as relative to the perspectives of their classmates. A Christian student, who reflected on her SERVICE-LEARNING experiences at the end of her undergraduate career, perhaps experienced this most poignantly, saying,

> Ever since I was young, I have tried to center my life on the Christian principle of putting others before myself—my high school motto was actually "JOY," which stood for "Jesus, Others, Yourself." I have always desired to dedicate my life in some shape or form to the service of others, yet as selfless

as I may have felt, the truth is that my thoughts revolved around what I wanted to do for me—not where my place was in relation to my community and to others around me. Several years later, I still have the same dream and drive that I did before. Now, though, I see myself as a new person.

One of the biggest lessons that I have learned . . . is that in order to truly make a change in a community, I need to work with people—not for people. It seems like such a simple concept right now, but it absolutely boggled my mind when we first talked about it. Back in high school, I went on several mission trips around the world in which our goal was to go into impoverished places and "bring light into the dark," or help those who are less fortunate than us. Now, I see how that only perpetuates a problem. By going into a situation acknowledging that I am "above" a person in a way, then I am just reinforcing their disadvantage, disability, or minority status.

Another student articulated a similar change in perspective on a more interpersonal level but still used the language of faith. Although usually associated with the Judeo-Christian tradition, the so-called Golden Rule has many parallels in other traditions, including but not limited to Baha'i Faith, Buddhism, Confucianism, Hinduism, Islam, Jainism, Sikhism, Taoism, and Wicca.

I myself never questioned [the fundamental pillar "treat others the way you want to be treated"] until recently when an 11-year-old product of Detroit Public Schools provided me with a new perspective. "Instead of treating people how you would want to be treated, you should treat people how THEY want to be treated," she told me. I'll always remember this as the moment I truly understood the definition of empathy. It's moments like these—the moments that challenge the very fiber of your being, from the most unlikely of sources—in which the most learning can occur.

An Anishinaabe student developed a metaphor with me about her SERVICE-LEARNING: "walking with a moccasin in two worlds," a cluster of experiences all centered on creating access to higher education for under-represented communities but grounded in her belief that she consider the impact of her work on the next seven generations.

These selected examples, alongside my teaching strategies, challenge the SERVICE-LEARNING literature, where the dominant view is that the goal of instruction is to move students across a continuum, from individual-level direct service to social change. Keith Morton (1995) dissented, positing instead three distinct paradigms of service, which he defined as *charity*, *project*, and *social justice*. My practice of integrative pedagogy, at least with respect to religion and spirituality, aligns itself with that of Morton, notably his observation that students tend to move within given paradigms and not between them, and that movement, borrowing from anthropologist Clifford Geertz, is to develop a thick versus thin culture of service. I would argue that in this view student growth is deep, instead of wide, and has more ideological nuance and internal connectedness than political suasion.

Charles Strain (2006) added a framework to Morton's, taken from his discipline of developmental psychology. Could students' movement within the three paradigms be informed by their existing moral and spiritual development? Personally, I think of Eboo Patel (2007). Anticipating his meeting with the Dalai Lama, Patel believed the Dalai Lama would want him to become a Buddhist. He was pleasantly surprised to be encouraged to become the best Muslim he can possibly be. Similarly, these strategies for teaching the spirit are designed for a student to become the best Anishinaabe she can be—or Christian, or Jew, or Muslim.

Finally, I should note that it is possible to be spiritual without being religious. More than 20 years ago, with students' permission, I edited and published "Reflectors Anonymous: Six Recovering Service-Learners Share Their Experience, Strength, and Hope" (Galura, 1993). I still correspond with "Matt," who went on to successful careers as both a substance abuse therapist and the author of four novels, critically reviewed as "the Stephen King" of his subgenre. Once a year, I invite him to speak to my students about long-term recovery from addiction. Matt makes it clear to me—and the class—that this is how he chooses to live out the 12th step of Alcoholics Anonymous:

> Having had a spiritual awakening as the result of these steps, we tried to carry this message to alcoholics and to practice these principles in all our affairs.

Matt would add that he sees opportunities to educate others regarding addiction as service to the recovering community. This is a majority view within 12-step groups. What is unique and compelling to college students about Matt's story is that his recovery began as an undergraduate who enrolled in my SERVICE-LEARNING class.

Conclusion: Teaching Mind, Heart, Spirit, and e-Portfolios?

On the TV comedy *The Big Bang Theory* (Prady, Engel, & Murray, 2008), Leonard prepares for his presentation at a physics conference and decides to open with a joke: "I have a solution but it only works for spherical chickens in a vacuum." Contrast this punch line with the iterative process in a SERVICE-LEARNING course: Students engage in action and reflection, cocreating applications of knowledge that they implement immediately at their placements, in their classroom, perhaps in their personal life, and even in their career choices. Because this iterative process casts students as active learners within and beyond traditional academic borders, a SERVICE-LEARNING course is an ideal setting for integrative pedagogy—teaching the whole student: mind, heart, and spirit. To that end, this chapter has suggested strategies for classroom interactions with students about pedagogy, boundaries, and invitation, which roughly correspond, respectively, to teaching the mind, heart, and spirit.

It should be noted that some of the conversations with students I have quoted are taken from my capstone course, where seniors reflected back on their engagement in the community over the span of their undergraduate years. Kuh (2008) identified both capstones and SERVICE-LEARNING as "high-impact practices" (pp. 17–20) and recommended undergraduates experience at least one per academic year. It would be an interesting topic for further research to investigate whether the effect of formally combining these two high-impact practices within an academic program is cumulative or synergistic. Data are just now beginning to emerge, examining metareflection or structured student reflection on previous reflections (Peet et al., 2011).

Regardless of the outcome, in my small sample there does appear to be some benefit to students in reflecting back on their SERVICE-LEARNING experiences at multiple points in time. Technology, specifically the capacity for students to archive their best work in an electronic portfolio throughout their undergraduate years, seems to facilitate this process. Intentionally engaging the whole student, the mind, heart, and spirit—it is this reflective and perhaps metareflective process, over and above any specific product, that is quintessential to both SERVICE-LEARNING and integrative pedagogy.

Reflection Questions

1. Service-learning is a powerful, engaged pedagogy as described in this chapter. What have been your experiences, if any, with service-learning courses? Have you experienced any of the challenges of balancing service with learning that are outlined here? How did you address them?

2. If you have never experimented with service-learning, what aspects of students' learning of the *content* of the courses you typically teach might be improved by including a service-learning component? How might service-learning integrate students' understanding of course content with their heart, mind, and spirit?

3. Tatum's (2007) "Where I'm From" activity is meant to make aspects of a person's culture visible: "familiar items found around their homes, sights, sounds, and smells from their neighborhoods, names of foods and dishes enjoyed at family gatherings, familiar family sayings, and names of relatives or other people who are a link to their past" (p. 120). What would your poem look like? Would you consider sharing some portion of your completed "Where I'm From" poem with your students, and if so, under what circumstances?

4. In what ways do the courses you teach attempt to bring about social change? To what extent do you use reflection to help students understand the connection between theory and action? How do your assignments creatively engage students in the critical self-reflective process of understanding oneself in society?

5. The core values of social work are service, social justice, dignity and worth of the person, importance of human relationships, integrity, and competence. How do these align with your personal values? How do these core values of social work fit or not fit with the core values of your discipline? Is a discussion of values—personal, discipline specific, professional, other—built into your syllabus, and if so, how would you, as the instructor, frame and facilitate that conversation?

6. One key point made in this chapter concerns *boundaries*—the careful definition of what the service-learning class is and what it is not. Why are boundaries important? What kinds of boundaries do you think might help students, community members, and yourself as an instructor have a positive and productive experience?

7. In what ways can you imagine bringing students' spiritual experiences and religious identities into your service-learning classroom? How might discussion of students' core values deepen their understanding of course content and their ability to integrate their learning of course content with their social identities and career aspirations (who they are and what they do)?

8. In this chapter, e-portfolios are discussed as one means by which students can integrate more fully their experiences in service-learning courses. What other high-impact, metacognitive strategies could you use to help students create and represent meaning from engaged learning?

9. How do you envision your last day of class? If you are teaching a service-learning course, what specific strategies are you using to address closure, especially as students exit the community? If you are not teaching a service-learning class, what are you planning that will engage the mind, heart, and spirit during your last meeting?

References

AA Grapevine, Inc. (n.d.). *About us.* Retrieved from http://www.aagrapevine.org/content/about-us

Bloom, B., & Krathwohl, D. R. (1956). *Taxonomy of educational objectives: The classification of educational goals, by a committee of college and university examiners. Handbook 1: Cognitive domain.* New York, NY: Longmans.

Boyte, H. (2009). Repairing the breach: Cultural organizing and the politics of knowledge. *Partnerships: A Journal of Service Learning and Civic Engagement, 1*(1), 1–29.

Canda, E. (2009, June). *Spiritually sensitive social work: An overview of American and international trends.* Plenary address at the International Conference on Social Work and Counseling, Hong Kong.

Chesler, M., Galura, J. A., Ford, K., & Charbeneau, J. (2006). Peer facilitators as border crossers in community service learning. *Teaching Sociology, 34*(4), 341–356.

Chin, T., Rabow, J., & Estrada, J. (2011). *Tutoring matters: Everything you always wanted to know about tutoring* (2nd ed.). Philadelphia, PA: Temple University Press.

Dewey, J. (1929). *Experience and nature.* New York, NY: Grave.

Dunlap, M. (2000). *Reaching out to children and families: Students model effective community service.* Lanham, MD: Rowman & Littlefield.

Freire, P. (1970). *Pedagogy of the oppressed.* New York, NY: Continuum.

Galura, J. (Ed.). (1993). Reflectors Anonymous: Six recovering service-learners share their experience, strength, and hope. In J. Galura, R. Meiland, R. Ross, M. J. Callan, & R. Smith (Eds.), *Praxis II: Service-learning resources for university students, staff and faculty* (pp. 365–393). Ann Arbor, MI: OCSL Press.

Galura, J., & Lawsin, E. (2002). *Filipino women in Detroit, 1945–1955: Oral histories from the Filipino American History Project of Michigan.* Ann Arbor, MI: OCSL Press.

Galura, J., Raudenbush, S., Denzin, J., Kai, N., Balogh, N., Brady, K., . . . Wargel, C. (2004). LUCY: The Lives of Urban Children and Youth Initiative. In J. Galura, P. A. Pasque, D. Schoem, & J. Howard (Eds.), *Engaging the whole of service-learning, diversity, and learning communities* (pp. 51–72). Ann Arbor, MI: OCSL Press.

Gopnik, A. (2009). *Angels and ages: A short book about Darwin, Lincoln, and modern life.* New York, NY: Random House.

Hall, M., & Raudenbush, S. (2005). *Wisdom teachings: Lessons learned from gatherings of elders.* Saint Paul, MN: National Youth Leadership Council.

Howard, J. (1997, November). *Michigan Campus Compact Faculty/Staff Community Service-Learning Award Recognition.* Colleagues in Service Dinner, Kellogg Center, East Lansing. MI.

Howard, J. (2014). *Discussion in the college classroom: Get your students engaged and participating in person and online.* San Francisco, CA: Jossey-Bass.

Jackson, K. (2014). Social worker self-care: The overlooked core competency. *Social Work Today, 14*(3), 14–17.

Kuh, G. D. (2008). *High-impact educational practices: What they are, who has access to them, and why they matter.* Washington, DC: Association of American Colleges & Universities.

Lynskey, D. (2011). *33 revolutions per minute: A history of protest songs, from Billie Holiday to Green Day.* New York, NY: HarperCollins.

Matney, M. (2007). *2006 entering student profile, community service.* Ann Arbor: University of Michigan Division of Student Affairs.

Matney, M. (2013). *Factbook: Activities.* Ann Arbor: University of Michigan Student Life. Retrieved from http://studentlife.umich.edu/files/research/activities2012.pdf

Morton, K. (1995). The irony of service: Charity, project and social change in service-learning. *Michigan Journal of Community Service Learning, 2*(1), 19–32.

National Association of Social Workers. (2008). *Code of ethics of the National Association of Social Workers.* Washington, DC: Author.

Palmer, P. (1987). Community, conflict, and ways of knowing: Ways to deepen our educational agenda. *Change, 19*(5), 20–25. Retrieved from http://www.couragerenewal.org/parker/writings/community-conflict

Patel, E. (2007). *Acts of faith: The story of an American Muslim, the struggle for the soul of a generation.* Boston, MA: Beacon Press.

Peet, M., Lonn, S., Gurin, P., Boyer, K. P., Matney, M., Marra, T., . . . Daley, A. (2011). Fostering integrative knowledge through ePortfolios. *International Journal of ePortfolio, 1*(1), 11–31.

Prady, B. (Writer), Engel, S. (Writer), & Murray, J. (Director). (2008). The Cooper–Hofstadter polarization [Television series episode]. In C. Lorre & B. Prady (Executive producers), *The Big Bang Theory.* New York, NY: CBS Television.

Raudenbush, S., & Galura, J. (2000). We made the road by talking: Teaching Education 310, "Service-Learning With Multicultural Elders" at the University of Michigan. In C. R. O'Grady (Ed.), *Integrating service learning and multicultural education in colleges and universities* (pp. 153–168). Mahwah, NJ: Lawrence Erlbaum.

Sigmon, R. (1994). *Serving to learn, learning to serve: Linking service with learning.* Washington, DC: Council for Independent Colleges Report.

Smith, S. (2001). *Dancing in the street: Motown and the cultural politics of Detroit.* Cambridge, MA: Harvard University Press.

Strain, C. (2006). Moving like a starfish: Beyond a linear model of student transformation in service learning classes. *Journal of College and Character, 8*(1), 1–12.

Sugrue, T. (2012). *Expert report of Thomas J. Sugrue: The compelling need for diversity in higher education:* Gratz v. Bollinger *and* Grutter v. Bollinger. Retrieved from http://www.vpcomm.umich.edu/admissions/legal/expert/sugrutoc.html

Tatum, B. (2007). *Can we talk about race? And other conversations in an era of school resegregation.* Boston, MA: Beacon Press.

PART THREE

INTEGRATIVE PEDAGOGY

8

TEACHING AND LEARNING THAT MAKE A DIFFERENCE

James L. Heft

In late 2006, as president of the Institute for Advanced Catholic Studies at the University of Southern California (USC), I gathered in Boston with an international group of Jewish, Christian, and Muslim scholars. The institute is a freestanding 501(c)3 corporation with its own board of trustees, located at USC. Its mission is "to create dialogue, spark ideas, inspire deep thinking, and support important and profound interdisciplinary and inter-faith research rooted in the rich Catholic intellectual tradition" (Institute for Advanced Catholic Studies at the University of Southern California, n.d.). One way it does this is by welcoming people of all religions and no religion to enter dialogues that last an academic year.

I had worked for over a year with a Jewish, a Catholic, and a Muslim scholar to identify and organize this group. In preparation for the confer-ence, I thought it would help the weeklong dialogue we planned to have in Jerusalem in 2007 about "learned ignorance" and "intellectual humility" if we met first for two days and got to know each other on a personal level. In preparation for that meeting, I asked each of the scholars to prepare a three-page response to the following questions: (a) Why did you accept the invitation to join in this dialogue?; (b) What do you think are the greatest obstacles to interreligious understanding?; and (c) What do you hope will be accomplished through our research project and dialogue? Their answers were so thoughtful and personally revealing, so honest and hopeful, that more clearly than ever before I realized that our research project had tapped into some of the deepest longings and the most personal experiences of these scholars.[1] They seemed more than willing to describe their spiritual and reli-gious commitments, especially as they related to the research that we had proposed for them to do. They all seemed quite at ease describing how their own faith commitments blended, even strengthened, the quality and depth of their research. In short, they transcended the advocacy versus objectivity dichotomy.

As a consequence, after writing our papers and discussing them in Jerusalem, I asked each of them, in preparation for the publication of the volume, to write a short autobiography, including the answers they gave to the questions I had asked them. We included their personal statements as introductions to each of their essays, which made up the heart of the book.

A moment of grace fell on us during the last day of the dialogue in Jerusalem. One of the participants asked, "According to your own religious tradition, what is the point of what we have been doing here for the past five days? What do you believe is the purpose of interreligious dialogue?" There followed a thoughtful silence. Then, for the next two hours, the 15 of us wrestled with his question. Were we really trying to convert each other? Foster mutual understanding? Collaboration? Were we just comparing our traditions? So important was this discussion that we decided to add to the volume an epilogue in which the three editors, a Jew, a Christian, and a Muslim, tried to recapture some of the richness and honesty of that discussion. Each of us was invited to state what he thought was the purpose of interreligious dialogue, and then the other two, after reading that statement, posed a question that the author then tried to answer. Although that epilogue to *Learned Ignorance* (Heft, Firestone, & Safi, 2011) could not reproduce that spontaneous and searching conversation we had in Jerusalem, it does convey to the reader something of what happens when scholars, deeply immersed in the careful study and appropriation of their own religious traditions, try to answer questions that make them personally vulnerable. Neither of these moments could have been predicted at the outset of the project, but both show, I believe, what happens when scholars open themselves to difficult and personal questions in the presence of other scholars and learn once again, but now at a deeper, more integrated level, what they had already thought but rarely, if ever, articulated.

This is not the only scholarly dialogue in which I've participated that was blessed with graced moments of unplanned openness and insight, but these examples show how such a personal and integrated, but no less intellectually rigorous, approach to learning and research leads not only to new understanding but also to personal transformation for faculty and the students they teach. It is about such genuine and deep encounters that I wish to write in this chapter.

I have structured my reflections as follows. After describing some early personal experiences, even before experiences as a college and graduate student had affected me, I describe some of the integrative pedagogical approaches I have taken to teaching, in the oft-used phrase the "whole student." I then describe some of the many faculty development seminars I have designed and led and the lessons they have taught me about the importance of engaging faculty around questions of deeply held values and spiritual commitments. I hope that all of this will show that subjectivity is not the same as subjectivism, that attention to one's own experience need not end in solipsism, that affirming beliefs that are not able to be scientifically proven is not to act irrationally, and that interdisciplinary research need not result in becoming incompetent in two disciplines.

Growing Up "Catholic"

My parents were farmers from central Ohio, my mother a Catholic and my father a Protestant. When they married in 1935, neither side of the family was happy. My parents were, after all, entering into a "mixed marriage." No one from my father's side of the family attended the ceremony, and the Catholic priest refused to witness the wedding in the church, choosing instead to conduct a bare-bones ceremony in the rectory, his residence. Of course, neither any of my four siblings nor I knew about any of this until years later. Not long after my parents married, they moved to Cleveland, Ohio, where a wonderful Jew hired my father, for whom he worked for the next 26 years. I did not realize until college that I had personally been living out sociologist Will Herberg's classic 1955 book *Protestant, Catholic, Jew*. Had I been raised in an Irish Catholic ghetto in Boston, I think my experiences would have been quite different.

With my father's support, my mother passed on the Catholic faith to all of us, supporting us all through Catholic elementary and secondary school. But in the second grade, I had an experience that shaped me for the rest of my life. I was tall even then, seated therefore in the back of the room. The teacher, a Catholic sister, announced, "If you are not Catholic, you will not go to heaven." I knew that my father, to whom I was especially close, was a good man, even if he rarely went to church with the rest of the family on Sundays. The teacher's comment made me angry. I immediately stood up, hit my fist on the desk, and shouted, "That's not true!" Then I hit my fist even harder on the desk and, pointing my finger at her, shouted even louder, "That's not true. My daddy's going to heaven!" I have no memory of what happened after that. Nor did I have the vocabulary then to clothe adequately with words that graced moment. But even then I knew that if persons, even those in positions of religious authority, said something that contradicted my lived and trusted experience of love, I would not accept what they said.

Another important experience was the theatre. In grade school, high school, and college, I acted in various plays; the most powerful, for me at least, was when in college I played the role of Thomas More in *A Man for All Seasons* (Bolt, 1960). Although I don't think I ever became that good at acting, I know that trying to act forced me to do my best to enter into someone else's shoes, to imagine what he or she experienced, and to portray that person in as authentic a way as possible. Some roles were more of a stretch than others. All of them, however, forced me to try to feel what someone else felt. Acting broadened my range of empathy.

I began graduate studies in philosophy at Georgetown University. After two years, my interest in philosophy waned. I found that I had become more interested in the life and formation of the philosophers than in their philosophy, in their times rather than their ideas. I switched my course of studies to history and theology. Theology alone can be abstract; history alone can become a numbing string of facts. Historical theology was about people, their beliefs and times. This switch did not disappoint. I also began to study the relationship between Judaism and Catholicism and discovered already as a college student the long, shameful treatment of the Jews by the Catholic Church, culminating in the horrors of the *Shoah*. In one form or another, I have been involved in interreligious dialogue ever since.

Years later, successive experiences in university administration forced me to expand further my range of empathy. At the end of my first year as chair of a rather large and contentious department, I wrote, with tongue only slightly in cheek, what the job had forced me to do:

> I no longer have the luxury of belonging to a clique; I can't pass on gossip about certain members of the department; I have to find ways to be helpful to individuals whom I don't particularly like; and I have to keep a certain distance from all the members of the department, even my close friends, so as to remain equally accessible and at least appear fair to everyone. I hate this job; it is forcing me to be virtuous! (Heft, 2011, p. 91)

After six years of chairing that department, I spent eight years as provost of the university. In that capacity, during very much of the months of January and February, I interviewed all the final candidates for faculty positions, which could number as many as 100. At the University of Dayton, we had a college of arts and sciences; schools of business, education, engineering, and law; library faculty; and a large research institute. There were many fields of study about which I knew very little. Yet, I worked hard at learning about them through reading résumés and interviewing the candidates. I asked them all kinds of questions about their discipline and about their reasons for going into academia. I asked them what they would have chosen to do if they had not gone into academia. I asked them to help me understand why their discipline fascinated them. I learned a great deal not just about the candidates but also about the incredibly rich variety of disciplines, and I began to discern areas of overlap and of connection that should be made between disciplines but all too often were not.

Finally, the position of provost forced me to think about the university as a whole, not only as a university but also as a Catholic university, one with a distinctive, long, rich, and complex intellectual history. I found myself asking how that tradition might be integrated with the faculty's research and the university's curriculum. I knew, of course, that scholars who pursued their own discipline with passion and rigor made a real contribution to the fund of knowledge. Obviously, serious research in neuroscience or the French Revolution is valuable in itself, and not everyone needs to be doing interdisciplinary work. But I was convinced that a fuller understanding of the Catholic intellectual tradition and its major contributions to civilization, along with its dark moments, could enrich the thinking of the faculty and might actually push some of them beyond the narrow confines of their disciplines, so as to enrich them, their research, and their teaching.

My family life, my studies, my love of theatre, and my administrative experiences (I will not add the lessons, valuable as they also were, learned navigating between faculty and members of the university's board of trustees) often pushed me beyond my comfort zone, forcing me to understand persons and realities with which I had not yet become familiar. In a word, these kinds of expansive, integrative experiences made me more "Catholic."

Teaching as a Learning Experience

From early childhood, I watched my father tell stories. He was very good at it. I think from him I learned how telling a good story can capture the attention of others. Later, I realized that the more I knew of history and of the people who shaped it, the more interesting the stories I could tell. Subjects that I have taught at the college level, such as ethics and doctrines, have a content whose integrity needs to be respected. But I also realized that if I couldn't illustrate through examples and stories what I was talking about, I rarely made an educational connection with my students. Moreover, if I didn't get the students to ask their own questions, to discover what they might have been hesitant to ask because of embarrassment or shyness, they did not really learn as much as they might otherwise. Faculty can make students feel stupid; that is easy to do. It is much more worthwhile to help students discover that they have a mind, that they can ask good questions, and that their own ideas are worth talking about. A mentor of mine once remarked, "Meet students where they are, but don't ever let them stay there." To that bit of good advice, I would add, "Help students value learning, but also teach them to pay close attention to their own experiences." Though limited, the ranges of experiences that young people have can often be underestimated. Taking experience to a level of adequate articulation is at the heart of integrative pedagogy. One must both think and live. If "the unexamined life is not worth living," then the "unlived life is not worth examining." We must both live and think; neither takes care of itself without personal discipline.

Faculty mentors have an important role to play in encouraging students to bring together their lived experiences with their learning and reflection, and we can do this powerfully through the personal connections we make with students. For nearly 30 years, I taught an undergraduate course in Christian ethics at the University of Dayton. During my first year of teaching, at the very beginning of the semester, I interviewed all my students individually, a practice I have continued to this day, even now at a large secular university. These short, 15-minute interviews open up communication, create a more personal relationship, and help me understand something about my students I would not otherwise know. In that particular course, I also asked all the students to write what I called a spiritual autobiography. These essays, sometimes 12 to 15 pages in length, were incredibly valuable for me and, I hope, for the students. I asked them to be honest about themselves and their journey, the people who have been helpful to them and those who have not. I assured them that I would keep their papers in the strictest confidence; I would not grade them, either. Students who did not want me to read their story had only to write on the cover sheet "Do Not Read." In 30 years, I think only about five students asked me not to read their essay; I did not read their essay. I encouraged all the students to keep these essays for the rest of their life and reread them in the years to come, promising them that they would find fascinating what they thought as a college student. Over the years, students have told me that I can read their mind; not really, because they often tell me what's on their mind, and I simply tell them what they've told me as a way of helping them reflect on and integrate their living with their learning.

Service-Learning and Leadership

For the past few decades, much has been written about service-learning, less about service leadership. One of the major hurdles in running a good service-learning program for students is the reluctance of faculty to put in the time it takes to mentor students so that the service really fosters integrative, engaged learning. That is why I think that for service-learning to thrive among students, service leadership among faculty needs to be offered. Faculty often need support and incentives to provide this leadership, but the positive learning outcomes from a combination of service and classroom or laboratory are well documented. Twenty-five years ago, the University of Dayton received a major endowment gift to make service-learning an integral part of its undergraduate honor's program, the Berry Scholars. The endowment supports the service leadership by faculty needed for an especially rich service-learning experience for the students. The extraordinary results have been documented for years.

Even without asking students to reflect on their personal experiences, it is possible to structure learning activities that help them integrate their own and others' perspectives with course material. One course I teach at USC is a history of the issues that Catholic immigrants to the United States dealt with in the nineteenth and twentieth centuries. I require the students to write several research papers about some issue related to the course that interests them. Five pages of their paper describe what they have found through their research; on the last page, however, I ask them to write out their own opinions about what they've learned. Again, this opens both to them and to me how they are thinking and increases their engagement with course material.

I also like to create "mini" case studies in the form of a story and then ask the students what they would do if they were to play a certain role within the story. For example, in discussing mid-twentieth-century Supreme Court decisions on prayer in public schools, I'd ask them to imagine themselves as a devout Christian, or a Jew, or an atheist, or parents, or a school principal and ask them what they would do. Or, I'd ask them to oppose a position that I think they'd naturally want to support, such as gay marriage, religious freedom, or the separation of church and state.

Finally, when I present issues, I do my best to describe several sides of an issue, as fairly as I can, to present the complexities of the issue and to be open about my own questions. I think it is important to let students know what you as a teacher don't know or understand, to admit, in the face of a good question posed by a student, "I just don't know. Would someone be willing to research that?" Pope Francis (2013) caused a media sensation when to a reporter's question about gay priests he answered, "If a priest is gay and does his best to follow the Lord, who am I to judge?" Most people expect popes and teachers to have authoritative answers, clear ones about everything. When was the last time any pope in history said, "Who am I to judge?"

Nothing of what I have described here as teaching the "whole student" is unique. Many good teachers have developed similar engaged pedagogical approaches.[2] What is surprising is how many teachers don't learn how to do things that open up the communication between them and the students and, as a result, deepen the learning process for themselves and their students.

Interdisciplinary Faculty Seminars

Probably one of the most valuable forms of learning for me has been the work I have been privileged to do in leading interdisciplinary faculty seminars that ask faculty to experience, consider, and integrate a variety of perspectives on larger questions about the nature and purpose of higher education. Some faculty have difficulty learning from their students, and some faculty, often the same ones, have difficulty learning from their colleagues. Faculty spend years "mastering" a discipline. Many faculty talk mostly to other faculty within their discipline, their teaching is judged by colleagues in the same discipline, and their publications are judged by faculty from their own discipline. It takes a lot of energy and time to keep up with developments in one's discipline. Is it advisable for faculty to push beyond their own discipline, to pursue relevant questions that their own discipline has overlooked or not even asked? For the sake of precision, rigorous academic methodologies understandably exclude whatever is judged to be extraneous to the particular knowledge being sought. But there is, of course, more knowledge than what can be examined through a particular methodology. And more important, the limits created by certain methodologies can exclude knowledge important to the discipline itself. Faculty who rely exclusively on already established methodologies within their disciplines may prematurely dismiss important questions they don't yet know how to answer. In the words of philosopher Denys Turner (2002), they "reverse the traffic between questions and answers so as to permit only such questions to be asked as we already possess predetermined methodologies for answering, cutting the agenda of the questions down to the shape and size of our given routines for answering them" (p. 136). Interdisciplinary faculty development seminars can move faculty out of familiar ways of thinking and engage them in conversations that raise new questions that help them grow in exciting and creative ways.

A Hyphenated Identity and the "Whole Student"

For the past decade, occupying an endowed professorship at a secular university, I've lived an especially hyphenated existence as a professor–priest. At first, I rarely wore my Roman collar on campus until I realized how wearing it opened up seldom explored channels of communication. In a typical class of 25 students, I might have 5 or 6 students who are Catholic, most of whom are in the "spiritual but not religious" period of their lives. The courses I teach have to do with religion. For example, most recently, I have taught a general education course, as mentioned earlier, on the history of the issues Catholic immigrants to the United States faced in the nineteenth century and led a senior seminar designed for majors in the School of International Relations on the subject of religions and violence. My wearing a clerical collar allows students to project immediately an identity on me, which in a time of exposed sexual abuse among priests might make a priest think again about being "public" about his identity. Nevertheless, after the students begin to realize that I am not an ideologue and have a brain and welcome their questions, the "whole student" begins to appear. That is to say, they do ask many questions about what I believe and why, as well as relate some of their own struggles, doubts, and confusions about religion. In other words, who I am, not just how I teach, opens up a dimension in the classroom that is for me and the students very important. The students know they are free to disagree with what I believe, but they often wonder "why an intelligent person like you" believes at all. We stay focused on the syllabus but don't duck these types of questions and discussions. Several times a semester I invite my students to dinner with my religious community two blocks from campus. It is obvious that students are really curious about spirituality and religion, seek honest responses to their own questions, and value an informed perspective that transcends the false dichotomy between advocacy and objectivity. A few years ago, Sandy Astin at the University of California, Los Angeles, did a study (Astin, Astin, & Lindhom, 2010) that showed that students were much more interested in spiritual questions than professors were in addressing them. The academy is averse not only to the study of religion but also to the spiritual dimension as well, both important parts of any student considered as "whole."

After serving as provost at the University of Dayton, I became a university professor who, in addition to teaching and doing my own research, was responsible for some faculty development programs. From 1997 to 2006, I designed, with the help of faculty, interdisciplinary seminars that focused on the following themes: (a) the history of Catholic higher education in the United States, (b) the history of the disciplines of the faculty who participated in the seminar, and (c) the themes in the Catholic intellectual tradition that might contribute a distinctive character to research and teaching at the university.[3] I had the liberty to invite faculty to these seminars, typically tenured, academically productive faculty who were willing to spend considerable time in such discussions. During the fall, we developed a semester-long syllabus of readings, and during the spring, benefiting from a one-course reduction, we met two hours a week. We were also able to offer small grants for summer research projects related to the seminar. Early in the fall, we held an all-day symposium where faculty shared their summer research. We concluded the evening with a festive dinner with spouses and university administrators.

These seminars included faculty not only from different disciplines but also from different faiths and from those who had no faith. For example, in one of these seminars, besides some Catholics, there were also a Muslim; an atheist; a Coptic Christian; a Jew; and a person who described himself as "non-religious," which he distinguished from both atheism and agnosticism. Of the attendees, five were women and seven were men. In nearly all these seminars, similar dynamics unfolded, whatever the diversity of the participants. At the beginning of the 14 weeks of meetings, participants usually spoke from within their disciplines. Then, from around weeks 6 to 8, they began to share their questions and what they had trouble understanding and to ask other faculty members to help them understand and teach them. At this same time, faculty would say, "You know, I never understood . . ." Or, "One of the things that I think is really a problem in my discipline is . . ." Or, "I have no clue how to answer that!" and "I often feel very inadequate when . . ." Such moments led to the creation of a real community of shared, integrative questioning and learning. Their honesty, vulnerability, and openness created bonds that were often stronger than those they experienced in their own academic departments.

Some of the most significant results of these seminars were new forms of research, the creation of new courses, and friendships that sustained new intellectual interests. One educational researcher found in the Catholic tradition of social justice cogent arguments for making public schools more accessible. Another professor, a social scientist, began working with another member of his department (someone who was not in the seminar) to explore the "free market" theory and its impact on school choice. He and his colleague established connections between "liberation theology" and better education for the poor in the publication of several articles. And this same professor published a widely acclaimed book (see St. John, 2009) that explored creative ways to integrate moral reasoning in professional education.

Among the law faculty who participated in this seminar, one professor of constitutional law began doing research on jurisprudence and how it relates to a more philosophical approach that looks not just to precedents but also to whether a particular law is just. Another professor began a study of restorative justice. He also designed a seminar for law students that would help them interact more effectively and helpfully with clients. A third professor was encouraged through the seminar to begin a major research program in environmental law, which he now teaches.

In the field of engineering, a popular and creative professor who describes himself as an atheist developed a course with a Christian theologian on sustainable design that they have continued to teach together for more than a decade. Another Christian historian produced a book on the religious influence on medieval architecture. Several engineering professors organized an international conference on engineering, the environment, and sustainable design.[4]

Catholic Engineering?

The Dayton engineering professors, especially those in mechanical engineering, continued to work together after the very successful international conference they organized. They began to collaborate with professors in biology and physics on designing interdisciplinary courses that focused on the environment. Some of these professors were Catholic; some were not religious. But together they also began to explore Catholic social teaching, which includes issues of justice, concern for the poor, protection of the environment, and taking on design challenges that help people with disabilities. Engineers need not be Catholic to see the importance of these priorities, but it was a rich educational experience for the Catholics and others to see how integral these priorities are to Catholic social teaching. They began to publicize their innovative approaches to courses and research. Several years ago, a donor gave the university a multimillion-dollar gift to establish an interdisciplinary Center on Sustainable Development. Sometimes the stars align, and doing good leads also to doing well!

The previous paragraphs are only a partial description of the results of some of these faculty seminars. Many good things came out of them, especially for the participants who discovered integral dimensions of their disciplines that they had overlooked. Each of these seminars costs between $75,000 and $100,000, money that was contributed by the university, from outside grants, and from the budgets of various deans. The cost included replacement faculty for the course reduction of the seminar participants, summer research support, and partial support for initiatives that grew out of seminars (e.g., the development of new courses). That faculty had released time to enter such conversations and explore new avenues of research showed that the university was serious about these interdisciplinary conversations and the value they brought to learning and teaching. The faculty very much appreciated that support.

A Catholic Catholicism

I think it is important to clarify that in these discussions I embodied a "hybrid" existence, which is to say I was both a Roman Catholic priest and a respected academic. For faculty predisposed to believe that faith and reason inevitably must oppose each other, such hybridity evokes cognitive dissonance. I think more faculty at a secular university like USC than at a Catholic university assume that someone like me couldn't credibly be both a believer and an academic. This perception often colored some of the earlier discussions in the seminars. Participants were initially hesitant to raise questions they thought might offend me or put me in an uncomfortable place. Gradually, they learned that I too had my own questions and recognized gray areas in life that official church teaching did not recognize and that change in the church can and should take place in many more ways than is commonly understood.

My studies in medieval history helped me understand that many things have changed in the Catholic Church over the centuries. Studying doctrines, especially in their historical context, underscored the critical importance of the historical and cultural context. Among Catholics, for example, the very word *dogma* is commonly understood as a teaching that explains a truth of the faith. A dogma cannot be questioned. Rightly understood, however, a dogma does not explain but embodies an affirmation of the faith. Moreover, as the members of our interreligious dialogue on "learned ignorance" knew well, no verbal formulation can capture adequately the transcendent. As Thomas Aquinas taught in the thirteenth century, in making an act of faith, the words a believer uses do not in themselves reach the reality affirmed: "The act of the believer does not reach its end in the proposition, but in the revealed reality itself." Even more striking, his contemporary Bonaventure, also recognized as a Doctor of the Church (a great teacher), wrote of the "mystical wisdom" bequeathed by the Holy Spirit:

> If you ask how such things can occur, seek the answer in God's grace, not in doctrine, in the longing of the will, not in the understanding; in the sighs of prayer, not in research; seek the bridegroom not the teacher; God and not man; darkness not daylight; and look not to the light but rather to the raging fire that carries the soul to God with intense fervor and glowing love. (as cited in Mahoney, 1975, p. 36)

Is Bonaventure inviting academics to abandon all that is important to them: reason, freedom, research, knowledge, and objectivity? I do not think so. Rather, Bonaventure is underscoring the limits of rationality in facing the transrational. Reasoning is very important but goes only so far. People who acknowledge the transrational may not be irrational. A nonbeliever in one of our seminars agreed, saying that, for her, love provides important pathways difficult to articulate—pathways to knowledge that she, as a scientist, valued. These faculty discussions create "space" precisely in areas where many academics tend to think there is none, especially the space to admit ignorance and raise questions.

I wrote earlier that a dogma does not explain but affirms what a believer accepts as truth. For example, Christians believe that Jesus is both human and divine but not schizophrenic, or in the words of the Council of Chalcedon, Jesus has two natures but is one person. If a Christian denies the humanity or divinity of Jesus or claims that they are parallel but not intimately connected in a single person, he or she distorts the revelation. Many questions can be raised about this dogma. For example, what is "humanity," and even more, what is "divinity"? And how does it work that divinity does not swallow up humanity or that a single person can be both human and divine? A non-believer may well think that anyone who believes this dogma is irrational. My only point is to say that the dogma affirms rather than explains—and usually raises lots of questions.

Moreover, dogmas leave lots of room for development—a sort of unfolding of new understandings that grow out of the affirmation. In an age when ecological questions have become critically important, the Christian doctrine of creation can be tapped for resources in responding to this new awareness. Each age raises new questions. In our global world, when Christians meet more and more good people who are not Christians, they ask themselves how it can be claimed that only through Jesus is anyone saved. That is not an easy question to answer.

One of the things I learned through these seminars is that there are many really good questions that would not be raised if I stayed in my own comfort zone, my own discipline, and my own religious faith. I also learned that not being able to answer certain questions about what one believes is not in itself sufficient reason to reject that belief. John Henry Newman (1989), the great nineteenth-century British theologian, once wrote, "Truth is the daughter of time" (p. 47). Some excellent questions can be posed long before an adequate response can even be given. In the meantime, scholars need to continue to be open, to listen, to criticize, and to realize that there are thoughtful explanations as to why not everything can be explained.

I also have learned that genuine disagreement is rare. Usually, disagreements come from misunderstandings. The famous Dominican theologian Herbert McCabe often entered into public debates with atheists who, after they stated all their reasons for not believing, would stand up and say, "I completely agree!" When I have taught some course about the Christian tradition, I've told my students that my purpose in teaching is to raise them to the level of "informed rejection."

The examples that I have used describe some of the ways in which there exists, in a religious tradition like Catholicism, space for questions and exploring the beliefs that are established as dogmas. But something similar can be said about many of the assumptions and "settled" conclusions held by academics in different disciplines. Studying the history of one's discipline makes clearer how "settled" conclusions have since become quite unsettled. I am often struck by the number of academics who are "presentists," or people who do not know even the history of their own discipline. One need only think of racial theories of the early 1900s, eugenics assumptions of the 1930s, and Catholic positions on religious freedom and the separation of church and state before 1960 to realize that things change. When historians, theologians, and law, engineering, and business professors who are open to new learning come together, some wonderful things happen. The participants not only learn from each other and grow in their calling to be teachers and researchers but also form friendships that many continue for years.

Serious interdisciplinary conversations are not designed to dismantle disciplinary learning; rather, such conversations enrich the disciplines by often raising questions heretofore not raised from within a specific discipline, and when attended to, these questions actually broaden the scope of the discipline and extend its range of explanation.

Conclusion

In my introduction, I wrote that interdisciplinary studies that engage scholars not only as academics but also as persons need not result in subjectivism or loss of competence in one's chosen field of study or descend into some radical form of postmodernism that asserts that only the self exists with its assertions fully explained by gender, location, and power. Nor are we limited to only abstract ideas and generalizations. Language, even the sophisticated language of academic disciplines, lacks the capacity to illuminate all the questions we confront. Competence without vulnerability places efficiency above morality. There are many ways to learn intellectual humility. Teaching that engages the whole student, research that pursues important questions, and faculty development that brings faculty from different disciplines and backgrounds into real conversations about significant questions all promote integrative learning; sustain intellectual humility; and, for these reasons alone, should be treasured.

Reflection Questions

1. This chapter opens with a description of an interreligious dialogue that creates an opportunity for faculty to examine their own deeply held

beliefs and integrate them with their identities as teachers and scholars. What opportunities have you had to engage in similarly meaningful dialogue with your colleagues, and what did you gain from that experience? If you haven't had this opportunity, what kinds of dialogues do you think would be meaningful to you? How?

2. How have your early experiences—academic, extracurricular, social, and emotional—shaped the way you approach teaching and learning?

3. In your experience, what role does empathy play in teaching and learning? What experiences have broadened your "range of empathy"? How does your teaching provide opportunities for students to broaden theirs?

4. How have interdisciplinary connections and conversations enhanced your own teaching and research?

5. In what ways could you be seen to embody a hybrid identity as a teacher and researcher? What are the gifts this identity provides? What are some of the challenges? In what ways do you address students' hybrid identities in your teaching?

6. As this chapter suggests, certainty about a field can be an important aspect of a teacher's authority—and also a trap that limits learning and growth. Creating an open space for questions, particularly ones that step outside disciplinary boundaries, can enable both faculty and students to deepen their understanding by identifying "gray areas." How do you make space for questioning in your teaching and research?

Notes

1. The research project was published by Oxford University Press in 2011 as *Learned Ignorance: Intellectual Humility Among Jews, Christians, and Muslims*, edited by James L. Heft, Reuven Firestone, and Omid Safi. My chapter is titled "Humble Infallibility."

2. See Roche (2010), especially chapter 3, for many excellent examples on teaching at an undergraduate level.

3. I published a number of articles on these seminars. See, for example, Heft (2000) and Heft (2002).

4. See Heft and Hallinan (2012), chapter 1, for a description of the interdisciplinary seminar.

References

Aquinas, T. (1947). *Summa theologia* (Vol. II, II-II, Q. 2, Art. 2). New York, NY: Benziger Brothers.

Astin, A. W., Astin, H. S., & Lindholm, J. A. (2010). *Cultivating the spirit: How college can enhance students' inner lives*. San Francisco, CA: Jossey-Bass.

Bolt, R. (1960). *A man for all seasons*. New York, NY: Vintage International.

Heft, J. L. (2000). Ethics and religion in professional education: An interdisciplinary seminar. In J. R. Wilcox & I. King (Eds.), *Enhancing religious identity: Best practices from Catholic campuses* (pp. 175–199). Washington, DC: Georgetown University Press.

Heft, J. L. (2002). A study of Catholicism: An interdisciplinary faculty seminar. *Horizons, 29*(1), 94–113.

Heft, J. L. (2011). *Catholic high schools: Facing the new realities*. Oxford, UK: Oxford University Press.

Heft, J. L., Firestone, R., & Safi, O. (Eds.). (2011). *Learned ignorance: Intellectual humility among Jews, Christians, and Muslims*. Oxford, UK: Oxford University Press.

Heft, J. L., & Hallinan, K. (2012). *Engineering education and practice: Embracing a Catholic vision*. South Bend, IN: University of Notre Dame Press.

Herberg, W. (1955). *Protestant, Catholic, Jew: An essay in American religious sociology*. Chicago, IL: University of Chicago Press.

Institute for Advanced Catholic Studies at the University of Southern California. (n.d.). *About us*. Retrieved from ifacs.com/about-the-institute-for-advanced-catholic-studies

Mahoney, J. P. (Ed.). (1975). *The liturgy of the hours according to the Roman Rite III: Ordinary time, weeks 1–17* (International Commission on English in Liturgy, Trans.). New York, NY: Catholic Book.

Newman, J. H. (1989). *An essay on the development of Christian doctrine*. Notre Dame, IN: University of Notre Dame Press.

Pope Francis. (2013, July 28). *Press conference after World Youth Day, Rio de Janeiro, Brazil*. Retrieved from http://w2.vatican.va/content/francesco/en/speeches/2013/july/documents/papa-francesco_20130728_gmg-conferenza-stampa.html

Roche, M. (2010). *Why choose the liberal arts?* South Bend, IN: University of Notre Dame Press.

St. John, E. P. (2009). *Action, reflection, and social justice: Integrating moral reasoning into professional education*. Cresskill, NJ: Hampton Press.

Turner, D. (2002). *Faith seeking*. Norwich, UK: SCM Press.

9

INTEGRATIVE APPROACHES FOR SUSTAINED DIVERSITY ENGAGEMENT IN THE EARLY YEARS OF COLLEGE

Angela M. Locks

My grandparents started the first public school for African Americans in rural, central Louisiana in the 1940s. My grandfather served as its only principal until desegregation reached that part of the South in 1973, prompting his retirement. Although the progress and efforts of my grandfather are certainly to be admired, that progress had costs. When my mother and other Creole-speaking schoolchildren entered the new school system for Blacks, they were demoted one or two grade levels and were told to speak English immediately. This was my first introduction to the connection among culture, learning, and the educational experiences of students of color. The educational experiences of my mother led to my first academic interest: understanding and helping marginalized and minority groups develop strategies to manage feelings of isolation within educational environments in ways that lead to their success. These strategies are linked directly to the themes of teaching the whole student, engaged learning, and integrative pedagogy.

Attending a public high school in the San Francisco Bay Area during the 1980s meant attending a high school whose student body was a global community before the concept became a buzzword. Coming to the University of Michigan (UM) in 1991 put me in a different world. The UM community struck me as a divided one. I quickly learned I was no longer in the Bay Area. My high school experiences left me wholly unprepared for how I would have to negotiate the terrain of race, gender, and class at UM and how they would shape my undergraduate experience. The rules were discordant. *Rule 1:* "Don't trust White folks." *Rule 2:* "Blacks were admitted to UM solely because of a quota system." *Rule 3:* "Blacks don't mix with Asians. Asians don't mix with Latinos." *Rule 4:* "You can't get to Detroit on a subway!"

The clear lines of segregation and low numbers of faculty and students of color in certain environments made feelings of racial and ethnic resentment between groups run deep. The physical barriers between Ann Arbor and Detroit created a sense of isolation from the largest African American community in the area and made for a challenging transition. My first opportunity to redefine these rules for myself came when I became an Undergraduate Research Opportunity Program (UROP) student in the psychology department. Having the opportunity for engaged learning, working with a diverse research team, and being connected to a community of other students were defining moments in my undergraduate experience. UROP's engaged pedagogy and the program's recognition that my bringing my authentic, whole self was valuable afforded me the opportunity to deepen my learning and awareness and to change the rules I had encountered as a first-year student. *Rule 1:* "White folks," on my research team and part of the UROP staff, were actually helping me, invested in my development, and listening to what I had to say. *Rule 2:* The quota theory regarding the admission of Black students to UM was not accurate. There were too many Black students and other students of color in my research peer group and in the program for *all* of us to have been admitted because of a quota system. *Rule 3:* I knew all along that relationships across communities of color existed, and this rule was not correct. The relationships I developed as a UROP peer adviser were reminiscent of my precollege experiences. *Rule 4:* I still could not get to Detroit on a subway. However, as part of the engaged learning approach to community-based research, to facilitate social skills groups and conduct interviews with elementary school students about their coping skills, I was trusted to drive a UM car with my fellow UROP students to Detroit twice a week.

My academic interests stem from the drastic changes in my educational environment and the academic and personal challenges I faced during my early years at UM. I was not only making the traditional first-year transition to college but also learning a new set of rules about culture, race, and ethnicity in the radically different midwestern culture. Over time, I developed a strong interest in answering the following questions: How do college students learn about diversity? How are students' lives affected by their precollege experiences, and how do their subsequent college experiences affect their outlook on their educational experiences and postgraduate choices in employment, education, and civic life?

Several years ago, I completed a study titled "Institutional Commitment to Policies and Practices That Support Racial and Ethnic Diversity in the Post–Affirmative Action Era." This chapter focuses on the part of that study that examined the relationships among (a) precollege environments and dispositions, (b) student engagement with diverse others in college, and (c) students' engagement in integrative cocurricular diversity programs. By focusing on these interrelationships, this chapter explores through a research model what prompts students to engage with diverse others, formally and informally. Furthermore, it explores group differences among African American, Latina and Latino, and White students. It also argues for the importance of meaningful, sustained engagement in diversity programs with the implicit understanding that such positive programs help students understand themselves and others as authentic and whole in a college environment.

The findings in this chapter support previous research, which found that having meaningful engagement with diverse others was important. Moreover, the results shed more light on the relationships between college students' engagement with their peers and their engagement in campus activities. Engagement with diverse peers during the first two years of college is particularly key for sustained engagement with diversity activities.

Background

Social science research examining how students develop the necessary skills to participate in a diverse democracy provided key pieces of evidence considered by the Supreme Court in the affirmative action case *Gratz et al. v. Bollinger et al.* (2003) and was used extensively in amici curiae briefs in the *Fisher v. University of Texas* case. Gurin, Dey, Hurtado, and Gurin (2002) completed one of the primary studies cited in this area of research, weaving together Erikson's (1946, 1956) work on identity, Newcomb's (1943) work on political and social perspectives, and Piaget's (1971, 1985) theories on disequilibrium. These theories were the foundation of their assertions about how interactions with diverse peers in college environments challenge students' perspectives in and beyond the classroom, particularly when students come from racially and socially homogeneous precollege environments. Gurin and colleagues proposed three definitions of *diversity*—structural, classroom, and informal interactional—that they used to assess learning and democracy outcomes for African American, Asian American, Latina and Latino, and White students. This work is part of a now well-established body of research on the effects of diverse higher education environments on college students. Students' cognitive development and their development of democratic skills are the primary focus of this body of research (Hurtado, 2003).

In 2005, the Association of American Colleges & Universities created an initiative titled Making Excellence Inclusive: Diversity, Inclusion, and Institutional Renewal, through which it commissioned several papers examining the connection between diversity and excellence in academe. In one of these papers, Milem, Chang, and Antonio (2005) updated Hurtado, Milem, Clayton-Pedersen, and Allen's (1999) conceptualization of the campus climate for racial and ethnic diversity to include an *organizational–structural dimension*. This dimension includes diversity of the curriculum, tenure policies, organizational decision-making policies, and budget allocations; this represents a growing acknowledgment that concrete institutional actions are important to college student experiences with diversity. The model has interconnected dimensions and provides a framework within which to understand how institutions may foster cross-racial relational interactions in dynamic internal and external sociopolitical environments.

Such relational interactions can help develop multicultural competencies, which have become part of the skill set college students need to function in the workplace; colleges have a role in preparing such students for globally interdependent realities (Engberg, 2004; Jayakumar, 2008). If institutions are to continue to prepare students for leadership positions and the workforce in the twenty-first century, they must create opportunities for students to develop these multicultural skills and competencies (Chesler, 2002). Curricular and cocurricular engaged learning initiatives that help college students develop core competencies necessary for participation in an increasingly interconnected world and changing society are receiving increased attention. Central to this area of research and practice are the specific conditions under which meaningful interactions with racially and ethnically diverse others occur and the effects such interactions have on college students, the educative benefits of which were highlighted in the Supreme Court's decision in *Grutter v. Bollinger et al.* (2003) and again in friend of the court briefs submitted by a range of social institutions.

Previous Research

Gurin and colleagues (2002) found distinct racial and ethnic group differences in their examination of the educational benefits of diverse college environments. Although interactions that allow students to share their authentic, whole selves with diverse others in and outside of the classroom have positive effects on learning and democracy outcomes for all four racial and ethnic groups included in their analyses, informal interactional diversity that occurs outside of the classroom is more important to students' learning and democracy outcomes. This research strongly suggests that positive outcomes associated with a diverse learning environment are not achieved through traditional academic learning alone, underscoring the importance of integrative approaches to college student learning. Moreover, the types of encounters with diverse peers that have been found to affect college students must be substantive and meaningful if they are to mediate perceived racial tension on campus and anxiety with diverse peers (Gurin et al., 2002).

As previously mentioned, well-established psychological and social psychological theories shape the growing higher education literature on the impact of racial and ethnic diversity on students (e.g., Gurin, Gurin, and Hurtado's [2003] use of Erikson [1946, 1956], Newcomb [1943], and Piaget [1971, 1985]). Gurin and her colleagues offered a new conceptualization of why race and ethnicity matter in college by adding Allport's (1954) intergroup contact hypotheses and Feldman and Newcomb's (1969) accentuation theory, providing a framework from which to understand what happens when college students engage informally with diverse peers or engage in more formal campus-sponsored programs and activities focused on racial and ethnic diversity.

Allport's (1954) theory on intergroup relationships shapes much of the literature on cross-racial interactions in the college context. Although not using the language of the whole person, these concepts related to understanding oneself and honoring others are embedded in Allport's conditions that, once met, lead to greater cross-racial liking and respect: (a) equal group status, (b) common goals, (c) cooperation across groups, and (d) sanctions and support from authority. Allport argued that interactions across racial and ethnic boundaries could facilitate mutual liking and respect and under certain conditions ameliorate racial tension. In the college context, Allport's conditions suggest interactions must be directed and meaningful, and the work of Gurin and her colleagues (2002) supports this notion. Feldman and Newcomb's (1969) accentuation theory has also shaped the growing body of higher education literature on college student interactions with diverse others. Feldman and Newcomb hypothesized that students enter college predisposed to certain values and attitudes and that students seek out peers and activities that fit their preexisting perspectives. This in turn accentuates and reinforces their predispositions over the course of their time in college. Thus, institutional programming is necessary to provide sanctioned support for such engaged, diversity-focused programs that provide students with opportunities for cross-racial interactions.

In the past 10 years, a number of scholars have explored aspects of Feldman and Newcomb's (1969) accentuation theory relative to students' experiences with racial and ethnic diversity in college. Pascarella, Edison, Nora, Hagedorn, & Terenzini (1996) found that students' initial openness to diversity, as measured by the College Student Experiences Questionnaire, was related to integrative learning experiences, including their courses, study habits, residential environment, peer interactions, and specific college environment. Another study, conducted at a large public research institution, found that first-year students had high levels of campus engagement and openness to diversity (as measured by Pascarella et al.'s [1996] scale). Summers, Svinicki, Gorin, and Sullivan (2002) found that most first-year students at a large research university had high levels of engagement. Last, a number of studies have affirmed the effects of homogeneous precollege experiences and environments on choices students make in their college years. Although educational segregation is no longer legal in the United States, de facto racial segregation in housing and education endures (Orfield, Bachmeier, James, & Eitle, 1997; Orfield & Lee, 2006). Previous research has shown that the racial composition of precollege neighborhoods, high schools, and peer groups affects how students interact with their peers in college (Locks, Hurtado, Bowman, & Oseguera, 2008; Núñez, 2005; Saenz, 2005; Saenz, Ngai, & Hurtado, 2007). Such segregation *does* affect the college experience, supporting Feldman and Newcomb's (1969) accentuation theory.

Being in a diverse college environment challenges perceptions held by students coming from racially and ethnically homogeneous backgrounds (Gurin et al., 2002). This is related to Piaget's assertion about cognitive disequilibrium: Interactions with diverse others are capable of interrupting students' existing notions about their racially and ethnically diverse peers. In the *Gratz v. Bollinger* decision, it was noted that a critical mass of underrepresented minority students is necessary to realize the educational benefits of a diverse student body and for underrepresented students to feel comfortable being their authentic, whole selves on campus. The importance of a critical mass of historically underrepresented students of color is supported by the literature pertaining to the campus racial climate (see Cabrera, Nora, Terenzini, Pascarella, & Hagedorn, 1999; Davis et al., 2004; Hurtado, 1992; Morley, 2003; Reid & Radhakrishnan, 2003; Rendón, Jalomo, & Nora, 2000; Tierney, 1992). Such compositional diversity allows for students of color to be their whole selves in ethnic-specific spaces and those that foster cross-racial interactions.

Campus climate has important effects on students' ability (or lack thereof) to be their whole, authentic selves and to persist in college. As Harper and Hurtado (2007) emphasized in their review of campus climate research borne out of the initial model by Hurtado and colleagues (1999), the growing body of research on undergraduate interactions with diverse others is very much connected to the body of research on campus racial climates. Although students of color encounter racial microaggressions (Solórzano,

Ceja, & Yosso, 2001) from their peers, faculty, and staff, they have reported that such interactions occur most frequently with their peers (D'Augelli & Hershberger, 1993). Cabrera and colleagues (1999) found that sensitivity to prejudice was found to have an impact on the social experiences for students of color and had a large, direct effect on their commitment to staying at their institution. In addition, several studies have linked a perception of a negative racial campus climate to lower rates of sense of belonging for Latina and Latino students (Hurtado & Carter, 1997) and academic achievement for African Americans at primarily White institutions (Allen, 1992). When students receive messages in their campus environment that who they are as a whole person is not valued by members of their campus community, it shapes their sense of belonging. This latter finding remained persistent in qualitative studies that addressed how microaggressions undermine students' "sense of self" (Fries-Britt & Turner, 2001) and in more recent studies, such as that of Museus, Nichols, and Lambert (2008), using advanced statistics techniques like structural equation modeling (*SEM*). There are real and serious consequences for students on campuses where attention is not paid to improving the racial climate; these consequences are especially negative for students of color. Thus, it is important to understand how anxiety about diverse peers and perceived racial tension on campus affects the college student experience.

C. W. Stephan and Stephan's (1992) theory of intergroup contact posits that prior intergroup relationships, prior cognitive judgments about others, and the nature of specific lived situations dictate the levels of anxiety individuals experience around intergroup engagement. Research has found that intergroup anxiety mediates how intergroup engagement affects racial attitudes on stereotypes and subsequent intergroup contact (W. G. Stephan et al., 2002). Previous negative contact was the strongest precursor for anxiety with diverse others. C. W. Stephan and Stephan (1992), for example, found that Latina and Latino students' perceptions of having lower status and being subject to negative stereotyping led to higher levels of intergroup anxiety. This suggests that a poor campus climate, where Latina and Latino students are targets of discrimination, will produce higher degrees of anxiety about cross-racial interactions among Latina and Latino students. This is significant because other research has demonstrated the importance of positive interactions with diverse peers in college, and intergroup anxiety is an important predictor and mediator of negative racial attitudes (see Engberg, 2004, 2007; Locks et al., 2008; Saenz et al., 2007). Negative racial attitudes may have a dampening effect on students' willingness to engage in activities that might foster skills needed to function in diverse groups and settings. If negative perceptions of racially and ethnically diverse others are not counteracted, students may miss opportunities to develop the skills necessary to function in an increasingly globally interdependent world.

Recent large-scale, longitudinal studies like the National Survey of Student Engagement represent a major effort to assess college student engagement. This body of research reveals specific encounters associated with positive outcomes and underscores the importance of out-of-classroom interactions that shape the overall integrative college experience (Kuh, Kinzie, Buckley, Bridges, & Hayek, 2007). Faculty–student interactions, engagement with one's peers outside of the classroom, and involvement with cocurricular activities while in college are ways students become connected to their campuses (Astin, 1993; Kuh et al., 2007). Although curricular and cocurricular activities such as writing-intensive courses, undergraduate research, service-learning, and learning communities have long histories in higher education, they are increasingly considered high-impact practices and have begun to receive much attention as the desirable form of cocurricular engagement (see www.aacu.org/leap/hips). Curricular diversity programs and activities often foster positive cross-racial interactions. For example, Nagda, Kim, and True-love (2004) found that nontraditional integrative pedagogical approaches to learning, such as their specially designed enlightenment-encounter curricular intervention, have positive effects on students' motivation and engagement with learning across racial and ethnic differences. In addition, Nelson-Laird (2005) found that students' engagement with diversity-oriented course work and interactions with racially and ethnically diverse others affects students' academic self-confidence and critical thinking skills. Despite recent research that has highlighted the importance of the inclusion of diversity in the formal curriculum (see Nelson-Laird, Engberg, & Hurtado, 2005), out-of-class encounters remain a key part of the college experience. It may be that the integration of formal *and* informal contexts for cross-racial interactions must be available to students for them to access the benefits of a racially and ethnically diverse student body.

Students from different racial and ethnic backgrounds vary in their engagement with diversity-related activities. For example, Chavous (2005) found a positive relationship for White students between perceptions of intergroup contact and level of engagement in student organizations with diverse sets of students. Chavous suggested that because African Americans are more likely to have contact with Whites in precollege environments simple contact in a college environment is not enough to influence these students' interactions with diverse others in college; the engagement must be substantive to be meaningful. Other studies have suggested that despite students' involvement in cultural awareness programs aimed at increasing sensitivity, their racial and cultural background may explain more about their perspectives on race than any college intervention (Neville & Furlong, 1994). An example of these racial and ethnic differences is Núñez's (2005) finding that although Latina and Latino and White students both benefited in terms of their sense of belonging from cross-racial interactions and engagement in cocurricular activities, this effect was stronger for Latinas and Latinos.

In their review of research on how Whiteness operates in the college context, Reason and Evans (2007) called for support for White students as they navigate college contexts that are racially charged. They argued that although all students need support to navigate and engage with the racialized context of college, this is especially important for White students in overcoming challenges such as color blindness, pervasive White privilege, and the sense of entitlement some White students display. Furthermore, they argued that the responsibility to provide such support rests with institutions. Reason and Evans's work suggests that students from various racial and ethnic backgrounds need variant types of support. Their argument is supported by the many studies showing the influence of precollege environments on choices students make in college. Milem, Umbach, and Liang (2004) found that White students' frequency of interactions with diverse others in precollege environments, as well as their plans to engage in diversity activities while in college, had direct significant and positive effects on their substantive engagement with diverse others in college. Others have found similar patterns of relationships between such precollege experiences for students of color and for White students (Locks et al., 2008; Malaney & Berger, 2005; Saenz, 2005; Saenz et al., 2007).

Many primarily White institutions continue to face challenges with racial tension among students. Previous research has shown that students of color are particularly sensitive to perceived racial tension on campus (Gloria, Hird, & Navarro, 2001; Smedley, Myers, & Harrell, 1993). One way to ameliorate such tensions is to demonstrate a commitment to diversity: Institutions that sponsor diversity awareness workshops and host discussions on racial and ethnic issues send a message that diversity is valued on their campuses. Research has demonstrated that participation in diversity workshops, even those that are short term, decreases students' negative perceptions of their diverse peers (Springer, Palmer, Terenzini, Pascarella, & Nora, 1996). Such onetime activities may include diversity-themed lectures or ally trainings or workshops. Integrative cocurricular diversity programs and engaged activities often help students establish common goals and encourage group cooperation and thus may be another way colleges can counteract the continuing influence of precollege environments. Institutional programs that continue for a full semester or academic year are one way campuses can meet Allport's (1954) call for authoritative sanctions and provide students with the opportunity to have their preconceived notions of diverse others challenged. In regard to Allport's conditions, the crucial question is how students' precollege experiences influence their participation in college cocurricular experiences.

Research Question

As higher education continues to be a contested area of U.S. society in regard to access at state flagships and other top-tier institutions, there has been a renewed focus on diversity and student outcomes. Different outcomes for students of color and White students have consistently been found. Although the benefits of diversity hold true for all students, White students are more likely to benefit than students of color (Gurin et al., 2002). Another body of research relevant to this chapter is the literature on the climate for students of color at primarily White institutions. The specific question guiding the study featured in this chapter is as follows: "What precollege and college experiences with diverse peers affect participation in integrative and engaged cocurricular diversity programs for African American, Latina and Latino, and White students in the second year of college?"

Many factors may contribute to students' participation in cocurricular diversity programs. For example, C. W. Stephan and Stephan (1992) found that students of color experience anxiety when interacting with White students. Saenz and colleagues (2007) suggested that students of color who come from predominantly White precollege environments may be more likely than students from more homogeneous backgrounds to seek opportunities for cross-racial interactions at the beginning of college but less likely to do so after being in the college environment for two years. Higher education literature gives strong indications that the campus climate for racial diversity is critically important for how students engage with one another across racial and ethnic groups (Chang, 1996, 2003; Engberg, 2007; Nelson-Laird et al., 2005; Saenz et al., 2007); this may be especially true for students of color (Cabrera et al., 1999; Hurtado, 1992; Rendón et al., 2000; Tierney, 1992). Previous research has also demonstrated that positive engagement with diverse others has implications for a variety of student outcomes (see Chang, 1999, 2003; Engberg, 2007; Locks et al., 2008; Nelson-Laird et al., 2005; Saenz et al., 2007). In combination, these findings guide the selection of variables included in the hypothesized relationships outlined next and the use of *SEM* techniques. Specifically, the use of *SEM* allows for the testing of latent factors, which include most campus climate and cross-racial interactions measures; in addition, the method allows for multigroup comparison in ways that test for invariance across groups (Byrne, 2006). Although personal testimony and anecdotes about the value of educating the whole student through engaged learning and integrative pedagogy are powerful, it is critical to also provide research-based scientific evidence to demonstrate the importance of such experiences as part of undergraduate education. The latter is particularly useful in understanding why diversity-related gains vary across racial and ethnic groups.

Theoretical Structural Model and Hypotheses

My hypotheses were as follows:

1. The proportion of Whites in precollege environments will have direct and indirect effects on students' engagement in integrative cocurricular diversity programs (negative for African Americans and Latinas and Latinos; positive for Whites).
2. For all students, a predisposition to participate in diversity-related activities should have positive direct and indirect effects on their engagement with diverse peers in college and their participation in integrative cocurricular diversity programs.
3. The proportion of Whites in precollege environments will have indirect and direct effects on students' positive engagement with diverse peers in college (positive for African Americans and Latinas and Latinos; negative for Whites).
4. Positive engagement with diverse others will mediate the negative effects of both students' anxiety about interacting with diverse others and perceived racial tension on campus on participation in cocurricular diversity programs and have a direct effect on students' engagement in these programs. Note the direct positive effect of positive interactions with diverse others on students' sustained diversity engagement.

Methods

Data and Sample

I used data from the Diverse Democracy Project, undertaken in 2000 and 2001 under the direction of Sylvia Hurtado, supported by a Field Initiated Studies Program grant from the Office of Educational Research and Improvement at the U.S. Department of Education (Hurtado, 2003). Data were collected at two points, first in 2000 (at the beginning of the first college year) and second in 2002 (at the end of the second college year), and examined students' diversity-related perspectives and experiences. Nearly 4,500 students completed both the first- and second-year surveys, and I used a sample of 3,950 students from 9 of the 10 campuses who participated in the study. Confirmatory analyses were performed on the entire subsample, which included only African American, Latina and Latino, and White students (N = 3,950, unweighted); 5% of participants were Hispanic/Latina/ Latino/Chicano/Chicana, 8% were African American/Black, and 85% were White (see Table 9.1). I used a weight to correct for any response bias and to reflect each campus's total first-year population. Because *SEM* requires a complete data matrix, I used an expectation-maximization (EM) algorithm to replace missing data from less than 10% of the cases (Dempster, Laird, & Rubin, 1977, cited in Allison, 2002; McLachlan & Krishnan, 1997).

Outcomes of Interest

I was interested in understanding any distinction between what affects short-term diversity engagement compared to the more sustained engagement recommended by Gurin and colleagues (2002, 2003). The items that comprise these two factors are detailed in Table 9.1. In modeling my suppositions about what predicted diversity engagement, I included both predispositions to participate in diversity-related activities and positive interactions with diverse peers in college. I also included a factor that captured students' predisposition to participate in diversity-related activities (as a six-item factor) and perceived racial tension on campus as an endogenous observed variable. The model that I used to examine sustained diversity engagement also included anxiety with diverse peers in college as an endogenous variable (see Table 9.2).

Previous research has demonstrated the lasting impact precollege segregation has on college students' educational experiences (see Jayakumar, 2008; Locks et al., 2008; Orfield et al., 1997; Orfield & Lee, 2006; Saenz et al., 2007). Thus, I included this precollege diversity measure as the only exogenous variable included in the cocurricular diversity programs model, also detailed in Table 9.2. In addition, at this stage of analyses, anxiety with diverse peers in college was an exogenous variable with paths to factors *positive interactions with diverse peers* and *participation in cocurricular diversity programs*, depicted in Figures 9.1 and 9.2. Because White students and students of color often have different experiences and college outcomes, each racial group was assigned a number for the three-group comparison model that allowed me to detect differences across racial and ethnic groups (1 = African American, 2 = Latina and Latino, and 3 = White).

TABLE 9.1

Means and Standard Deviations of Cocurricular Diversity Engagement Variables by All Students, African Americans, Latinas and Latinos, and Whites (N = 3,950)

Variables and Factors	All Students			African American			Latina and Latino			White		
	M	SD	n	M	SD	n	M	SD	n	M	SD	n
Proportion of Whites in precollege environments												
Racial composition of neighborhood grew up in	4.05	1.04	3,919	2.77	1.33	219	3.14	1.25	366	4.24	0.87	3,334
Racial composition of high school	3.77	1.01	3,905	2.96	1.17	217	3.04	1.11	364	3.90	0.93	3,324
Racial composition of friends in high school	3.87	1.00	3,899	2.65	1.07	217	3.02	1.11	363	4.04	0.88	3,319
Precollege predispositions to participate in diversity activities in college												
Participate in activities of my culture in college	2.21	0.94	3,899	3.17	0.75	218	2.73	0.90	366	2.09	0.90	3,315
Take diversity course in first year of college	2.26	0.94	3,896	2.70	0.94	216	2.40	0.90	366	2.21	0.94	3,314
Join cultural diversity organization in college	2.27	0.85	3,867	2.93	0.87	214	2.55	0.92	364	2.20	0.81	3,289
Anxiety with diverse peers in college	1.66	0.61	3,693	1.68	0.56	200	1.64	0.61	355	1.66	0.61	3,138
Positive interactions with diverse peers in college												
Dined or shared a meal	3.56	1.17	3,774	3.88	1.16	208	3.88	1.20	358	3.51	1.16	3,208
Had meaningful and honest discussions about race/ethnic relations outside of class	2.84	1.20	3,773	3.19	1.16	208	3.13	1.26	359	2.79	1.18	3,206
Shared personal feelings and problems	3.21	1.24	3,766	3.40	1.19	207	3.42	1.23	359	3.17	1.24	3,200

(Continues)

TABLE 9.1 (*Continued*)

Variables and Factors	All Students			African American			Latina and Latino			White		
	M	SD	n	M	SD	n	M	SD	n	M	SD	n
Studied or prepared for class	3.28	1.24	3,762	3.82	1.00	207	3.58	1.17	356	3.21	1.25	3,199
Socialized or partied	3.53	1.14	3,766	3.59	1.16	207	3.63	1.21	359	3.51	1.13	3,200
Had intellectual discussions outside of class	3.19	1.19	3,739	3.39	1.07	205	3.36	1.19	356	3.16	1.19	3,178
There is a lot of racial tension on the university campus	1.71	0.75	3,759	2.07	0.85	205	1.65	0.78	360	1.69	0.73	3,194
Participation in cocurricular diversity programs												
Participated in campus discussions on racial issues	1.49	0.81	3,762	2.01	1.11	207	1.53	0.89	359	1.46	0.76	3,196
Participated in diversity awareness workshops	1.42	0.77	3,756	1.83	0.99	208	1.48	0.88	358	1.38	0.74	3,190
Sustained cocurricular diversity engagement												
Attended events sponsored by other racial/ethnic groups	1.75	0.63	3,950	2.03	0.67	220	1.92	0.72	370	1.71	0.63	3,360
Sustained participation in diversity	1.75	0.70	3,950	2.08	0.69	220	1.86	0.77	370	1.71	0.69	3,360

TABLE 9.2

Factor Loadings and Reliabilities for Independent Variables

Factor Scales and Item Wording	Factor Loadings and Reliabilities			
	All Students N = 3,950 (alpha)	African American n = 220 (alpha)	Latina and Latino n = 370 (alpha)	White n = 3,360 (alpha)
Proportion of Whites precollege environments[a]	(.844)	(.766)	(.845)	(.807)
Racial composition of neighborhood grew up in	.743	.594	.750	.792
Racial composition of high school	.824	.762	.853	.820
Racial composition of friends in high school	.844	.848	.819	.679
Precollege predispositions to participate in diversity activities in college[b]	(.672)	(.643)	(.769)	(.633)
Participate in activities of my own culture in college	.570	.579	.658	.517
Take diversity course in first year of college	.593	.661	.693	.580
Join cultural diversity organization in college	.766	.608	.830	.739
Positive interactions with diverse peers in college[c]	(.883)	(.851)	(.878)	(.884)
Dined or shared a meal	.743	.677	.753	.741
Had meaningful and honest discussions about race/ethnic relations outside of class	.704	.720	.750	.694

(Continues)

TABLE 9.2 (*Continued*)

Factor Scales and Item Wording	Factor Loadings and Reliabilities				
	All Students N = 3,950 (*alpha*)	African American n = 220 (*alpha*)	Latina and Latino n = 370 (*alpha*)	White n = 3,360 (*alpha*)	
Shared personal feelings and problems	.794	.735	.780	.798	
Studied or prepared for class	.663	.478	.623	.672	
Socialized or partied	.731	.775	.702	.735	
Had intellectual discussions outside of class	.850	.802	.821	.857	
Participation in cocurricular diversity programs	*(.774)*	*(.769)*	*(.809)*	*(.761)*	
Participated in campus discussions on racial issues[c]	.794	.792	.823	.784	
Participated in diversity awareness workshops[c]	.794	.792	.823	.784	
Sustained cocurricular diversity engagement	*(.426)*	*(.547)*	*(.423)*	*(.397)*	
Attended events sponsored by other racial/ethnic groups[d]	.521	.613	.518	.498	
Sustained participation in diversity[e]	.521	.613	.518	.498	

[a]Five-point scale: From *all people of color* = 1 to *all White* = 5.

[b]Four-point scale: From *very unlikely* = 1 to *very likely* = 4.

[c]Five-point scale: From *never* = 1 to *very often* = 5.

[d]Five-point scale: From *never* = 1 to *very often* = 5, recoded into 1 = *none*, 2 = *moderate*, 3 = *frequent*.

[e]Mark all that apply; count variable recoded into 1 = *none*, 2 = *moderate*, 3 = *frequent*.

Figure 9.1. Theoretical structural model for participation in cocurricular diversity programs.

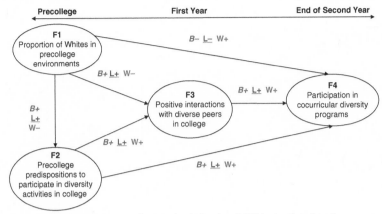

Note. Black (italicized text), Latina and Latino (underlined text), White (unaltered text).

Figure 9.2. Modeling participation in cocurricular diversity discussions and workshops.

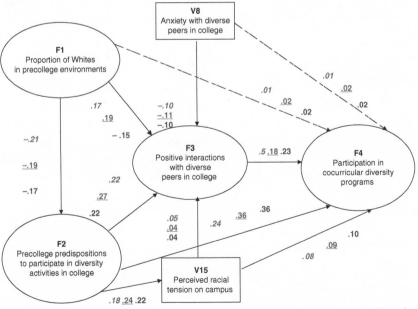

Note. Black (italicized text), Latina and Latino (underlined text), White (unaltered text). The relationship between diversity experiences and participation in diversity discussions and workshops. Structural model three-group comparison: NFI = .935, NNFI = .947, CFI = .951, RMSEA = .049, χ^2/df = 3.74. Paths in bold text were released based on EQS output recommendations. Standardized coefficients shown. Nonsignificant coefficients are indicated with a dashed path.

Figure 9.3. Modeling sustained participation in cocurricular diversity engagement.

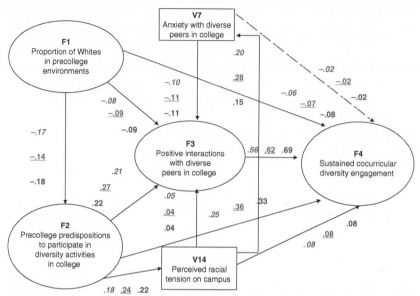

Note. Black (italicized text), Latina and Latino (underlined text), White (unaltered text). The relationship between diversity experiences and participation in cocurricular diversity programs. Fully constrained structural model three-group comparison: NFI = .932, NNFI = .942, CFI = .948, RMSEA = .051, χ^2/df = 3.95. Standardized coefficients shown. Nonsignificant coefficients are indicated with a dashed path.

Analyses

For both models, I used *SEM* techniques and completed analyses on a measurement model, and the entire multiethnic sample was used to test both full structural models. The final models represent fully constrained three-group comparison analyses of the following subsamples: African American (n = 220), Latina and Latino (n = 370), and White (n = 3,360) (see Figures 9.1 and 9.2).

Summary of Results

The results are depicted in Figures 9.1 and 9.2 and Tables 9.3 and 9.4 and in summary are as follows:

    1. My first hypothesis that the proportion of Whites in precollege environments will have direct and indirect effects on students' engagement in cocurricular diversity programs (negative for African Americans and

Latinas and Latinos; positive for Whites) was partially supported, and in Model II, there was a significant direct negative effect of the proportion of Whites in precollege environments on sustained diversity engagement for all three racial and ethnic groups included in this chapter.

2. My second hypothesis that for all students a predisposition to participate in diversity-related activities will have positive direct and indirect effects on their interactions with diverse peers in college and their engagement in integrative cocurricular diversity programs was supported by the results shown in Figures 9.1 and 9.2.

3. My third hypothesis that the proportion of Whites in precollege environments will have indirect and direct effects on students' positive engagement with diverse peers in college (positive for African Americans and Latinas and Latinos; negative for Whites) was partially supported. There was a negative effect of the proportion of Whites in precollege environments on students' engagement with diverse others, yet this is consistent for all three racial and ethnic groups included in this chapter.

4. My fourth hypothesis that positive engagement with diverse others will mediate the negative effects of students' anxiety about interacting with diverse others as well as perceived racial tension on campus on participation in integrative cocurricular diversity programs and have a direct effect on students' participation in these programs was supported. Note the direct positive effect of positive engagement with diverse others on students' sustained diversity engagement (see Figure 9.3).

Discussion

This chapter examines the interrelationships between students' precollege and college experiences with diversity and the effects such factors and relationships have on students' engagement in integrative cocurricular diversity programs through the second year of college. To explore these differences, I disaggregated the *SEM* analyses by race to test for group variance and tested two distinct conceptualizations of student engagement with cocurricular diversity programs. Model I's dependent measure comprised students' participation in campus-organized discussions on racial and ethnic issues and diversity awareness workshops. Model II included a more complex dependent measure, which captured sustained engagement with diversity through living in culturally themed residence halls and/or involvement in student organizations that promote cultural diversity. The results affirm the importance of positive engagement with diverse others in accord with previous

TABLE 9.3

Direct, Indirect, and Total Effects of Three-Group Comparison Model for Participation in Cocurricular Diversity Discussions and Workshops (*N* = 3,950)

Direct effects	African Americans n = 185			Latinas and Latinos n = 334			Whites n = 2,918		
	b	*B*	*R²*	*b*	*B*	*R²*	*b*	*B*	*R²*
V15 Perceived racial tension on campus			.032			.059			.047
F2 Precollege predispositions to participate in diversity activities in college	.259***	.179		.259***	.243		.259***	.217	
F2 Precollege predispositions to participate in diversity activities in college			.046			.034			.028
F1 Proportion of Whites in precollege environments	-.137***	-.213		-.137***	-.185		-.137***	-.167	
F3 Positive interactions with diverse peers in college			.077			.110			.094
F1 Proportion of Whites in precollege environments	.179***	.172		.179***	.186		-.198***	-.146	
F2 Precollege predispositions to participate in diversity activities on campus	.353***	.218		.353***	.273		.353***	.215	
V8 Anxiety with diverse peers in college	-.167***	-.101		-.167***	-.114		-.167***	-.102	
V15 Perceived racial tension on campus	.054*	.048		.054*	.044		.054*	.039	
F4 Participation in cocurricular diversity programs			.112			.215			.246
F1 Proportion of Whites in precollege environments	.011	.014		.011	.018		.011	.016	
F2 Precollege predispositions to participate in diversity activities in college	.300***	.243		.300***	.356		.300***	.356	
F3 Positive interactions with diverse peers in college	.116***	.153		.116***	.179		.116***	.227	
V8 Anxiety with diverse peers in college	.017	.014		.017	.018		.017	.020	
V15 Perceived racial tension on campus	.072***	.084		.072***	.091		.072***	.101	

Indirect effects	African Americans n = 185		Latinas and Latinos n = 334		Whites n = 2,918	
	b	B	*b*	B	*b*	B
V15 Perceived racial tension on campus						
F1 Proportion of Whites in precollege environments	−.036***	−.038	−.036***	−.045	.036***	−.036
F3 Positive interactions with diverse peers in college						
F1 Proportion of Whites in precollege environments	−.050***	−.048	−.050***	−.052	−.050***	−.037
F2 Precollege predispositions to participate in diversity activities in college	.014*	.009	.014*	.011	.014*	.008
F4 Participation in cocurricular diversity programs						
F1 Proportion of Whites in precollege environments	−.029**	−.036	−.029**	−.046	−.073***	−.105
F2 Precollege predispositions to participate in diversity activities in college	.061***	.050	.061***	.073	.061***	.073
V8 Anxiety with diverse peers in college	−.019***	−.016	−.019***	−.020	−.019***	−.023
V15 Perceived racial tension on campus	.006*	.007	.006*	.008	.006*	.009
Total effects	*b*	*B*	*b*	*B*	*b*	*B*
F4 Participation in cocurricular diversity programs						
F1 Proportion of Whites in precollege environments	−.018	−.022	−.018	−.028	−.062***	−.089
F2 Precollege predispositions to participate in diversity activities in college	.361***	.293	.361***	.428	.361***	.429
F3 Positive interactions with diverse peers in college	.116***	.153	.116***	.179	.116***	.227
V8 Anxiety with diverse peers in college	−.002	−.002	−.002	−.002	−.002	−.003
V15 Perceived racial tension on campus	.078***	.092	.078***	.098	.078***	.110

Note. All paths were constrained to be equal across groups with exceptions noted by differences in unstandardized coefficients (freely estimated paths). Three-group comparison structural model fit indices: NFI = .935, NNFI = .947, CFI = .951, RMSEA = .049, X^2/df = 3.74.

*p < .05. **p < .01. ***p < .001.

TABLE 9.4

Direct, Indirect, and Total Effects of Three-Group Comparison Model for Sustained Cocurricular Diversity Engagement
($N = 3{,}950$)

Direct effects	African Americans $n = 186$			Latinas and Latinos $n = 335$			Whites $n = 2{,}939$		
	b	B	R^2	b	B	R^2	b	B	R^2
V7 Anxiety with diverse peers in college			.041			.077			.021
V14 Perceived racial tension on campus	.138**	.202		.230***	.278		.122***	.146	
V14 Perceived racial tension on campus			.033			.057			.048
F2 Precollege predispositions to participate in diversity activities in college	.267*	.182		.252***	.239		.261***	.220	
F2 Precollege predispositions to participate in diversity activities in college			.029			.021			.033
F1 Proportion of Whites in precollege environments	−.143***	−.171		−.143***	−.144		−.143***	−.181	
F3 Positive interactions with diverse peers in college			.068			.099			.077
F1 Proportion of Whites in precollege environments	−.118***	−.083		−.118***	−.090		−.118***	−.093	
F2 Precollege predispositions to participate in diversity activities in college	.352***	.207		.352***	.265		.352***	.218	
V7 Anxiety with diverse peers in college	−.172***	−.101		−.172***	−.113		−.172***	−.106	
V14 Perceived racial tension on campus	.054*	.046		.054*	.043		.054*	.039	
F4 Participation in cocurricular diversity programs			.477			.691			.742

	African Americans n = 186		Latinas and Latinos n = 335		Whites n = 2,939	
	b	B	b	B	b	B
F1 Proportion of Whites in precollege environments	−.031**	−.059	−.031**	−.071	−.031**	−.081
F2 Precollege predispositions to participate in diversity activities in college	.159***	.252	.159***	.359	.159***	.325
F3 Positive interactions with diverse peers in college	.207***	.559	.207***	.619	.207***	.685
V7 Anxiety with diverse peers in college	−.010	−.017	−.010	−.021	−.010	−.021
V14 Perceived racial tension on campus	.035***	.081	.035***	.083	.035***	.084
Indirect effects						
V7 Anxiety with diverse peers in college						
F1 Proportion of Whites in precollege environments	−.005	−.006	−.008**	−.010	−.005***	−.006
F2 Precollege predispositions to participate in diversity activities in college	.037	.037	.058**	.066	.032***	.032
V14 Perceived racial tension on campus						
F1 Proportion of Whites in precollege environments	−.038	−.031	−.036***	−.034	−.037***	−.040
F3 Positive interactions with diverse peers in college						
F1 Proportion of Whites in precollege environments	−.051***	−.036	−.051***	−.039	−.051***	−.040
F2 Precollege predispositions to participate in diversity activities in college	.008	.005	.004	.003	.009	.005

(Continues)

TABLE 9.4 (Continued)

	African Americans n = 186		Latinas and Latinos n = 335		Whites n = 2,939	
	b	B	b	B	b	B
Indirect effects						
V14 Perceived racial tension on campus	-.024*	-.020	-.040***	-.032	-.021***	-.015
F4 Participation in cocurricular diversity programs						
F1 Proportion of Whites in precollege environments	-.059***	-.112	-.059***	-.134	-.059***	-.153
F2 Precollege predispositions to participate in diversity activities in college	.083***	.132	.082***	.184	.083***	.170
V7 Anxiety with diverse peers in college	-.036***	-.056	-.036***	-.070	-.036***	-.072
V14 Perceived racial tension on campus	.005	.011	.000	.001	.005	.013
Total effects	b	B	b	B	b	B
F4 Participation in cocurricular diversity programs						
F1 Proportion of Whites in precollege environments	-.090***	-.171	-.090***	-.205	-.090***	-.234
F2 Precollege predispositions to participate in diversity activities in college	.243***	.384	.241***	.543	.243***	.496
F3 Positive interactions with diverse peers in college	.207***	.559	.207***	.619	.207***	.685
V7 Anxiety with diverse peers in college	-.046***	-.073	-.046***	-.091	-.046***	-.094
V14 Perceived racial tension on campus	.039***	.092	.035***	.084	.040***	.098

Note. All paths were constrained to be equal across groups. Three-group comparison structural model fit indices: NFI = .932, NNFI = .943, CFI = .949, RMSEA = .049, X^2/ df = 3.78.

*p < .05. **p < .01. ***p < .001.

research (Antonio, 2004; Engberg, 2004, 2007; Gurin et al., 2003; Saenz et al., 2007). Moreover, such interactions can mediate the potential negative effects of predominantly White precollege environments and perceived racial tension (see Gloria et al., 2001; Locks et al., 2008; Milem, Umbach, et al., 2004; Núñez, 2005; Orfield et al., 1997; Orfield & Lee, 2006; Saenz, 2005; C. W. Stephan & Stephan, 1992).

I hypothesized that the relationship between the proportion of Whites in the precollege environments and a precollege predisposition to engage in diversity activities would be negative for White students and positive for African American and Latina and Latino students based on previous research (Locks et al., 2008). However, results revealed that this relationship is negative and statistically significant for all students. In other words, the higher the number of White students in a student's neighborhood, high school, and adolescent peer group, the less likely the student is to engage in diversity activities during college. This finding supports previous research about the effects of segregated secondary educational environments and suggests that such effects are long term and follow students into their college environments (see Orfield et al., 1997; Orfield & Lee, 2006). Nonetheless, the proportion of Whites in the precollege environments did not have a significant direct relationship to students' engagement in integrative cocurricular diversity workshops and discussions. However, the proportion of Whites in precollege environments did have negative effects on students' *sustained* engagement with cocurricular diversity programs. College students growing up in predominantly White neighborhoods with mostly White peers in mostly White high schools are less likely to participate in organizations that promote cultural diversity or to live with diverse others. In addition, the proportion of Whites in the precollege environments had an effect on engagement in integrative cocurricular programs, mediated by meaningful interactions with diverse peers. Furthermore, having meaningful engagement with diverse others mediated both anxiety about engaging with diverse others and perceived racial tension on campus. As with previous research, this chapter highlights the positive outcomes college students experience because of engaging with diverse others (see Antonio, 2004; Engberg, 2007; Locks et al., 2008). Given the number of factors mediated by positive engagement with diverse others, the importance of such interactions is amplified because of the multilayered benefits.

I hypothesized that for African American and Latina and Latino students, the number of Whites in their precollege peer groups, high schools, and neighborhoods would have a positive effect on these students' predisposition to engage in diversity activities. This hypothesis was based on the notions that African American and Latina and Latino students who had spent more time with their White peers before college would be more inclined to engage in diversity activities in college and that the reverse would be true of White students coming from predominantly White precollege environments (see C. W. Stephan & Stephan, 1992). My hypothesis was supported for White students but not for African American and Latina and Latino students, as this relationship was negative for all students in both models.

Both models supported my initial hypothesis that the relationship between students' precollege orientation toward diversity activities and their engagement in such activities in college would be direct and positive for African American, Latina and Latino, and White students. Although I did not hypothesize about indirect effects, the sustained diversity *SEM* results for both models revealed that an indirect effect of predisposition to engage in diversity-related activities in college on anxiety with diverse peers existed for Latina and Latino and White students but not for African American students. This is important given that students' predispositions to engage in diversity activities at the beginning of college serves as a control measure for the dependent measure of students' engagement with diversity activities during the second year of college. The inclusion of students' precollege orientation toward diversity activities in the model allows for a stronger test of the relationship between positive interactions with diverse peers and students' engagement in diversity activities at the end of the second year in college.

In both models, positive interactions with diverse peers in college had a positive effect on diversity engagement for all three racial and ethnic groups, supporting my hypothesis. In contrast to the findings in previous research (Locks et al., 2008) and findings for Model I, in Model II predispositions to participate in diversity activities, which served as a control measure, did not have the strongest effect on the outcome. For Model II, the factor with the strongest effect on the outcome was positive engagement with diverse others in college. This distinction signals the relative influence of precollege predisposition to engage in cocurricular diversity activities and highlights the critical importance of institutions fostering cross-racial interactions as a way to counteract the negative effects of segregated precollege environments.

The study featured in this chapter revealed a distinct set of relationships that further explore Gurin and colleagues' (2002) emphasis on the importance of substantive and meaningful engagement with diverse peers in college. Because sustained engagement may be necessary to evoke changes in students' perspectives on diverse others, it may be that meaningful interactions are a proxy for sustained engagement. Students having meaningful interactions may be contingent on such interactions being sustained over time, keeping with Gurin and colleagues' assertions that engagement must be substantive for students to educationally benefit from diversity. For example, students in culturally themed residential programs are regularly engaged with diversity in an integrative cocurricular setting and may receive a greater benefit from engagement with racially and ethnically different peers. By contrast, students who attend a onetime campus workshop or discussion on race may receive fewer educational benefits from engaging with their diverse peers because their interactions are not sustained over time. The latter group of students may be less likely to develop sustained relationships with diverse others. The intimacy of living with diverse others, where being one's authentic, whole self is valued, and interacting with them to complete tasks associated with sustained involvement in a student organization may be keys to the educational benefits of diversity. These results should be interpreted with caution, as the survey data used in this study did not measure *how* students came to live with diverse others or participate in culturally themed student organizations.

These analyses sought to extend the work of previous research (Locks et al., 2008) by completing a three-group comparison rather than comparing White students with an aggregated group of students of color. However, disaggregating by racial ethnic group did not help to explain Gurin and colleagues' (2002) finding that White students received the most benefits from being in diverse learning environments and campuses. The group differences found were between African American students and their Latina and Latino and White counterparts. Based in part on previous research findings, which demonstrated differences between students of color and White students, my hypothesis reflected an assumption that African American and Latina and Latino students would have more in common with one another than with their White counterparts, which was not supported by this study. The number of Whites in students' precollege environments did not have the hypothesized effect on positive interactions with diverse others or engagement in diversity activities for African American, Latina and Latino, and White students. My hypothesis posited that African Americans and Latinas and Latinos would be similar across all relationships. This was true for Model I. However, Model II revealed one set of relationships that was inconsistent for African American and Latina and Latino students. The indirect effects of proportion of Whites in students' precollege environments on both anxiety with diverse others in college and perceived racial tension were detected for Latinas and Latinos and Whites but not African Americans. This difference is subtle but worth exploring in future studies. It may be that African Americans' culturally distinct precollege life experiences translate into equally distinct college experiences in regard to their perception of the campus climate for race and ethnicity.

As indicated earlier, the findings in this chapter reveal that having meaningful engagement with diverse others is important. Furthermore, the results of both models, individually and collectively, shed more light on the relationships between college students' engagement with their peers and their engagement in campus activities. Interactions with diverse peers during the first two years of college are particularly key for sustained engagement with diversity activities. Although each model tested for differences across racial and ethnic groups, differences between students of color and their White counterparts noted in Gurin and colleagues (2002) and other research (Locks et al., 2008) were not illuminated. Although these findings did not reveal anticipated group differences, these results should not be interpreted to mean that African American, Latina and Latino, and White students have homogeneous college experiences. Nonetheless, these findings extend Nelson-Laird and colleagues' (2005) examination of the importance of sanctioned support for engaged, integrative approaches for racial and ethnic diversity through the formal curriculum by suggesting how critical and important sanctioned support is for activities outside of the formal classroom.

It is clear in comparing the two models that when engagement with integrative cocurricular diversity activities is more sustained in nature, interactions with diverse peers in college become key to facilitating student engagement, nearly doubling the effects. This may be due to integrative cocurricular diversity programs meeting Allport's (1954) conditions for intergroup contact that results in increased racial understanding and awareness. Given W. G. Stephan and colleagues' (2002) findings about the effect of negative contact on students' racial attitudes, it may be that providing students with opportunities to engage with diverse others over time is what is needed for students to experience Piaget's disequilibrium cited by Gurin and colleagues (2002). Opportunities to engage with diverse others in a sustained manner may be a key piece of the puzzle of why students experience educational benefits from racial and ethnic diversity.

Conclusion and Significance

With recent Supreme Court rulings restricting the use of race and ethnicity in K–12 education but upholding diversity in higher education as a compelling interest, more research is needed to understand how students' precollege engagement with diverse others affects their college experiences and outcomes. Moreover, further empirical investigations are needed on the effectiveness of specific programs and initiatives designed to facilitate cross-racial and ethnic engagement and the educational benefits to students engaged in campus diversity programs and initiatives. More research is needed to understand the complexities of how meaningful engagement with diverse peers that supports the authentic, whole student may result in other key outcomes for college student learning.

Cocurricular diversity programs represent a realization and nexus of the broader evidence from higher education scholarship on the educational value of a diverse learning environment and also support the importance of engagement in out-of-classroom activities and experiences with overall college engagement. A significant aspect of these findings is the importance of meaningful, quality engagement with diverse others. Most critics of educationally diverse environments are not aware that advocates for diversity argue that engagement must be purposeful and situated within positive racial contexts and climates. This, and previous research, supports that merely situating a group of dissimilar individuals together in the college context will not result in beneficial educational results for students; instead, such interactions must be meaningful. In addition, meaningful interactions with diverse peers mediate anxiety with diverse peers, also supported by previous research. Positive interactions with diverse peers also have a positive relationship to engagement in integrative cocurricular diversity programs, highlighting the critical responsibilities institutional actors have for creating opportunities for students to have sustained and meaningful cross-racial engagement through programs such as integrative, culturally themed living–learning programs and encouraging students to join student organizations that focus on racial and ethnic diversity.

Understanding more about distinct types of cocurricular diversity engagement would allow administrators and practitioners more insight into the types of programs students are attached to and become engaged in and which programs make a difference in students' ability to interact effectively across race and ethnicity. This is a key piece of information in a context where budgets are restricted and student affairs professionals must justify integrative programs. There is a hostile climate for race-related and diversity programs, and those responsible for facilitating meaningful cross-racial engagement or directing race-related programs may find this information useful, as it underscores the importance of their programs in helping students take advantage of the benefits associated with being engaged in a college environment with a diverse student body.

In fall 2012, the educational legacies my grandparents left me and the opportunities my parents, classroom instructors, and other educators worked to ensure were available to me came full circle. An article I had written with several colleagues about college students' diverse engagement with others and the campus climate was in *Fisher v. University of Texas* in a friend of the court brief filed in this U.S. Supreme Court case. I had achieved a personal goal for my scholarship, yet more important, my father cried tears of joy and pride when I shared this news with him, saying, "All of your grandparents' hard work has paid off, and they would be so proud of you."

Reflection Questions

1. In what ways have your own educational experiences—particularly related to gender, race, class, and sexual orientation—shaped your teaching and/or research interests?
2. What are the "unwritten rules" that guide relations between marginalized and privileged students, faculty, and staff on your campus? To what extent do you, or others, actively work to rewrite those rules?
3. This chapter described research that indicates that interactions with diverse peers in educational environments are important for effective learning and for workplace success. To what extent have you, from your own observations, seen the benefits of interaction with diverse peers for marginalized and privileged students on your campus? Have you observed differences in benefit between classroom interactions and informal, structured interactions?
4. In what ways have you seen your campus climate affect White students and students of color differently? What intentional, substantive activities have helped White students overcome color blindness and students of color experience inclusion on your campus?
5. This chapter indicated that sustained interaction with diverse peers is important. How does your campus foster this kind of interaction? If it doesn't do so already, what kinds of cocurricular programs or activities might support students' interactions with each other over time?

References

Allen, W. R. (1992). The color of success: African-American college student outcomes at predominantly White and historically Black public colleges and universities. *Harvard Educational Review, 62*(1), 26–44.

Allison, P. D. (2002). *Missing data.* Thousand Oaks, CA: Sage.

Allport, G. (1954). *The nature of prejudice.* Cambridge, MA: Addison-Wesley.

Antonio, A. L. (2004). The influence of friendship groups on intellectual self-confidence and educational aspirations in college. *The Journal of Higher Education, 75*(4), 446–471.

Astin, A. W. (1993). *What matters in college: Four critical years revisited.* San Francisco, CA: Jossey-Bass.

Byrne, B. M. (2006). *Structural equation modeling with EQS: Basic concepts, applications, and programming* (2nd ed., Multivariate Applications Series). New York, NY: Routledge.

Cabrera, A. F., Nora, A., Terenzini, P. T., Pascarella, E. T., & Hagedorn, L. S. (1999). Campus racial climate and the adjustment of students to college: A comparison between White students and African-American students. *The Journal of Higher Education, 70*(2), 134–160.

Chang, M. J. (1996). *Racial diversity in higher education: Does a racially mixed student population affect educational outcomes?* (Unpublished doctoral dissertation). University of California, Los Angeles.

Chang, M. J. (1999). Does racial diversity matter? The educational impact of a racially diverse undergraduate population. *Journal of College Student Development, 40*(4), 377–395.

Chang, M. J. (2003). Racial differences in viewpoints about contemporary issues among entering college students: Factor or fiction? *NASPA Journal, 40*(4), 55–71.

Chavous, T. A. (2005). An intergroup contact-theory framework for evaluating racial climate on predominantly White college campuses. *American Journal of Community Psychology, 36*(3–4), 239–257.

Chesler, M. (2002). Effective multicultural teaching in research universities. In J. Chin, C. W. Berheide, & D. Rome (Eds.), *Included in sociology: Learning climates that cultivate racial and ethnic diversity* (pp. 21–51). Washington, DC: American Association for Higher Education.

D'Augelli, A. R., & Hershberger, S. L. (1993). African American undergraduates on a predominantly White campus: Academic factors, social networks, and campus climate. *Journal of Negro Education, 62*(1), 67–81.

Davis, M., Dias-Bowie, Y., Greenberg, K., Klukken, G., Pollio, H. R., Thomas, S. P., & Thompson, C. L. (2004). "A fly in the buttermilk": Descriptions of university life by successful Black undergraduate students at a predominantly White southeastern university. *The Journal of Higher Education, 75*(4), 420–445.

Dempster, A. P., Laird, N. M., & Rubin, D. B. (1977). Maximum likelihood from incomplete data via the EM algorithm. *Journal of the Royal Statistical Society: Series B, 39*, 1–38.

Engberg, M. (2004). Educating the workforce for the 21st century: The impact of diversity on undergraduate students' pluralistic orientation. (Doctoral dissertation). Retrieved from ProQuest. 3138145.

Engberg, M. (2007). Educating the workforce for the 21st century: A cross-disciplinary analysis of the impact of the undergraduate experiences on students' development of a pluralistic orientation. *Research in Higher Education, 48*(2), 283–317.

Erikson, E. (1946). Ego development and historical change. *Psychoanalytic Study of the Child, 2*, 359–396.

Erikson, E. (1956). The problem of ego identity. *Journal of the American Psychoanalytic Association, 4*, 56–121.

Feldman, K., & Newcomb, T. (1969). *The impact of college on students*. San Francisco, CA: Jossey-Bass.

Fisher v. University of Texas, 570 U.S. ___ (2013).

Fries-Britt, S. L., & Turner, B. (2001). Facing stereotypes: A case study of Black students on a White campus. *Journal of College Student Development, 42*(5), 420–429.

Gloria, A. M., Hird, J. S., & Navarro, R. L. (2001). Relationships of cultural congruity and perceptions of the university environment to help-seeking attitudes by sociorace and gender. *Journal of College Student Development, 42*(6), 545–562.

Gratz et al. v. Bollinger et al., 539 U.S. 244 (2003).

Grutter v. Bollinger et al., 539 U.S. 306 (2003).

Gurin, P., Dey, E., Gurin, G., & Hurtado, S. (2003). How does racial/ethnic diversity promote education? *Western Journal of Black Studies, 27*(1), 20–29.

Gurin, P., Dey, E. L., Hurtado, S., & Gurin, G. (2002). Diversity and higher education: Theory and impact on educational outcomes. *Harvard Educational Review, 72*(3), 330–366.

Harper, S., & Hurtado, S. (2007). Nine themes in campus racial climates and implications for institutional transformation. *New Directions for Student Services, 120*, 7–24.

Hurtado, S. (1992). The campus racial climate: Contexts of conflict. *Journal of Higher Education, 63*(5), 539–569.

Hurtado, S. (2003). *Preparing college students for a diverse democracy: Final Report to the U.S. Department of Education, OERI, Field Initiated Studies Program*. Ann Arbor, MI: Center for the Study of Higher and Postsecondary Education.

Hurtado, S., & Carter, D. F. (1997). Effects of college transition and perceptions of the campus racial climate on Latino college students' sense of belonging. *Sociology of Education, 70*(4), 324–345.

Hurtado, S., Milem, J., Clayton-Pedersen, A., & Allen, W. (1999). *Enacting diverse learning environments: Improving the climate for racial/ethnic diversity in higher education* (ASHE-ERIC Higher Education Report, Vol. 26, No. 8). Washington, DC: George Washington University.

Jayakumar, U. (2008). Can higher education meet the needs of an increasingly diverse and global society? Campus diversity and cross-cultural workforce competencies. *Harvard Educational Review, 78*(4), 615–651.

Kuh, G. D., Kinzie, J., Buckley, J. A., Bridges, B. K., & Hayek, J. C. (2007). *Piecing together the student success puzzle: Research, propositions, and recommendations* (ASHE-ERIC Higher Education Report, Vol. 32, No. 5). Washington, DC: George Washington University.

Locks, A. M., Hurtado, S., Bowman, N. A., & Oseguera, L. (2008). Extending notions of campus climate and diversity to students' transition to college. *The Review of Higher Education, 31*(3), 257–285.

Malaney, G. D., & Berger, J. B. (2005). Assessing how diversity affects students' interest in social change. *Journal of College Student Retention, 6*(4), 443–460.

McLachlan, G. J., & Krishnan, T. (1997). *The EM algorithm and extensions*. New York, NY: Wiley.

Milem, J. F., Chang, M. J., & Antonio, A. L. (2005). *Making diversity work on campus: A research-based perspective.* Washington, DC: Association of American Colleges & Universities. Retrieved from https://www.aacu.org/publications-research/publications/making-diversity-work-campus-research-based-perspective

Milem, J. F., Umbach, P. D., & Liang, C. T. H. (2004). Exploring the perpetuation hypothesis: The role of college and universities in desegregating society. *Journal of College Student Development, 45*(6), 688–700.

Morley, K. M. (2003). Fitting in by race/ethnicity: The social and academic integration of diverse students at a large predominantly White university. *Journal of College Student Retention, 5*(2), 147–174.

Museus, S. D., Nichols, A. H., & Lambert, A. (2008). Racial differences in the effects of campus racial climate on degree completion: A structural model. *The Review of Higher Education, 32*(1), 107–134.

Nagda, B. A., Kim, C., & Truelove, Y. (2004). Learning about difference, learning with others, learning to transgress. *Journal of Social Issues, 60*(1), 195–214.

Nelson-Laird, T. F. (2005). College students' experiences with diversity and their effects on academic self-confidence, social agency, and disposition toward critical thinking. *Research in Higher Education, 46*(4), 365–387.

Nelson-Laird, T. F., Engberg, M. E., & Hurtado, S. (2005). Modeling accentuation effects: Enrolling in a diversity course and the importance of social action engagement. *The Journal of Higher Education, 76*(4), 448–476.

Neville, H., & Furlong, M. (1994). The impact of participation in a cultural awareness program on the racial attitudes and social behaviors of first-year college students. *Journal of College Student Development, 35*(5), 371–377.

Newcomb, T. L. (1943). *Personality and social change: Attitude formation in a student community.* New York, NY: Dryden Press.

Núñez, A.-M. (2005). *Modeling college transitions of Latina/o students* (Unpublished doctoral dissertation). University of California, Los Angeles.

Orfield, G., Bachmeier, M., James, D. R., & Eitle, T. (1997). Deepening segregation in American public schools: A special report from the Harvard Project on School Desegregation. *Equity and Excellence in Education, 30*(2), 5–24.

Orfield, G., & Lee, C. (2006). *Racial transformation and the changing nature of segregation.* Cambridge, MA: The Civil Rights Project at Harvard University.

Pascarella, E. T., Edison, M., Nora, A., Hagedorn, L. S., & Terenzini, P. T. (1996). Influences on students' openness to diversity and challenge in the first year of college. *The Journal of Higher Education, 67*(2), 174–195.

Piaget, J. (1971). The theory of stages in cognitive development. In D. R. Green, M. P. Ford, & G. B. Flamer (Eds.), *Measurement and Piaget* (pp. 1–111). New York, NY: McGraw-Hill.

Piaget, J. (1985). *The equilibrium of cognitive structures: The central problem of intellectual development.* Chicago, IL: University of Chicago Press.

Reason, R. D., & Evans, N. J. (2007). The complicated realities of Whiteness: From color blind to racially cognizant. *New Directions for Student Services, 120,* 67–75.

Reid, L. D., & Radhakrishnan, P. (2003). Race matters: The relationship between race and general campus climate. *Cultural Diversity and Ethnic Minority Psychology, 9*(3), 263–275.

Rendón, L. I., Jalomo, R. E., & Nora, A. (2000). Theoretical considerations in the study of minority student retention in higher education. In J. M. Braxton (Ed.), *Reworking the student departure puzzle* (pp. 127–156). Nashville, TN: Vanderbilt University Press.

Saenz, V. B. (2005). Breaking the cycle of segregation: Examining students' pre-college racial environments and their diversity experiences in college. (Doctoral dissertation). Retrieved from ProQuest 3188367.

Saenz, V. B., Ngai, H. N., & Hurtado, S. (2007). Factors influencing positive interactions across race for African American, Asian, American, Latino, and White college students. *Research in Higher Education, 48*(1), 1–38.

Smedley, B. D., Myers, H. F., & Harrell, S. P. (1993). Minority-status stresses and the college adjustment of ethnic minority freshmen. *The Journal of Higher Education, 64*(4), 434–452.

Solórzano, D. G., Ceja, M., & Yosso, T. J. (2001). Critical race theory, racial micro-aggressions, and campus racial climate: The experiences of African American college students. *Journal of Negro Education, 69*(1–2), 60–73.

Springer, L., Palmer, B., Terenzini, P. T., Pascarella, E. T., & Nora, A. (1996). Attitudes toward campus diversity: Participation in a racial or cultural awareness workshop. *The Review of Higher Education, 20*(1), 53–68.

Stephan, C. W., & Stephan, W. G. (1992). Reducing intercultural anxiety through intercultural contact. *International Journal of Intercultural Relations, 16*(1), 89–106.

Stephan, W. G., Boniecki, K. A., Ybarra, O., Bettencourt, A., Ervin, K. S., Jackson, L. A., . . . Renfro, C. L. (2002). The role of threats in the racial attitudes of Blacks and Whites. *Personality and Social Psychology Bulletin, 29*(9), 1242–1254.

Summers, J. J., Svinicki, M. D., Gorin, J. S., & Sullivan, T. A. (2002). Student feelings of connection to the campus and openness to diversity and challenge at a large research university: Evidence of progress. *Innovative Higher Education, 27*(1), 53–64.

Tierney, W. G. (1992). An anthropological analysis of student participation in college. *The Journal of Higher Education, 62*(6), 603–618.

IO

ASSESSMENT

Rethinking the Role of Integrative Pedagogies

Kimberly A. Kline, Edward P. St. John, and Annie E. Connors

Development of formal systems of assessment and accountability over the past three decades has marginalized core values of teaching reflective citizens. The problem is complicated by the coevolution of these formal systems and the development of new, more inclusive measures of student development. We began to reflect on the limitations of assessment schemes earlier this century because of the inequalities in higher education being created by data-driven accountability (St. John, Kline, & Asker, 2001). This volume has provided reflective assessments of inclusive, integrative pedagogies by diverse faculty. This chapter focuses on the integration of professors' reflective assessment with formal systems of evaluation. We discuss whole student development, reflect on engaged learning as a missing link, and use integrative pedagogies as a means of improving diversity and inclusion. We include a case study of teaching assessment as content to further encourage readers to rethink how integrative pedagogies can be used to promote diversity and inclusion in higher education classrooms.

Aligning Assessment With Whole Student Development

Since the 1980s, the study of student learning and development has devolved from studying the whole student to treating students and the higher education population as a commodity. Wall, Hursh, and Rodgers (2014) noted, "Assessment has become a tool of social control within managed (higher education) professional culture, rather than a component of shared governance" (p. 5). Indeed, there was a shift from an emphasis on institutional autonomy coupled with mission-oriented planning in the public sphere (Glenny, 1959, 1971; Halstead, 1974) to budget strategies that integrate funding with systemic approaches to public and institutional accountability (Banta, Rudolph, Van Dyke, & Fisher, 1996). These practices have also been deeply embedded in the planning and budgeting practices in public universities as they have adapted practices from private universities (Paulsen & St. John, 2002; Priest & St. John, 2006). We examine the implications these practices have on teaching the whole student before providing guidance about strategies for practitioners.

The Whole Student, Equity, and Public Accountability

Contributors to this volume have provided new conceptions of the whole student being transformed in the contemporary context of education. Three authors explicitly addressed core challenges related to evolving conceptions of the whole student in contemporary universities: Pattengale's discussion in Chapter 1 of *students' personal sense of purpose* can be integrated into liberal arts education delivery using *web-based technologies* in Chapter 8; Heft reflected on the ways *faith-based and humanistic values*, once at the core of liberal arts education (Marsden, 1994; Thelin, 2004), can be reintegrated into education emphasized in universities that increasingly respond to *students' and professors' career interests*; and Manning explicitly addressed *challenges aspiring administrators encounter* as they address emerging challenges related to *diversity and inclusion* in Chapter 2. Each of these challenging chapters addresses intersections between the purposes of and the context for higher education as a means to address holistic student development and growth.

Unfortunately, reflections on the purposes of undergraduate education are seldom the basis for rethinking public accountability, but it is essential that we reconsider accountability within the broader rubric of the purposes of undergraduate liberal arts education. When a mission-oriented perspective dominates in the public sphere, there is discursive space to focus on whole student development and essential outcomes. Unfortunately, the rush by state and federal agencies to hold universities accountable has pushed consideration of student development nearly out of the public discourse.

Inequalities in Opportunity Have Grown Along With Public Accountability

The public accountability movement converges in a complex way with policy arguments about equity, diversity, and fairness, the pillars of social justice in higher education. The primary methods used in public accountability are related to diversity and completion rates, whereas national ranking focuses on test scores (i.e., student achievement prior to admission). Unfortunately, this combination of incentives too often results in a narrowing of admissions standards, causing a decline in diversity in elite universities. Specifically, reviews of public data systems developed as part of the movement toward public accountability (e.g., Advisory Committee on Student Financial Assistance, 2013; Giacoda & Kahlenberg, 2016; St. John, Daun-Barnett, & Moronski-Chapman, 2013) consistently indicate there has been improvement in minority access, largely due to increased requirements and standards for high school graduation, yet there is growing inequality in representation of underrepresented people of color in leading public and private colleges, due to increases in net cost for low-income students and admissions policies that overemphasize standardized tests.

This contrast of expanding access to higher education, on one hand, and the decline in diversity in universities that educate elites, on the other hand, provides a starting point for reconsidering both student development and diversity in undergraduate education, two intertwined problems that probably require simultaneous solutions.

Research on Outcomes Related to the Purposes of Higher Education Has Slowly Adapted to the Necessity of Recognizing Growing Diversity in College Students

The methods historically used to measure development of the whole student as an outcome of higher education did not recognize student diversity. The development of broader conceptions of the whole student remains an elusive goal, but new methods are evolving.

Moral development has been a widely studied concept in the research on college students (Colby & Kohlberg, 1987; Pascarella & Terenzini, 2005). However, the underlying theory (e.g., Kohlberg, 1981, 1984) has treated as universal a framework appropriate for the study of White males. One critique of the theory pertains to gender (Gilligan, 1982, 1998). There are also substantial variations in conceptions of human, community, and moral constructs across racial groups (Siddle Walker & Snarey, 2004). The religious diversity on college campuses also complicates conceptions and measures of student moral development: Christian, Jewish, Islamic, and nonbelievers (spiritualist) all have different conceptions of conventional moral reasoning and the morally developed individual (Small, 2011).

Most of the common measures of student outcomes, including psychological and sociological measures, were originally based on studies of male students (Feldman & Newcomb, 1969; Pascarella & Terenzini, 1991). As is the case with moral development, traditional measures of student development have long histories in research on college students. The process of deconstructing older universal measures is not only evident in research on moral development but also under way in other psychological and sociological measures of student development (e.g., Strayhorn, 2016).

Teaching the Whole Student With Heart, Mind, and Spirit

Unfortunately, current calls for accountability are in part the result of higher education and student affairs professionals allowing external stakeholders to dictate ways in which we facilitate learning and development in students. Students, in turn, increasingly demand more for their money, along with a guarantee of job placement. This departure from teaching the whole student with heart, mind, and spirit has far-reaching consequences, which extend well beyond the college years. As a profession, we have drifted away from the original intent of U.S. higher education, which was to promote the public good. It is important to pause and examine the impact of our actions as professionals and—consciously—to strive to better create situations and opportunities that benefit the students we serve. It is possible to combine habits of the mind, heart, and spirit in the ways in which we coconstruct learning, reflection, and action in an assessment in a higher education course that trains students to become student affairs professionals. Students can learn to critically interpret research findings and apply those findings to an action research focus group project. Giving students safe spaces to reflect on current practices, distinguish ethical research from unethical research, and then apply those new understandings in a real-world situation may be a first step toward reframing this current dilemma.

Reflecting on the ways in which we measure how students learn and grow is directly related to social justice and social agency issues within higher education. Reflection, social justice, and social agency are indeed integral to each other and should be explored more deeply in tandem for several reasons:

1. Viewing ways in which we teach students about assessment through a social justice and social agency lens can help engage students in real work dilemmas.

2. Using reflection and integrative and applied learning as outcomes in an assessment course allows students to directly see the application and impact of a student-centered learning outcome (see also Association of American Colleges & Universities, n.d.).

3. It is crucial that we create a paradigm shift from simply developing students as a commodity to treating students we are assessing as whole humans from the time that they arrive on our campuses until the time that they leave.

Engaged Learning: A Missing Link in Assessment

Research informing litigation of affirmative action cases can inform system reforms in assessment, as well as provide a starting point for student-centered assessment by teaching faculty. Diversity is a legally defensible goal in American universities in spite of their increasing elitism. This emphasis was reinforced by the research used in the defense of affirmative action (i.e., Gurin, Dey, Hurtado, & Gurin, 2002), which supported an agreement that White students benefit educationally from having diverse dialogues in their classrooms and on their campuses. Locks extended this conception in Chapter 9 in this volume to focus on the benefits to minority students. Clearly, the social skills for working with diverse groups are increasingly necessary for leadership and professional practice in both the public and private sectors, including the military.

Actualizing learning environments that support development of these skills relies on creating and maintaining an inclusive climate that supports the sense of belonging by students of color on campus and in the classroom. Researchers are now focusing on the educational outcomes of intergroup dialogues for students of color and Whites (Jayakumar, 2008; Winkle-Wagner & Locks, 2013). Several authors have addressed issues related to classroom discourse among diverse students, especially Dessel, Malnarich, and Schoem in this volume (Chapter 6, Chapter 3, and Chapter 4, respectively).

The capacity to maintain diversity on campus and in classrooms depends on having inclusive climates that enable students to develop a sense of belonging among minority students (Hurtado & Carter, 1997; Hurtado, Milem, Clayton-Pedersen, & Allen, 1998). Dealing with these difficult issues is related not only to the numeric problems of diverse representation but also more fundamentally to learning environments that support diverse values and cultures. The authors in this volume discussed strategies for building dialogues that support learning about values across cultures.

Systemic Change in Assessment

There is also now a legal basis for using noncognitive measures—including problem-solving, the ability to deal with racism, and other strengths-based indicators of capacity to work in diverse settings—as admissions criteria (Bowman, 2011; Sedlacek, 2004, 2011). These approaches hold up as legal, post–affirmative action strategies for actualizing diversity in admissions. Furthermore, American College Testing (ACT) and Educational Testing Service (ETS) have invested in new instruments that measure these noncognitive items for undergraduate and graduate school admissions (Burkum, Robbins, & Phelps, 2011; Burrus, MacCann, Kyllonen, & Roberts, 2011). These trends reinforce the argument that teaching the whole student, inclusive of the skills necessary for leadership in a diverse democracy, merits attention.

Limited Uses of Data in Public Accountability

Tracking the numbers of students entering and completing colleges and programs—and especially numbers in science, technology, engineering, and math (STEM) fields—has been the primary means of reporting on higher education outcomes (Hossler, Dunbar, & Shapiro, 2013). Both enrollment and completion are intertwined with student engagement in learning. Student support services can help attract and retain students, but the underlying issues related to attracting and retaining students in STEM and other demanding fields depend largely on improving engagement in learning within classrooms through discussion, supplemented by research opportunities, internships, and service activities.

However, the measurement of the quality of collegiate learning environments has long been linked to the capacity of colleges to promote engaged learning. For example, the freshman surveys, started by the American Council on Education and continued at the Higher Education Research Institute at UCLA (Astin, 1975, 1985, 1993), and the National Survey of Student Engagement (Hu & Kuh, 2003; Kuh, Kinzie, Schuh, Whitt, & Associates, 2005) use indicators of engaged learning and civic engagement to compare institutions. These indicators are included in the assessment information considered by students in selecting colleges. Many selective colleges actually use this type of information when marketing to students.

Engaged learning is typically measured by the extent to which students work in groups and discussion-based activities. These represent measures of the way classroom learning environments develop the skills necessary for a diverse democracy. In contrast, questions used to measure civic engagement include those regarding community service, reflection of cultures, and participation in religious activities. These questions indirectly relate to students' experiences in the classroom and directly relate to college climates and interactions between campuses and their diverse communities. Therefore, engaged learning is fundamentally related to the core values of higher education. Codification of learning into content bits, what could be the outcome of massive open online courses (MOOCs) and tightly regulated curriculum through corporate or state accountability, could systematically exclude these humanistic values. But scholarship by national associations and testing agencies continues to value the broader view. However, computer-based curriculum can enhance humanistic values, as Pattengale's discussion of extended learning illustrates in this volume.

Linkages to Diversity and Social Justice

Students of color ofen find it difficult to find faculty advisers and face exclusion in formation of groups and learning teams in classrooms, especially in STEM fields, where they are extremely underrepresented (St. John & Bigelow, 2012). Racial prejudice is exacerbated in STEM classrooms by majority students' perceptions that students of color are there because of equal opportunity programs (St. John, 2009; St. John & Bigelow, 2012). These conditions are further complicated by the role of economic privilege in enabling student engagement.

Studies of high-achieving, low-income students of color have found that those whose financial needs are met are more engaged in classrooms, internships, and civic projects than equally prepared peers who lack this financial support (Allen, Epps, & Haniff, 1991; Allen, Harris, & Dinwiddie, 2008; Hune & Gomez, 2008; Tippeconnic & Faircloth, 2008). In interviews, students have explained that working to pay college costs makes it substantially more difficult for them to engage in internships and service activities (St. John, Hu, & Fisher, 2011).

Inclusive engagement of diverse students begins with organizational environments that support and encourage engaged learning for underrepresented students. Frequently, professors of color and professors who advocate for underrepresented students face chilly environments themselves, making it difficult to reach out to and support students (Constantinople, Cornelius, & Gray, 1988). Indeed, there is a long history of marginalizing faculty of color (Tierney & Bensimon, 1996). Although mentoring can help innovative faculty navigate academic systems, high barriers to success still loom in many institutions (Turner & González, 2014). These challenges not only permeate the classroom but also make it difficult for students of color to find trustworthy advisers (St. John et al., 2011).

Using Reflection in Student Assessment

Another theme in this volume has been about integrating reflection on engaged learning into curriculum. Crowfoot (Chapter 5) illustrated curriculum and pedagogy for sustainability. Dessel (Chapter 6) focused on the role of intergroup dialogue in conflict resolution and peace work. Galura (Chapter 7) reflected on the development of service-learning in social science curriculum. Schoem (Chapter 4) illuminated a strategy for integrating these pedagogies in a living–learning community.

These authors used reflection on teaching to illustrate the development of integrative approaches to experiential learning. Later, Kimberly Kline, the first author of this chapter, introduces a reflective case on strategies for integrating a focus on assessment into preparation of student affairs administrators.

Integrating Reflection Into Assessment

Reflection is an important skill shared through whole student teaching but currently absent from many classrooms. Students are consistently offered the opportunity to experience growth and development; however, they are not often given the time or skills to reflect on these experiences. *Reflection* has been defined as "a process or activity that is central to developing practices" (Dewey, 1933, 1938/1973; in Leitch & Day, 2000, p. 180). Osterman (1990) elaborated on this definition, indicating that although reflection is a process, it also requires intentional action. Osterman drew from previous scholarly work on reflective thinking (Dewey, 1933, 1938/1973); assumptions of stage-related development (Piaget, 1960, 1970, 1973); and sequential development in college students' underlying assumptions about truth, knowledge, and values (Perry, 1981; Perry et al., 1968).

In this area of literature, Schön (1983, 1987, 1991) expanded on Dewey's (1933) concept of thinking-in-action. Schön distinguished between two types of reflective thinking: *reflecting-on-action* and *reflecting-in-action*. When people reflect on their action, they take time to think back on what they experienced (Russell & Munby, 1992). Reflecting-in-action is a "way of making explicit some of the tacit knowledge embedded in action so that the agent can figure out what to do differently" (Argyris, Putnam, & Smith, 1985, p. 51).

Teaching students to think reflectively on and in their learning and experiences creates individuals who are capable of critical reflection on their environments, any new information they may receive, and their own day-to-day practices and beliefs. Coupling this concept with a dialogue on social justice and practices of social agency can foster the development of people with the skills and knowledge to work in a variety of situations, with a diverse range of individuals, through a critical lens.

The Field of Student Personnel

The Higher Education and Student Affairs Administration program at SUNY–Buffalo State creates situations for our students that allow them to practice being social advocates in safe spaces. The American College Personnel Association's (2006) *Statement of Ethical Principles and Standards* supports this practice, stating that student affairs professionals "have a responsibility to contribute to the improvement of the communities in which they live and work and to act as advocates for social justice for members of those communities . . . protect human rights and promote respect for human diversity within higher education." Higher education and student affairs graduate programs are particularly important for creating a mechanism for learning such behaviors, in that these programs prepare professionals who will later go on to manage, counsel, and train students in our nation's colleges and universities. Thus, higher education graduate programs could make significant strides in graduate training, particularly as they relate to promoting cultural awareness within college and university contexts.

Integrating Reflection Into Assessment Pedagogy

Using reflection and applied learning as outcomes in an assessment course allows students to see directly the application and impact of a student-centered learning outcome. In the Higher Education and Student Affairs Administration (HEA) program at SUNY–Buffalo State, we are fortunate to provide majors with a complete course titled "Assessment, Tests, and Measurement in Higher Education." Most master's programs do not devote an entire semester to the application of assessment. The course description is as follows:

> CSP 650 is the first of two courses in the core curriculum dealing with student/program assessment and research methodologies in higher education and student affairs administration. The course enables graduate students to learn important fundamentals in the area of assessment in order to be able to gather, analyze, and interpret evidence of program and course effectiveness. (hea.buffalostate.edu)

Multicultural competence is a learning and developmental outcome that HEA focuses on, and issues of social justice and social agency are woven intentionally throughout the assessment, tests, and measurements course. As students become integrated into the department, conversations take place regarding the role that HEA at Buffalo State plays in weaving the conversation of social justice and social agency into our work as lifelong learners and educators, and many of these discussions are centered on the role of student affairs professionals in creating a postsecondary experience that is socially just. Assessment is one major component in ensuring that students' postsecondary experience is socially just. The graduate program was originally founded in 1970 as a way to credential individuals who were being discriminated against because of their race, ethnicity, class, gender, sexual orientation, religion, ability, nationality, age, or size, along with other forms of oppression.

Integrative Pedagogies Improving Diversity Outcomes

The idea that faculty should pay attention to learning outcomes in schools and colleges is not a new concept. John Dewey (1927/1988, 1938/1973), a philosopher of education at the University of Michigan and University of Chicago, argued for inquiry into teaching as an alternative to a conventional scientific approach. However, the reduction of teaching to content bits and "best" teaching practices can be highly problematic, especially given the importance of a diverse democracy. We advocate use of the scholarship of teaching with an explicit focus on strategies for diversity and inclusion.

Building New Foundations for Reflective Assessment

Although reconceptualization of scholarship to include an emphasis on teaching is an ongoing issue, it is necessary to pursue practical means toward this goal (Paulsen & Feldman, 1995). Too often, the outcomes of research receive more emphasis than student learning outcomes (Braxton, 1996). Attention to teaching as a crucial part of the formation of scholars is particularly critical (Walker, Golde, Jones, Bueschel, & Hutchings, 2008).

Evaluation of teaching has become common practice, but overreliance on systemic approaches can discourage young faculty from addressing diversity issues in their classroom (Baldwin & Chronister, 2001). Teaching to indicators and pleasing the majority of students may be implicitly reinforced in formal systems. Majority opinions on standardized indicators can disguise racism within classrooms. For example, majority students may give higher evaluation scores when they have control over grouping for discussions and so forth. Inclusion of indicators of engaged learning and integrative teaching practices may be a necessary addition to standardized evaluation.

Breakdowns of data on teaching measures that address racial disparities in course evaluations remain elusive in the evaluation of teaching. Student identifiers are generally left out of evaluation information provided to teaching faculty, frequently a necessity given that this information should not lead to student identification. Given the small numbers of underrepresented students of color in upper-division courses in elite universities, especially in STEM fields (St. John & Bigelow, 2012; St. John, Massé, Fisher, Moronski-Chapman, & Lee, 2013), it simply is not possible to rely exclusively on formal evaluation to deal with diversity matters.

In addition to the formal evaluation mechanisms, faculty should be encouraged to reflect on their own pedagogical practices using evidence from observation (Van Manen, 2003). Reflective practice has long been integral to teaching professional fields that rely on artistic judgment, but it should be more broadly represented across fields (Schön, 1983, 1987, 1991). It is especially important that more serious attention be given to race and ethnicity, gender, and class differences in engagement in classrooms. Mentoring junior faculty so they are encouraged to pay attention to diversity matters is especially important.

Kline's Case Study of Reflective Assessment

Over the past two years, I have kept copies of papers and exams from students enrolled in the assessment, tests, and measurement course. The final exam contains a version of a reflective question to which students are to respond. One question posed that has garnered interesting responses is as follows: *Colleges and universities should be assessing the learning, development, and happiness of the 2014–2015 college student. You are the associate vice president for student affairs at your institution. Prepare a response outlining why this statement is important for the president's cabinet.* The question is open-ended by design. We try to gauge the degree to which students are making the connection between content that they are learning in the area of assessment; viewing this content through a social justice and social agency lens; and applying it to the college student, specifically what we hope the student becomes in society.

Jacqueline noted,

> As a campus it is our responsibility to ensure that the scholars who choose our institution are becoming engaged with faculty and staff to ensure they are developing, learning, and are happy at our institution. Our number one priority is to help students develop into responsible citizens and also leaders of tomorrow. We must also make certain that these students are learning information about themselves and society to make it a better thriving place for the future. We should be assessing to determine if students are achieving these goals to stay on the path of success . . . making sure that the students are learning by test taking and evaluating the services we are providing for them. Keeping our students happy at our institution will help to retain them on our campus. Assessing the learning development and happiness of our students will allow us to do a self-check at how we are serving the students that choose our institution. It would be a disservice for this institution to not ensure that we are providing a service that we have stated we will do.

Keshia reflected,

> Assessment is at the core of a successfully run institution. Assessment allows us to gather vital information that is instrumental in guaranteeing the healthy social, mental, and academic development of our students. Learning is essential to push forth and break boundaries. We should strive to make our students academically and socially just. Happiness is what makes prospective students choose our campus. No one would like to attend an institution that didn't afford them the happiness they deserve as human beings. By assessing these crucial services that our institution

provides, we gather data about the happiness and effectiveness of said programs. Assessment can provide us more information about our institution as a whole. . . . [The college] experience is a crucial milestone in life, and our institution plays a role in the successful completion of college for our students. . . . We should make this our inner voice urging us to keep this in mind because we, as a whole, have the opportunity to influence a great deal of people! Holistic development is crucial for the long-term progress of our students. They seek out our institution to provide them the "home away from home," which is what we do. Students expect to be safe, respected, cared for, and to learn new things. From a business standpoint, by having a campus that effectively assesses its programs and lives to fill their happiness and developmental needs, we will continue to garner more enrollment, which will lead to an increase in revenue. We will have a successful institution if we choose to keep these core values in mind!

And Jorge wrote,

In an era of data-driven decision-making, higher education institutions are expected to show evidence of ways in which their students learn and develop throughout their collegiate years. This is no doubt an expectation of every college administration from the top down. However, nearly half of all college students report having symptoms of depression. . . . A culture of high-stakes testing going back to grade schools is partly to blame for the rise in mental health issues among students, as well as the decline of self-efficacy, self-esteem, and critical thinking skills. . . . We are ignoring real barriers that students have and assume that they can persist to graduation. We set lofty learning outcomes for students and spend a lot of time measuring these goals but do not spend time helping them with the problems they face upon their arrival. A solution to this issue is to help students decrease stress and anxiety through proactive exercises in happiness and mindfulness, as these will help to create better learning environments for all students. Also, colleges should develop and implement manageable learning outcome assessment projects that weave together academic and student affairs. While this may be challenging, as lack of time, resources, and coordination between units makes things difficult, it is not impossible. If units insist on transparency of the process, creating a sense of community, the assessment process will be demystified for all involved stakeholders. Overall, accurately assessing student learning and development is a crucial process in helping high levels of college administrators make decisions. Accurate assessment results can help in the macro-level processes of budgeting, strategic planning, and curriculum development, as well as the micro-level processes of programming and related services to help students reach their dreams.

Although I believe that the connection is clear among social justice, social agency, and the responsibility as educators on college campuses to provide students with opportunities to soar in their adult life, I purposely asked a question about happiness without imposing the linkage to social justice and social agency issues on students. What is most fascinating to me is that the more students are given opportunities to question the fairness of life and their place in the world, the more they are able to make their own linkages between happiness and notions of equality. These linkages are important when looking at the promotion of approaches to assessment and evaluation that are fair and equitable for all members of a college community.

Conclusion

Postsecondary institutions are currently facing some common challenges. These challenges include greater numbers of students attending college, shrinking capital and human resources, and diminishing public confidence. This situation has resulted in higher demands for accountability by stakeholders across the board, not to mention increased numbers of remedial course offerings; faculty and administrators who are stretched too thin; and disdain for external calls for accountability at the state, federal, and local levels (Cohen & Brawer, 2008).

Yet, when assessment is viewed at a grassroots level, many individuals have successfully implemented learning outcome assessment projects that are manageable within the scope of their day-to-day job responsibilities. Other scholars and professional colleagues have also been able to implement promising practices that wed academic and student affairs. In some cases, they are able to build a culture of grassroots "buy-in" and have implemented professional development programs for learning and developmental outcomes assessments based on the past success of other colleagues.

At the program or department level, many colleagues have already identified potential challenges to the creation of effective assessment of program outcomes, and they also have been able to articulate methods for addressing those challenges. Some of these successes can be linked to outcomes-based assessment, "which goes beyond typical evaluation by examining the program improvements after they are implemented to determine whether the improvements enhanced or contributed to students' learning and development" (Bresciani, Moore Gardner, & Hickmott, 2010, p. 16). Getting to the point of examining program improvements is not always an easy task to achieve, in that authentic outcomes-based assessment is directed and informed by your organizational story (e.g., values, mission, goals), and it takes courage to tell your story. The following are seven tips and promising practices that colleagues are using to enhance and improve assessment of student learning and development:

1. Create buy-in and build a shared conceptual framework.

    a. Ensure the assessment process is one that is designed to be sustained over time and to yield relevant and useful results.
    b. Provide direction for the assessment process.
    c. Make the conceptual framework mission driven; informed by research; and, like the assessment process itself, continuously evaluated and modified when necessary.
    d. When fostered thoughtfully, a shared conceptual framework provides a sense of commonality and coherence with an institution, a department, or a program (Moore Gardner & Milliken, 2013; Senge, 1990).

2. Link assessment with what you are already doing at your institution.

    a. Connect assessment to current core documents, activities, and organizational priorities and demonstrate impact.
    b. Ask questions to which all members of the organization can relate to increase relevance and make establishing shared outcomes simpler and more sustainable.
    c. Involve all stakeholders in the planning, implementation, and leadership.

3. Realize that communication and transparency are keys to success.

    a. Communicating with and among all stakeholders involved in the process can increase motivation and improve understanding.
    b. Transparency through communication can lessen the fear of hidden agendas and suspicion of negative accountability measures.
    c. Communication can increase a sense of community as opposed to top-down directives.

4. Identify and evaluate the perceived value of assessment on your campus.

    a. Does the campus community value it?
    b. Does the institution or administration value it?
    c. Are faculty and staff rewarded for it?

5. Make assessment a key factor in decision-making at your institution.

   a. The transparent use of assessment results for improvement and change increases buy-in and the overall desire to engage in assessment.
   b. Actively using results to inform budgeting, strategic planning, curriculum development, and other major decisions will result in an increased understanding of the value of assessment.

6. Invest time and resources to educate professional staff, faculty, administrators, and students.

   a. Use respected colleagues who "get" assessment within your organization to help educate others.
   b. Create an assessment committee or office to spearhead educational efforts.
   c. Use in-house experts, webinars, conferences, books, and so on to assist in increasing understanding.
   d. Start at the beginning and build on knowledge base.

7. Have the courage to ask the following questions:

   a. What are we trying to accomplish?
   b. How well are we doing it?
   c. What needs to be improved?
   d. How can we enhance and improve student learning and development?
   e. Have we invested time, personnel, and money when needed to sustain a long-term process?
   f. How are we communicating?
   g. Why are we communicating?
   h. Does what we are communicating make sense?
   i. Are we sharing success stories?
   j. Do we have in-house experts we can use?
   k. Do we understand what it means to "close the loop," and are we doing that?
   l. Are there institution-wide resources we are not tapping into?
   m. What types of partnerships can we create (Moore Gardner, Kline, & Bresciani, 2013)?

With a desire to inform reauthorization conversations using outcomes-based assessment data, we continue to have one remaining question for all postsecondary educators: How do we address the learning and development of the whole student? Although we are doing a better job assessing learning and development now than we have in the past, it seems that there remains a part of undergraduate students that may still be ignored. We cannot get a complete and holistic picture of overall student growth and development during the postsecondary experience without assessing experiences that occur for our students both inside and outside the classroom.

Reflection Questions

1. How would you rethink your integrative pedagogical approach to promote diversity and inclusion?
2. What additional measures could you use to evaluate engaged learning strategies?
3. How could you use your reflection on your own teaching to more fully engage students through your courses?
4. How could you integrate your reflection on your own teaching, including formal evaluation and observations, to enhance your assessment work and the equity factor in the assessment of teaching?
5. What would allow you to be better able to make a clear connection between happiness and notions of equality?
6. Using this chapter's tips and promising practices for assessment, how might you improve your own assessment approach of student learning and development?

References

Advisory Committee on Student Financial Assistance. (2013). *Inequality matters: Bachelor's degree losses among low-income Black and Hispanic high school graduates; A policy bulletin for HEA reauthorization.* Washington, DC: Author.

Allen, W. R., Epps, E. G., & Haniff, N. Z. (Eds.). (1991). *College in black and white: African American students in predominantly White and in historically Black public universities.* Albany, NY: SUNY Press.

Allen, W. R., Harris, A., & Dinwiddie, G. (2008). Saving grace: Comparison of African American Gates Millennium Scholarship recipients and non-recipients. In W. T. Trent & E. P. St. John (Eds.), *Resources, assets, and strengths among successful diverse students: Understanding the contributions of the Gates Millennium Scholars Program; Readings on equal education* (Vol. 23, pp. 17–48). New York, NY: AMS Press.

American College Personnel Association. (2006). *Statement of ethical principles and standards.* Washington, DC: Author. Retrieved from http://www.myacpa.org/sites/default/files/Ethical_Principles_Standards.pdf

Argyris, C., Putnam, R., & Smith, D. M. (1985). *Action science: Concepts, methods, and skills for research and intervention.* San Francisco, CA: Jossey-Bass.

Association of American Colleges & Universities. (n.d.). *Essential learning outcomes.* Retrieved from www.aacu.org/leap/essential-learning-outcomes

Astin, A. W. (1975). *Preventing students from dropping out.* San Francisco, CA: Jossey-Bass.

Astin, A. W. (1985). *Achieving excellence in education.* San Francisco, CA: Jossey-Bass.

Astin, A. W. (1993). *Assessments for excellence: The philosophy of assessment and evaluation in higher education.* Phoenix, AZ: Oryx.

Baldwin, R. G., & Chronister, J. L. (2001). *Teaching without tenure: Policies and practices for a new era.* Baltimore, MD: Johns Hopkins University Press.

Banta, T. W., Rudolph, C. B., Van Dyke, J., & Fisher, H. S. (1996). Performance funding comes of age in Tennessee. *The Journal of Higher Education, 67,* 23–45.

Bowman, P. J. (2011). Diversity and merit in higher education: Challenges and opportunities for the 21st century. In P. J. Bowman & E. P. St. John (Eds.), *Diversity, merit, and higher education: Toward a comprehensive agenda for the twenty-first century; Readings on equal education* (Vol. 25, pp. 17–36). New York, NY: AMS Press.

Braxton, J. M. (1996). *Faculty teaching and research: Is there a conflict?* San Francisco, CA: Jossey-Bass.

Bresciani, M. J., Moore Gardner, M., & Hickmott, J. (2010). *Demonstrating student success: A practical guide to outcomes-based assessment of learning and development in student affairs.* Sterling, VA: Stylus.

Burkum, K., Robbins, S., & Phelps, R. (2011). Admissions, academic readiness, and student success: Implications for growing a diverse education pipeline. In P. J. Bowman & E. P. St. John (Eds.), *Diversity, merit, and higher education: Toward a comprehensive agenda for the twenty-first century; Readings on equal education* (Vol. 25, pp. 207–232). New York, NY: AMS Press.

Burrus, J., MacCann, C., Kyllonen, P. C., & Roberts, R. D. (2011). Noncognitive constructs in K–16: Assessments, interventions, educational and policy implications. In P. J. Bowman & E. P. St. John (Eds.), *Diversity, merit, and higher education: Toward a comprehensive agenda for the twenty-first century; Readings on equal education* (Vol. 25, pp. 233–274). New York, NY: AMS Press.

Cohen, A. M., & Brawer, F. B. (2008). *The American community college* (5th ed.). San Francisco, CA: Jossey-Bass.

Colby, A., & Kohlberg, L. (1987). *The measurement of moral judgment: Theoretical foundations and research validation* (Vol. 1). New York, NY: Cambridge University Press.

Constantinople, A., Cornelius, R., & Gray, J. (1988). The chilly climate: Fact or artifact? *The Journal of Higher Education, 59*(5), 527–550.

Dewey, J. (1933). *How we think.* New York, NY: Heath & Co.

Dewey, J. (1973). *Experience and education.* New York, NY: Collier Books. (Original work published 1938)

Dewey, J. (1988). *The public and its problems.* Athens, OH: Swallow Press. (Original work published 1927)

Feldman, K., & Newcomb, T. (1969). *The impact of college on students.* San Francisco, CA: Jossey-Bass.

Giacoda, J. G., & Kahlenberg, R. D. (2016). *True merit: Ensuring our brightest students have access to our best colleges and universities.* Lansdowne, VA: Jack Kent Cooke Foundation.

Gilligan, C. (1982). *In a different voice: Psychological theory and women's development.* Cambridge, MA: Harvard University Press.

Gilligan, C. (1998). Remembering Larry. *Journal of Moral Education, 27,* 125–140.

Glenny, L. A. (1959). *Autonomy of public colleges: The challenge of coordination.* New York, NY: McGraw-Hill.

Glenny, L. A. (1971). *Coordinating higher education for the 70s: Multi-campus and statewide guidelines for practice.* Berkeley, CA: Center for Research and Development in Higher Education.

Gurin, P., Dey, E., Hurtado, S., & Gurin, G. (2002). Diversity and higher education: Theory and impact on educational outcomes. *Harvard Educational Review, 72*(3), 330–366.

Halstead, D. K. (1974). *Statewide planning in higher education.* Washington, DC: U.S. Government Printing Office.

Hossler, D., Dunbar, A., & Shapiro, D. T. (2013). Longitudinal pathways to college persistence and completion: Student, institutional, and public. In L. W. Perna & A. Jones (Eds.), *The state of college access and completion: Improving college success for students from underrepresented groups* (pp. 140–165). New York, NY: Routledge.

Hu, S., & Kuh, G. D. (2003). Maximizing what students get out of college: Testing a learning productivity model. *Journal of College Student Development, 44,* 185–203.

Hune, S., & Gomez, G. G. (2008). Examining the college opportunities and experiences of talented, low-income Asian American and Pacific Islander Gates Millennium Scholars and non-recipients. In W. T. Trent & E. P. St. John (Eds.), *Resources, assets, and strengths among successful diverse students: Understanding the contributions of the Gates Millennium Scholars Program; Readings on equal education* (Vol. 23, pp. 73–106). New York, NY: AMS Press.

Hurtado, S., & Carter, D. F. (1997). Effects of college transition and perceptions of the campus racial climate on Latino college students' sense of belonging. *Sociology of Education, 70*(4), 324–345.

Hurtado, S., Milem, J. F., Clayton-Pedersen, A. R., & Allen, W. R. (1998). Enhancing campus climates for racial/ethnic diversity: Educational policy and practice. *The Review of Higher Education, 21*(3), 279–302.

Jayakumar, U. (2008). Can higher education meet the needs of an increasingly diverse global society? Campus diversity and cross-cultural workforce competencies. *Harvard Educational Review, 78,* 615–649.

Kohlberg, L. (1981). *The philosophy of moral development: Moral stages and the idea of justice.* San Francisco, CA: HarperCollins.

Kohlberg, L. (1984). *The psychology of moral development: The nature and validity of moral stages.* San Francisco, CA: Harper & Row.

Kuh, G. D., Kinzie, J., Schuh, J. H., Whitt, E. J., & Associates. (2005). *Student success in college: Creating conditions that matter.* San Francisco, CA: Jossey-Bass.

Leitch, R., & Day, C. (2000). Action research and reflective practice: Towards a holistic view. *Educational Action Research, 8*(1), 179–193.

Marsden, G. M. (1994). *The soul of the American university: From Protestant establishment to established non-belief.* New York, NY: Oxford University Press.

Moore Gardner, M., Kline, K. A., & Bresciani, M. J. (2013). *Assessing student learning in the two-year and community college.* Sterling, VA: Stylus.

Moore Gardner, M., & Milliken, B. (2013). Determining what you want to get out of the process. In M. Moore Gardner, K. A. Kline, & M. J. Bresciani (Eds.), *Assessing student learning in the two-year and community college* (pp. 1–17). Sterling, VA: Stylus.

Osterman, K. (1990). Reflective practice: A new agenda for education. *Education and Urban Society, 22,* 133–152.

Pascarella, E. T., & Terenzini, P. T. (1991). *How college affects students: Findings and insights from twenty years of research.* San Francisco, CA: Jossey-Bass.

Pascarella, E. T., & Terenzini, P. T. (2005). *How college affects students: A third decade of research.* San Francisco, CA: Jossey-Bass.

Paulsen, M. B., & Feldman, K. A. (1995). Toward a reconceptualization of scholarship: A human action system with functional imperatives. *The Journal of Higher Education, 66*(6), 615–640.

Paulsen, M. B., & St. John, E. P. (2002). Budget incentive structures and the improvement of college teaching. In D. M. Priest, W. E. Becker, D. Hossler, & E. P. St. John (Eds.), *Incentive-based budgeting systems in public universities* (pp. 161–184). Northhampton, MA: Edward Elgar.

Perry, W. G., Jr. (1981). Cognitive and ethical growth: The making of meaning. In A. W. Chickering & Associates (Eds.), *The modern American college* (pp. 76–116). San Francisco, CA: Jossey-Bass.

Perry, W. G., Jr., & others. (1968). *Patterns of development in thought and values of students in a liberal arts college: A validation of a scheme* (Final report). Cambridge, MA: Harvard University Press, Bureau of Study Counsel.

Piaget, J. (1960). *The psychology of intelligence.* Totowa, NJ: Littlefield Adams.

Piaget, J. (1970). *Science of education and the psychology of the child.* New York, NY: Orion Press.

Piaget, J. (1973). *Memory and intelligence.* New York, NY: Basic Books.

Priest, D., & St. John, E. P. (Eds.). (2006). *Privatization and public universities.* Bloomington: Indiana University Press.

Russell, T., & Munby, H. (Eds.). (1992). *Teachers and teaching: From classroom to reflection.* London, UK: Falmer Press.

Schön, D. A. (1983). *The reflective practitioner: How professionals think in action.* New York, NY: Basic Books.

Schön, D. A. (1987). *Educating the reflective practitioner: Toward a new design for teaching and learning in the professions.* San Francisco, CA: Jossey-Bass.

Schön, D. A. (Ed.). (1991). *The reflective turn: Case studies in and on educational practice.* New York, NY: Teachers College Press, Columbia University.

Sedlacek, W. E. (2004). *Beyond the big test: Noncognitive assessment in higher education.* San Francisco, CA: Jossey-Bass.

Sedlacek, W. E. (2011). Using noncognitive variables in assessing readiness for higher education. In P. J. Bowman & E. P. St. John (Eds.), *Diversity, merit, and higher education: Toward a comprehensive agenda for the twenty-first century; Readings on equal education* (Vol. 25, pp. 187–205). New York, NY: AMS Press.

Senge, P. M. (1990). *The fifth discipline: The art and practice of the learning organization.* New York, NY: Doubleday.

Siddle Walker, V., & Snarey, J. (Eds.). (2004). *Race-ing moral formation: African American perspectives on care and justice.* New York, NY: Teachers College Press.

Small, J. L. (2011). *Understanding college students' spiritual identities: Different faiths, varied world views.* Cresskill, NJ: Hampton Press.

St. John, E. P. (2009). *College organization and professional development: Integrating moral reasoning and reflective practice.* New York, NY: Routledge.

St. John, E. P., & Bigelow, V. (2012). STEM transfer students in research universities: A qualitative assessment of academic capital formation. In R. Winkle-Wagner, P. J. Bowman, & E. P. St. John (Eds.), *Expanding postsecondary opportunity for underrepresented students: Theory and practice of academic capital formation; Readings on equal education* (Vol. 26, pp. 255–290). New York, NY: AMS Press.

St. John, E. P., Daun-Barnett, N. J., & Moronski-Chapman, K. (2013). *Public policy and higher education.* New York, NY: Routledge.

St. John, E. P., Hu, S., & Fisher, A. S. (2011). *Breaking through the access barrier: Academic capital formation informing public policy.* New York, NY: Routledge.

St. John, E. P., Kline, K. A., & Asker, E. H. (2001). The call for public accountability: Rethinking the linkages to student outcomes. In D. E. Heller (Ed.), *The states and public higher education: Affordability, access, and accountability* (pp. 219–242). Baltimore, MD: Johns Hopkins University Press.

St. John, E. P., Massé, J. C., Fisher, A. S., Moronski-Chapman, K., & Lee, M. (2013). Beyond the bridge: Actionable research informing the development of a comprehensive intervention strategy. *American Behavioral Scientist, 20*(10), 1–20. doi:10.1177/0002764213515233

Strayhorn, T. L. (2016). *Student development theory in higher education: A social psychological approach.* New York, NY: Routledge.

Thelin, J. R. (2004). *A history of American higher education.* Baltimore, MD: Johns Hopkins University Press.

Tierney, W. G., & Bensimon, E. M. (1996). *Promotion and tenure: Community and socialization in academe.* Albany, NY: SUNY Press.

Tippeconnic, J. W., & Faircloth, S. C. (2008). Socioeconomic and cultural characteristics of high-achieving and low-income American Indian and Alaska Native college students: The first two years of the Gates Millennium Scholars program. In W. T. Trent & E. P. St. John (Eds.), *Resources, assets, and strengths among successful diverse students: Understanding the contributions of the Gates Millennium Scholars Program; Readings on equal education* (Vol. 23, pp. 107–142). New York, NY: AMS Press.

Turner, C. S. V., & González, J. C. (2014). *Modeling mentoring across race/ethnicity and gender: Practices to cultivate the next generation of diverse faculty.* Sterling, VA: Stylus.

Van Manen, M. (2003). On the meaning of pedagogy and its relation to curriculum and teaching. In D. Scott (Ed.), *Curriculum studies: Major themes in education* (Vol. 3, pp. 415–462). London, UK: Routledge.

Walker, G. M., Golde, C. M., Jones, L., Conklin Bueschel, A., & Hutchings, P. (2008). *The formation of scholars: Rethinking doctoral education for the twenty-first century.* Palo Alto, CA: Carnegie Foundation for the Advancement of Teaching.

Wall, A. F., Hursh, D., & Rodgers, J. W., III. (2014). Assessment for whom: Repositioning higher education assessment as an ethical and value-focused social practice. *Research and Practice in Assessment, 9*, 5–17.

Winkle-Wagner, R., & Locks, A. M. (2013). *Diversity and inclusion on campus: Supporting racially and ethnically underrepresented students.* New York, NY: Routledge.

II

TEACHING THE WHOLE STUDENT

Christine Modey, David Schoem, and Edward P. St. John

The teachers whose work appears in this volume share many similar approaches. Primary among them is a commitment to seeing students as whole people, who bring with them into the classroom a wide range of backgrounds and experiences, as well as varied social identities, and who learn not only with their minds but also with their emotions, their bodies, and their spirits. There is a radical people-centeredness among these teachers, a sense that the formation of people—students and teachers—is the primary task of college education. This is apparent in their emphasis on helping students identify and clarify their own core beliefs and values through reading, reflection, action, and dialogue with others. It is crucial for these teachers that their students consider their personal beliefs and values, as well as their social identities, together with the classroom material, to figure out not only what the course content means but also how it matters to them personally, how it can be integrated into their own worldview. For this reason, many of the faculty whose teaching practices are described in this volume emphasize integrative learning, which is specifically designed to connect the personal and intellectual with the ethical and social dimensions of course content and to connect various knowledge domains with each other. Such integrative approaches to learning also see student life and academic affairs as related and mutually reinforcing of curricular and cocurricular activities.

Integrative Pedagogy

Integrative pedagogy is deeply rooted in a particular view of human beings and what's required for us to learn, grow, and flourish. At its heart, integrative

246

pedagogy is deeply human and concerned with both our individual and collective human condition. Teachers who practice integrative pedagogy acknowledge that a holistic view of students and teachers demands a varied and extensive repertoire of teaching strategies. These strategies are grounded in the awareness that students and teachers enter classrooms as whole and complex people, that learning happens most successfully in the context of caring relationships between students and teachers, that empowering students requires that they test classroom knowledge in the wider world, and that learning from and about differences is essential if education is to attain its goal of effecting a more just society.

Relational Learning

As much as teachers view students as whole, they also strive to enter their classrooms as whole people; to acknowledge the full humanity of each student and teacher; and, significantly, to create communities of learners within their classrooms as part of the pedagogical practice of relational learning. Some teachers experience teaching as a spiritual practice, one that calls on them to intentionally integrate their deepest values and beliefs with their professional identities and to bring this integrated self into the classroom and every encounter with students. Other teachers represented in this volume teach from a variety of other ethical perspectives. For example, they tend to value equality between teachers and students and to work in a way that values partnership (among people and between people and nature) over domination. Such teachers practice pedagogy grounded in empathetic relationships, between teachers and students, and also among students. Often they value teaching, learning, and relating through human, face-to-face relationships over relating through or with technology. This emphasis on direct relationship leads teachers practicing whole student pedagogy to strive to create diverse learning communities built on a foundation of truth, scholarship, and belonging.

Connecting the Classroom to the World

The movement beyond the classroom is another philosophical underpinning of this approach to teaching. The teachers represented here place an emphasis on the application of theoretical work to real-world problems and experiences. They believe that learning should be experiential; that is, it should provide hands-on opportunities that require students to adapt and apply what they know. Just as they try to break down boundaries between the classroom and the world, these teachers break down divides between disciplines, asking students to find connections and relationships between seemingly disparate fields and disciplinary approaches to creating knowledge. This sense of disciplinary integration, coupled with an emphasis on integrative learning for students, leads to yet another important philosophy: the awareness that such an approach can connect students' interests and values to their life's purpose.

Diversity, Social Justice, and Democracy

Each teacher represented in this book helps students connect their learning to their identities and goals. The identification of these broader goals is yet another foundation of the whole student pedagogy outlined here. For example, many of these teachers see education for a diverse democracy as a key purpose of their work, and they strive to help students learn across and from differences within the classroom. They place great importance on helping minority students succeed, despite challenges, and also on helping all students learn about diversity and understand the long-term importance of cocurricular experiences in diverse groups of students for shaping attitudes toward diversity and difference. Ultimately, many of these teachers approach their classrooms with long-term social justice goals, whether those are environmental sustainability; economic equality; or racial, ethnic, and religious understanding.

Pedagogical Practices

Practitioners of an integrative pedagogy enact their philosophical principles in some pedagogical practices that are simultaneously innovative—and possibly countercultural in the context of higher education today—and highly traditional. For a student to truly understand and manifest what is being taught in the classroom, he or she must engage it in the real world; therefore, teachers use some form of engaged learning to help students apply and think critically about course content. Teachers emphasize the importance of classroom communities and empathetic relationships in a structured and intentional practice of dialogue that values all points of view, seeks understandings, and equips students for participation in deliberative democracy. Because integrative pedagogy emphasizes whole person development, various means of promoting reflection, particularly writing, are used to help students integrate course materials and their personal values.

Engaged Learning

The teachers whose work is represented in this book follow in the tradition of John Dewey, who emphasized the importance of experiential education and students' participation in their own learning. This type of education can take a variety of forms. One is service-learning, which connects students to local organizations—social service organizations, schools, and so forth. Students provide useful service to the community and make crucial connections between what they learn in the classroom and what they experience in their placements. This helps students develop as more complex and creative thinkers. Following Dewey's understanding that learning is profoundly social, teachers who practice engaged learning enable students to develop relationships through intentional collaborations. They also use community-based learning, in which the community itself becomes a classroom and where a learning community is created intentionally among a cohort of students who take interlinked classes together. In some cases, such a learning community may also be based in a living space, with cocurricular activities that help build community and foster learning goals, such as social justice, diversity, and environmental responsibility. Teachers may also develop integrative assignments, which ask students to bring together their experiences, readings, and class discussions and connect these to their own identities and vocational goals.

Intergroup Dialogue and Community

As noted previously, teaching through relationship is important to faculty who promote whole student education. We learn through our relationships with others. Thus, the teachers represented here engage in a variety of activities with their students intended to develop relationships and community. Most prominently, many faculty engage in intentional intergroup dialogue activities to promote understanding and awareness among students with varied backgrounds and identities and to build trust in the classroom. Intergroup dialogue may be a frequent classroom practice or an occasional exercise, but it is always meant to help create a safe space for open, honest, respectful, critical discussions. Often, ground rules and practices of active listening help establish this safe space, where students can engage in truth telling, analysis, and compassion, as well as confront difference and conflict with each other. Some teachers alternate between the use of affinity groups (where students share an important identity) and the use of inclusive groups (where students have diverse identities) to build trust and also to help promote honest, critical, and respectful conversations about what are often highly contentious issues. More broadly, such intergroup dialogue can build students' skills in democratic deliberation, a crucial practice in civic and community life in a diverse democracy.

These teachers also noted that it is important for faculty to communicate their care for students in this context, to build up students' ability to trust and care for each other, and to establish a sense of community in the classroom. They make an intentional effort to walk alongside their students, to share their own struggles and insights. They give students opportunities to both express and receive gratitude and also to acknowledge their own pain, suffering, and anger in light of personal and global challenges and injustices. Teachers also ensure that they make themselves available to their students by responding in detail to students' journals; holding—even requiring—office hours; and serving as informal mentors.

Course Content

Some faculty craft linked courses within learning communities, whereas others practice whole student pedagogy outside of any formal program. Regardless, common theories repeatedly come up in course content in such practices. For example, the critical pedagogy of Paulo Freire features prominently in whole student classrooms, along with connected concepts, such as a pedagogy of hope and developing and validating new ways of knowing about the world. Many of the faculty who describe their work here emphasize students' exploration of their own values and beliefs, social structures and inequalities, and issues of sustainability and unsustainability. These topics promote students' development of multicultural competencies and social justice identities and commitments. Many faculty also intentionally teach students to develop a sense of life purpose; many more expect that the exploration of various topics intimately connected to students' own identities and values will lead to a stronger sense of life purpose, through the practice of intentional reflection.

Reflection

The practice of self-reflection is crucial for students to learn and grow from their experiences by integrating them with classroom materials and background knowledge. Thus, many faculty assign reflective writing or other reflective activities to help students achieve this important goal of connecting theory to practice, the personal and the professional. Some, for example, use analytic and reflective journaling to encourage this reflecting-on-action. Others provide opportunities for personal and social identity exploration and development, through psycho-spiritual practices, such as silent walking in nature or guided meditation. As students develop their own sense of self (self-authorship) during their time in college, some faculty have found that electronic portfolios help students gather and reflect on examples of their work, as well as frame that work within their own system of personal and professional values and aspirations. Reflection is also a critical component of assessment for teaching the whole student, engaged learning, and integrative pedagogy, and many of the chapters in this book represent the best of reflective assessment.

Student Outcomes

Integrative pedagogy is an approach to education that taps into some of the deeply held values of its practitioners. The greater promise of integrative pedagogy, however, is demonstrated by student outcomes, and many practitioners who contributed to this volume have taken pains to evaluate the qualitatively or quantitatively measurable outcomes for students. Although students' reflective writing is an indicator of their intellectual growth and ability to learn how to learn, student retention, personal growth, and commitment to and participation in social change are also measurable in various ways and help to convince others of the efficacy of integrative learning for achieving student outcomes valued by the broader institution.

Learning Outcomes

When we examine outcomes for courses that emphasize whole student education, it is important to recognize that learning outcomes, particularly in areas of metacognition, remain important. Many of the faculty who contributed to this book put a premium on their students' ability to learn how to learn—for example, how to reevaluate their perspective in light of reading and classroom discussion or how to develop skills of integrative thinking that allow them to consider course topics from a variety of perspectives. Integrative thinking also permits students to integrate ethical and moral values with scholarly perspectives from the sciences, social sciences, and humanities, leading to a more interdisciplinary approach to learning and to knowledge creation. The application of knowledge, particularly from this broader perspective and in a wide variety of real-world situations, is also emphasized. This integrative perspective may privilege deep learning, from a variety of perspectives, over broad coverage of course material. The emphasis is on developing skills and knowledge and offering opportunities to pursue the big questions of life. Critical and analytical thinking and honest, open pursuit of answers to these questions are crucial to this process, as is reflection on oneself and development of an awareness of one's own self-presentation and learning style and how these affect classroom interactions.

Retention and Student Success

It is well known that students who experience a sense of community and also a sense of purpose and agency within their educational environment tend to stay in college and complete their degrees. Thus, whole student education is often pursued as a retention and student success strategy. Such pedagogical approaches, with their emphasis on values and identity, can help students develop a sense of vocation, of their life purpose or calling. These approaches empower students, offering them hopefulness, agency, and pathways toward their goals. Often, students who participate in such courses or programs learn more because what they learn is connected to their identities and their goals.

Personal Growth

Of course, beyond conventional definitions of *student success*, whole student education promotes various measures of personal growth for students. For example, many pedagogical strategies incorporate and train students in dialogue and listening skills, which are crucial for democratic deliberation and participation. Within such a controlled environment, students are less fearful of conflict and develop a stronger sense of identity and self-authorship and increased caring for others. In this context, many faculty put a special emphasis on multicultural competence, on extending one's comfort zone to include different views or different people. This is most effectively done through sustained and substantive diversity engagement. With or without the addition of a spiritual dimension—for example, centering meditation or spiritual relating to nature—these pedagogical practices point in the direction of personal, internal growth for students and further maturity, compassion, and understanding. In particular, many faculty hope that such personal growth leads to greater awareness and development of individual, social, and social justice identities for students.

Social Change

Ultimately, practitioners of whole student pedagogy may hope for social change through the individual change that happens in their students. Through education, they seek to turn despair and disengagement—all too common in the face of seemingly intractable social and environmental problems—into an active, critical hope and enable students to see clearly and act justly. These teachers aim to equip their students with the skills they need to take such action. They provide leadership opportunities on campus, in the community, and at academic conferences. Through dialogue, they teach their students to value the process of hearing and understanding different viewpoints in order to move forward together on social justice causes. These teachers help their students both understand and engage in social change practices. They immerse their students in a thick culture of service and point them toward solution-oriented action.

Gratitude and Inspiration

We are thankful, humbled, and inspired by these authors' honesty and expertise, their personal stories and experiences, and their immense commitment to student learning and excellence in teaching. We have learned deeply from their chapters and go forward ever more dedicated to our teaching, to our teachers, and to our students.

About the Editors

Christine Modey has taught in the Michigan Community Scholars Program at the University of Michigan and is a faculty member in the Sweetland Center for Writing, where she also directs the Peer Writing Consultant Program and teaches courses in new media writing for nonprofit organizations, peer tutor training, and first-year composition. Her research interests include spoken discourse of writing tutorials and history of the book. She holds degrees from Hope College (BA) and the University of Delaware (MA, PhD).

David Schoem is the founding faculty director of the University of Michigan's Michigan Community Scholars Program. He holds teaching appointments in the Sociology Department and University Courses Division and is an affiliated faculty member in Judaic studies. He has served as LSA assistant dean for undergraduate education and assistant vice president for academic and student affairs. A first-generation college student, Schoem holds degrees from the University of Michigan (BA), Harvard University (MEd), and the University of California, Berkeley (PhD).

Schoem has played a leadership role in many of the most important initiatives in student learning and undergraduate education at the University of Michigan, including developing learning communities, cofounding the Program on Intergroup Relations, serving as chair of the Committee for a Multicultural University, playing a critical role in the establishment of the LSA Race and Ethnicity Requirement, and implementing and growing the First-Year Seminar Program, and he has played a key role in community-based and engaged learning. Schoem has served as a PEW National Learning Communities fellow and has led faculty institutes on diversity issues and undergraduate education through the Association of American Colleges & Universities, the Ford Foundation, the Washington Center, and numerous colleges and universities. Schoem was recognized by the University of Michigan with the State Campus Compact Faculty Award for Community Service-Learning and by the National Center for Institutional Diversity with the Exemplary Diversity Engagement and Scholarship Award. Schoem has published extensively on topics in higher education, teaching, dialogue, diversity, social identity, students, student learning, and the American Jewish community. This is his 11th book.

Edward P. St. John, Algo D. Henderson collegiate professor (emeritus) at the University of Michigan's Center for the Study of Higher and Postsecondary Education, is concerned with education for a just society, an interest that stems from three decades of research on educational policy and practice. He is a fellow of the American Educational Research Association and has received awards for leadership and research from the Association for the Study of Higher Education. St. John is series editor for *Globalization and Social Justice*, a book series with AMS Press that addresses comparative issues in higher education. He serves as series coeditor for *Readings on Equal Education*, an annual volume focusing on initiatives seeking to reduce inequalities in K–12 and higher education, and *Core Issues in Higher Education*, topical texts for professors and graduate students with an interest in the field. His current research projects focus on strengthening pathways between high school and college for underrepresented students. His recent books include *Public Policy and Higher Education: Reframing Strategies for Preparation, Access, and Success* (Routledge, 2013) and *Research, Actionable Knowledge, and Social Change: Reclaiming Social Responsibility Through Research Partnerships* (Stylus, 2013).

About the Contributors

Annie E. Connors is currently the head academic adviser in the psychology department at the University at Albany. Prior to this role she served as an academic adviser in the School of Business and Technology at Excelsior College and as the college liaison in career services at Genesee Community College. Connors earned her MS from the higher education and student affairs administration master's program at SUNY–Buffalo State and earned a BA in anthropology with a concentration in indigenous studies. Her research focuses on inclusion, and she has been able to transfer many skills from the field of anthropology to the higher education and student affairs field. Connors has worked with a wide variety of students from diverse cultural and socioeconomic backgrounds including military, international, and first-generation. The career transition from anthropology to higher education and student affairs has ignited her passion in research that promotes human rights and social justice.

James Crowfoot is an emeritus professor of natural resources and urban and regional planning at the University of Michigan. He has an interdisciplinary educational background in organizational and social psychology, theology, and physics. His teaching and research focused on processes of socioenvironmental conflicts and change and their impacts on environmental sustainability and social and environmental justice. He is dean emeritus of the School of Natural Resources and Environment at the University of Michigan and former president of Antioch College.

Adrienne B. Dessel is co–associate director of the Program on Intergroup Relations (IGR) and lecturer in the School of Social Work at the University of Michigan. Dessel provides administrative support to IGR, curriculum leadership, and consultations to faculty and staff in higher education settings. She teaches courses on intergroup dialogue facilitation, the social psychology of prejudice and intergroup relations, and global conflict and coexistence. Her research focuses on attitudes and prejudice reduction and intergroup dialogue as a method of prejudice intervention and community building. Her recent research has examined motivations for engagement in dialogue and processes and outcomes of intergroup dialogue, around topics of conservative Christian religion and sexual orientation and of the Arab–Jewish conflict. Her community consultations include social justice education for public school teachers and evaluation of lesbian, gay, bisexual, and transgender education services.

Joseph A. Galura is a lecturer in the School of Social Work at the University of Michigan. He is also an academic adviser for the multidisciplinary undergraduate minor in community action and social change, which he helped launch. Previously, he developed, implemented, and taught service-learning courses in sociology (Project Community), education (the Lives of Urban Children and Youth Initiative), and Asian/Pacific Islander American Studies (the Filipino American Oral History Project of Michigan). Galura is the founder of the OCSL Press and has published five books on community service-learning.

James L. Heft is a priest in the Society of Mary and leader for more than 20 years in Catholic higher education. He spent many years at the University of Dayton, serving as chair of the theology department for 6 years, provost of the university for 8 years, and then chancellor for 10 years. He left the University of Dayton in the summer of 2006 to found the Institute for Advanced Catholic Studies at the University of Southern California (USC) in Los Angeles, where he now serves as the Alton Brooks Professor of Religion and president of the institute. He has written and edited 13 books and published more than 175 articles and book chapters. Most recently he edited *Learned Ignorance: Intellectual Humility Among Jews, Christians, and Muslims* (Oxford University Press, 2011), *Catholicism and Interreligious Dialogue* (Oxford University Press, 2011), and *In the Lógos of Love: Promise and*

Predicament in Catholic Intellectual Life (Oxford University Press, 2016). In 2011, he published *Catholic High Schools: Facing the New Realities* (Oxford University Press, 2011). He is currently working on a book on Catholic higher education. In 2011, the Association of Catholic Colleges and Universities awarded him the Theodore M. Hesburgh award for his long and distinguished service to Catholic higher education. Among the courses he teaches at USC is a senior seminar, "Religions and Violence," designed for majors in USC's School of International Relations.

Kimberly A. Kline serves as associate professor and chair of the higher education administration department at Buffalo State, State University of New York. Her research focuses on professional development, issues of social justice and agency in higher education, and student learning outcomes assessment. She had the privilege of serving as a 2012–2013 Fulbright scholar at the National University of Kyiv-Mohyla in Ukraine and returned as a 2014–2015 Fulbright scholar to study the student-initiated protests that led to the current revolution in Ukraine. Kline has more than 20 years of experience in higher education and student affairs, both as a faculty member and as a professional. She earned a PhD in higher education from Indiana University, an MS in student personnel administration from SUNY–Buffalo State, and a BA in political science from Slippery Rock University. Kline most recently published the text *Reflection in Action: A Guidebook for Faculty and Student Affairs Professionals* (Stylus, 2013) and was named a 2015 Diamond Honoree recipient by the American College Personnel Association Educational Leadership Foundation.

Angela M. Locks is an associate professor in the educational leadership department in the College of Education and the faculty director of the Undergraduate Research Opportunity Program, and she directs the Office of Undergraduate Research Services at California State University, Long Beach. She was a member of the University of Michigan community for 17 years, first as an undergraduate, then as a social science peer adviser and assistant director for the Undergraduate Research Opportunity Program (UROP). She left UROP to complete her doctorate at the University of Michigan's Center for the Study of Higher and Postsecondary Education. In 2008, she began her faculty position at Long Beach State, where she has developed a strong research agenda that explores institutional diversity praxis and the recruitment, retention, and experiences of students of color in colleges and universities. Locks's current research projects include an examination of college going from 7th grade through 12th grade and a quantitative campus climate study examining the experiences of diverse college students. Previously, Locks completed a three-part study titled "Institutional Commitment to Policies and Practices That Support Racial and Ethnic Diversity in the Post–Affirmative Action Era." In August 2013, Locks's first book, *Diversity and Inclusion on Campus: Supporting Racially and Ethnically Underrepresented Students* (Routledge, 2013), was published. Written with Rachelle Winkle-Wagner, this book examines how students of color get in, get through, and get out of college.

Gillies Malnarich taught in the Evening Weekend Studies program at The Evergreen State College during her tenure from 2000 to 2014 as codirector of the Washington Center for Improving the Quality of Undergraduate Education, the National Resource Center for Learning Communities. In this capacity, she co-developed, led, and wrote about learning community theory and practice, including the center's national action-research projects, and served as a consultant for national, regional, and campus-based educational reform initiatives. She is also a founding editor of *Learning Communities Research and Practice*, an open-access, peer-reviewed electronic journal. In addition, she has written about and worked to implement developmental education curriculum and pedagogy reforms at both campus and state levels. Before coming to Evergreen, she worked with educators in Canada on policy and system-wide practices related to professional development, institutional effectiveness, and abilities-based assessment from the classroom to the program level. Educated in the humanities and social sciences, she has taught adult literacy, developmental education, and sociology in multiple settings, including at community- and work-based popular education programs, universities, and a large urban community college.

Kathleen Manning served as a professor in the higher education and student affairs program at the University of Vermont from 1989 until her retirement in 2014. Her professional interests include social justice, international higher education, leadership, and organizational theory. A frequent contributor to the student affairs and higher education literature, Manning has published eight books and a number of articles and chapters. She was awarded the NASPA Outstanding Contribution to Literature and/or Research Award in 2007; the University of Vermont Kroepsch-Maurice Excellence in Teaching Award; the NASPA Pillar of the Profession; and on-campus awards for LGBTQA-, gender-, and race-related advocacy. She has taught and consulted in several international contexts including three voyages on Semester at Sea and three Fulbright awards. Manning has a PhD in higher education with a minor in anthropology from Indiana University, an MS in counseling and student personnel services from the State University of New York at Albany, and a BA in biology from Marist College. She is an avid sailor and skier, an advanced certified scuba diver, and a frequent international traveler.

Jerry A. Pattengale is Indiana Wesleyan University's first university professor and also has distinguished appointments at Excelsia College (Australia), the Sagamore Institute, Tyndale House, Cambridge, and Gordon–Conwell Theological Seminary. He is executive director for Nationalconversations .com and executive director of education at Museum of the Bible, in Washington DC (where he was one of the two founding scholars and developed an international research program for ancient texts [MOTB Scholars Initiative]). He received the National Student Advocate Award (University of South Carolina), two Professor of the Year Awards (Azusa Pacific University), and an NEH Award to Isthmia, Greece. He established the record viewership for *Teaching Professor* broadcasts (Madison, Wisconsin; "What Faculty Need to Know About Retention") and codeveloped the *Odyssey in Egypt* program. Some of his recent authored and edited books include *Why I Teach* (McGraw-Hill.Irwin; 2008), *Straight Talk: Clear Answers about Today's Christianity* (Triangle Publishing; 2008), *Helping Sophomores Succeed: Understanding and Improving the Second Year Experience* (Wiley; 2009), *The Purpose-Guided Student: The Purpose-Guided Student* (McGraw-Hill; 2010), *Biblical Evidence: Biblical Evidence* (Triangle Publishing; 2011), *Take Every Thought Captive: Forty Years of the Christian Scholar's Review* (Abilene Christian University Press; 2011), *Beyond Integration: Beyond Integration* (Abilene Christian University Press; 2012), *Book of Books: Book of Books* (Bible Lands Museum Jerusalem; 2013), *Buck Creek: True Stories to Tickle Your Mind* (Dust Jacket Press; 2013), *The Book* (2014, Hebrew; 2016, English), *Telling the Truth With a Smile: Telling the Truth With a Smile* (Dust Jacket Press; 2016), *Semitic Texts, Vol. 1* (2016, managing editor with Emanuel Tov), *Faith Made Real: Everyday Experiences of God's Power* (Wesleyan Publishing House; 2017), and *The World's Greatest Book: The World's Greatest Book* (Museum of the Bible Books; 2017, coauthored with Lawrence Schiffman). He contributes occasionally to national venues (e.g., *Washington Post, Wall Street Journal, Christianity Today, Books & Culture, Chicago Tribune, Patheos, Inside Higher Ed,* and *Christian Post*) and has appeared on various TV and radio broadcasts. He is associate publisher of the *Christian Scholar's Review* and board member for Religion News Service and Yale's Jonathan Edwards Center. Pattengale holds a PhD and MA from Miami University in ancient history, an MA from Wheaton College in interpersonal development, and a BS from Indiana Wesleyan University in history. In 2015 and 2016, the AP and Hoosier State Press Association gave his news column top awards, including "Best General Commentary."

INDEX

Association
of American
Colleges and
Universities

About AAC&U

AAC&U is the leading national association concerned with the quality, vitality, and public standing of undergraduate liberal education. Its members are committed to extending the advantages of a liberal education to all students, regardless of academic specialization or intended career. Founded in 1915, AAC&U now comprises nearly 1,400 member institutions—including accredited public and private colleges, community colleges, research universities, and comprehensive universities of every type and size.

AAC&U functions as a catalyst and facilitator, forging links among presidents, administrators, and faculty members who are engaged in institutional and curricular planning. Its mission is to reinforce the collective commitment to liberal education and inclusive excellence at both the national and local levels, and to help individual institutions keep the quality of student learning at the core of their work as they evolve to meet new economic and social challenges.

Information about AAC&U membership, programs, and publications can be found at www.aacu.org